DATELINE FREEDOM

By the same author
Special Correspondent

DATELINE FREEDOM

•

Vitali Vitaliev

HUTCHINSON
London Sydney Auckland Johannesburg

The right of Vitali Vitaliev to be identified as Author of this
work has been asserted by Vitali Vitaliev in accordance with the
Copyright, Designs and Patents Act, 1988

This edition first published in 1991 by
Hutchinson

Random Century Group Ltd
20 Vauxhall Bridge Road, London SW1V 2SA

Random Century Australia (Pty) Ltd
20 Alfred Street, Milsons Point, Sydney, NSW 2061, Australia

Random Century New Zealand Ltd
PO Box 40–086, Glenfield, Auckland 10, New Zealand

Random Century South Africa (Pty) Ltd
PO Box 337, Bergvlei, 2012, South Africa

British Library Cataloguing-in-Publication Data
Vitaliev, Vitali
Dateline freedom: Revelations of an unwilling
exile.
I. Title
920

ISBN 0–09–174677–9

Photoset by Speedset Ltd, Ellesmere Port
Printed and bound in Great Britain by
Mackays of Chatham PLC

*To my dear friends in the Soviet Union from whom I am
separated in space – but never in spirit.*

Where liberty dwells, there is my country.

Benjamin Franklin,
'Advice to a Young Tradesman'

Comrade, believe: joy's star will leap
upon our sight, a radiant token;
Russia will rouse from her long sleep;
and where autocracy lies broken,
our names shall yet be graven deep!

Alexander Pushkin (1799–1837),
To Chaadayev

Contents

Illustration Acknowledgements

Page 1
EAST COPIES WEST   As Macdonalds comes to Moscow, Russian women take part in an American-style Beauty Contest, 1989.

Pages 2–3
ARMS AND THE MEN   Broiler, former gangster leader; Almiashev, twice world classical wrestling champion; and one of the young team leaders, Stas; Brighton Beach in New York, stronghold of the Soviet mafia in exile, 1990.

Page 4
UNDER LENIN'S NOSE   In Perm 35, officially the last remaining labour camp for political prisoners in the Soviet Union.
(© Vitali Vitaliev)

Page 5
В. ВИТАЛЬЕВ   The poster advertising Vitali Vitaliev at Leningrad's Concert Hall, 1989.

Pages 6–7
VELVET GLOVE, IRON FIST   A tank crushing a protester in Vilnius, 1991.
© Popperfoto/AFP)
A poster in the Baltic Republics draws connections between President Gorbachev and Saddam Hussein.
(© Frank Spooner Pictures)
The dead laid out in Lithuania.
(© Magnum)
Demonstrators protesting against the KGB, Lithuania 1991.
(© Associated Press Ltd)

Page 8
DOWN UNDER   Vitali and his family in Sydney, 1990; with Clive James at the Australian High Commission; and with Peter Ustinov in Melbourne.

From the Author

'Have a good trip, Vitali!' Clive James said to me in London. 'You will like Australia, and Australia will like you!'

Monica, a slim Aussie woman at the Australian High Commission in Britain, liked to watch the *Saturday Night Clive* TV show. She confessed to me later that she immediately recognized me as Clive James' Moscow Man when I muttered into her window: 'I need a non-formal approach . . .' 'In the window you looked exactly like you do on TV,' she said.

I have been in Australia for several months now. Not long enough to make conclusions, but long enough to look back. I am living in Melbourne. Why? Simply because I like it. Am I happy? I really don't know. Happiness is an abstract category which mainly exists in the past. I think it was Jules Renard who said that at the station of happiness the biggest room is the waiting hall. But at least I am alive and working and writing, and getting lots of affectionate letters from the readers. And my wife Natasha and son Mitya are here with me.

Yes, I am missing Russia immensely. In my soul I have never left it at all.

I did not reject Russia; Russia did not reject me. I was rejected by the cruel and practically-unchanged system. I frankly believed in the possibility to change it and in the good intentions of its new leaders. I was wrong.

So, what is this book about? It is about one man's struggle with hypocrisy and fear, it is a story of disillusionment. Yes, I think we have all been duped by Gorbachev's propaganda. It was a case of conscious self-deception on the part of the people of the West and of the Soviet Union. After the long and dark years of the Cold War it was very tempting to think that at last the USSR was on its way to democracy and was no longer an immediate danger to peace and stability in the world. The events of the last two years have shattered these beliefs. It appears that Gorbachev is not a saviour, but a disaster. As soon as his power as an unelected leader was endangered by the progress of his own mild reforms, he put the whole mechanism into reverse and has travelled the whole way from vicious attacks on the progressive press at the end of 1989 to the bloody suppression of independence movements in the Baltic republics in the winter of 1990/91.

It is painful to have one's illusions shattered. It feels like being deceived by a trusted friend. But realism should prevail in the long run. So this is a book about how a dreamer was turned into a realist. I am not ashamed of my former beliefs.

In the Preface to my first book, *Special Correspondent,* I commented that books on Russia written by emigrants tended to be prejudiced. Now I've left Russia myself. But I do not think of myself as an emigrant. An emigrant is someone who has left his country of his own volition. I was thrown out – not by the country, but by the system. I am more an outcast than an emigrant.

It is also easy to accuse someone like me of being a disenchanted lover, trying to settle old scores with the former object of his affections. But my love for Russia has in no way been affected by my ordeal. Not a disenchanted lover, then, but a man forcibly separated from his sweetheart, a separation which makes my love even stronger.

In *Special Correspondent* I also promised to carry on with my investigations into miscarriages of justice in the Soviet Union. You will find those individual investigations here – camps for political prisoners, the workings of the KGB, punitive psychiatry, racism and anti-semitism. But what this book really shows is how the whole system is unjust. It is not a treatise or a political analysis. It is a cry; a cry of a dying country, a cry of pain and anger, a cry of a forced exile.

Initially I was planning to write about all the little things that would help you understand the atmosphere and conditions under which we were living. Some of these stories you will find investigated in more detail later, but here's just a selection so you can understand what it was like:

– the catastrophic state of the Soviet economy after over five years of Gorbachev's power – with 996 out of 1000 basic consumer goods missing from ordinary shops at the end of 1990;[1] with potentially the richest country in the world facing starvation and the worst winter since the Second World War; with food rationing introduced in all areas for the first time in nearly forty years;

– the unprecedented rise of crime in 1990 (12.3 per cent over 1989 and 45 per cent over 1988), when 775 militiamen were killed and 6799 wounded on duty;[2]

– the huge wave of ethnic unrest sweeping over the Soviet Union, when in Azerbaijan, Tajikistan, Kirgizia, Moldavia, Uzbekistan, Armenia and Georgia people were getting killed in hundreds during 1990 and

600,000 became refugees in their own country; when the freedom-loving Baltic republics were subjected to blockade and intervention by the Moscow government against a background of growing fear of a military takeover; when four paratroop divisions and two regiments were relocated to Moscow in September 1990;[3]

– the unseen number of emigrants using every opportunity to flee the imminent bloodbath, when over thirty days in June and July 1990 there were eleven attempts to hijack planes from the Soviet Union;[4] when the flow of Jewish emigrants arriving in Israel at a rate of between 2000 and 3000 a day kept growing, triggered by unfettered anti-semitism; when the Western countries – even Germany – expect millions of Soviet refugees in 1991;[5]

– when several hundred desperate Muscovites, fed up with their unsolvable problems, were simultaneously filing applications to emigrate to Lithuania, despite being a long way from real independence and suffering violent Communist Party pogroms;[6]

– when the atomic blast at a nuclear plant in Ust-Kamenogorsk (Kazakhstan) on 12 September 1990, where 120,000 people were contaminated and the consequences officially silenced for about a fortnight – as at Chernobyl in 1986;[7] the accidental release of a biological warfare agent from the secret testing site near Aralsk (also Kazakhstan) in mid-September 1990 with many casualties*;[8] the illicit underground nuclear test in Novaya Zemlya on 24 October 1990;[9] the hasty withdrawal of nuclear weapons from 'trouble spots' in the Soviet Union, when practically no 'untroubled spots' remained;[10]

– the continuing military build-up, disguised by the lip service paid to disarmament and 'the end of the Cold War', when in 1990 the Soviet Union developed four new long-range nuclear missiles[11] and three aircraft carriers[12] and allocated ninety-eight billion roubles (38 per cent of the annual budget) to 1991 military spending.[13] (In the first five years of Gorbachev's rule, there occurred a 45 per cent increase in military production. Five hundred and ninety intercontinental ballistic missiles – sixty-eight in the USA – have been made. Each year it produced about 3000 tanks – 20 per cent more than five years ago.) In 1989 the country built 700 short-range ballistic missiles (USA – none), 5700 armoured personnel carriers (USA – 725) and 1550 artillery installations (USA – 100);[14]

– the ongoing military and financial support to Cuba, Afghanistan and

* The development, production and stockpiling of biological weapons was outlawed by the 1972 Convention, to which more than a hundred countries – including the Soviet Union – are now signatories.

Iraq, when the main military might of the Iraqi army consisted of military technology, delivered by the USSR and serviced by several thousand Soviet military advisers;[15] when at the time of the Gulf Crisis, with the whole world joining efforts to curb the Iraqi aggressors, the USSR was continuing to train Iraqi troops at a naval base near Riga and frantically attempting to save Saddam Hussein's power.[16] An opinion poll conducted by the All-Union Public Opinion Studies Centre in August 1990 showed that 52 per cent of all Soviet people held the USSR 'largely or partly responsible for the Iraqi invasion of Kuwait'.[17] Against this background, the Nobel Committee's decision to award Gorbachev the 1990 Nobel Peace Prize looks, to put it mildly, preposterous. He has become an emperor without an empire, a dictator with enormous power, but without any authority, a leader without followers in his own country. This is the result of his indecisiveness, his playing possum and his frantic desire to preserve a doomed system;

– Tatiana Ivanova, the well-known Soviet literary critic, exclaimed in one of her articles addressing General Makashov, an outspoken hard-liner: 'What kind of a life is it that we are leading now? It's better to kick the bucket. Shoot us all, comrade General, to the devil's mother! Terminate our sufferings!';[18]

– in October 1990 the newspaper *Komsomolskaya Pravda* published letters in response to an article by a twenty-five-year-old who had made a failed suicide attempt. One of the letters ran: 'If our country is not capable of improving our lives, it might at least help us to end them';[19]

– Stanislav Govorukhin, a prominent Soviet film director, said in the commentary to his film *One Must Not Live Like This*:

The [Soviet] regime's most atrocious crime is the creation of a new human type. Seventy years of faulty genetic evolution cannot be corrected. It is a vast and rich country. Forests, waters, fish, fur, 50 per cent of the world's black earths, colossal mineral resources, oil, gas, gold – and appalling, shameful and humiliating poverty denigrating human dignity. When a country is rich, but the people live poorly – this is a crime – leaving nothing but vodka for the people, training them for years to drink heavily to forget their misery, to stop thinking, seeing or hearing anything – and then organising the distribution of two bottles per person in the most humiliating and outrageous form. Aren't they making other people behave like savages, criminal and barbarian savages themselves? There are also monstrous atrocities committed in this country: the genocide, the mass killings, the man-made famine which exterminated millions, the destruction of the economy and culture, the corruption of whole nations – [which] cannot be compared, in either scale or cruelty, with Hitler's crimes, especially because ours were committed against our own people.[20]

– G.F. Nikolayev, the editor-in-chief of the magazine *Zvezda* (The Star): 'Ideals – ideology – totalitarianism – crash. This is the inevitable result of the system which treats a human being not like its highest aim, but as a tool.'[21]

This is the system which Gorbachev was trying to save by giving the people a little bit of freedom. But freedom cannot be cut into bits. It is either there or it isn't. 'Half freedom' or 'quarter freedom' is nonsense. Halves and quarters are all right for pubs and McDonalds, but, if applied to freedom, meaningless and even ruinous. The collapse of the Soviet Union is the best proof of this. It is also a warning to those in the West who get easily carried away by Soviet political rhetoric.

So, now I'm out and there are many people to thank. Australia for me is like a pretty, sun-tanned teenage girl, still angular and immature, but one can see that she is going to grow into a real beauty. She is a very kind-hearted and cheerful country, with enough warmth for all her prodigal brothers and sisters. It is her whom I'd like to thank most of all for harbouring us, for giving us home and hope.

I am ever grateful to Monica Phlaum, Annabel O'Brien, Joe Rodigari and all the staff of the Migration Department of the Australian High Commission in London. Their trust and friendly, humane approach have enabled me to lead a normal life and hence to write *Dateline Freedom*. They will remain my friends for the rest of my days.

I am very much obliged to my new colleagues from the *Melbourne Age* and the *Sydney Morning Herald*, thanks to whom I quickly started feeling at home in Australia and came to grips with the personal computer, my new writing tool, as well as with my new duties as an Australian 'journo'. Here my special thanks go to Michael Smith, the editor of the *Age* and a personal friend whose taciturn, but warm, sincere and highly professional management of one of the world's biggest newspapers have won my deepest respect and admiration.

I have made lots of new friends in Melbourne, Sydney and Canberra, but here I'd like to name only two of them – Michael Danby, a young Melbourne editor, journalist and politician, and his wife Sandy. Without these two delightful people, this book would hardly have been possible. Their main concern was to help me negotiate the notorious 'tyranny of distance', which, it seems to me, is the biggest of Australia's problems. Michael and Sandy supplied me with books, magazines and newspaper clippings, and so kept me abreast of what was going on in the Soviet Union and around the world.

While writing I was constantly thinking of my two very best friends –

Martin Walker, a great British journalist and a wonderful person, and Alexander Kabakov, a great Russian writer and a wonderful person. I won't say anything more about them since they both are heroes of this book.

My wife Natasha and my ten-year-old son Mitya, who have been sharing with me the vicissitudes of our new life in new surroundings, are above all praise. My life would have been a misery without their support and understanding. They are my inseparable part, my heart, my brain and my soul.

My mother Rimma, who is still in Moscow waiting for permission to join us in Australia, had enough courage to give her maternal endorsement of my decision to leave. She gave it fully aware of the long period of solitude awaiting her. She is with me every minute – in my thoughts and in my dreams.

Kate Mosse, my sympathetic editor and publisher, Clarissa Rushdie, my faithful literary agent, and Alex Hippsley-Cox, my enthusiastic publicist deserve my gratitude and are to be commended for their sympathy, faith and enthusiasm.

Before I start my narrative, I'd like to thank one more person, someone I met only once. His name is John Gibson and he is a feature writer for the *Edinburgh Evening News*. He interviewed me in Edinburgh in February 1990 during the promotion tour for my first book, *Special Correspondent*. I was the 'first live, in-the-flesh Russian' he had ever met and in his interview, published on 1 March 1990, he wrote:

I don't know about you, but what's happening in Russia worries me. To the extent that I can't sleep sound for thinking that some morning I am going to wake up and find that the balloon has gone up. I walked him [ie me – VV] back to his hotel. He summoned an uneasy smile for the handshake. 'C'mon, you are thinking this is all traditional Russian gloom and doom but the true picture is much gloomier. If you're afraid to switch on your TV first thing in the morning, how do you think I feel?' Mark the man's words. I hope he lives to write another book.

Thank you for your hope, John. As you see, I've lived up to it.

Vitali Vitaliev

1

The Twists and Crazy Turns of Perestroika

She used to come every night, around ten o'clock. I could see her very well from my first floor window, dressed in an old red kerchief running threadbare all over her head and a flimsy blue overcoat with patches and holes. Looking around like a troubled bird, she stealthily approached the wall of our house where we kept the tin plate of rotten food for the stray cats. Having hastily snatched the plate with her shaking hands, she quickly emptied its contents into a plastic bag and, pressing it tightly to her breast, hurried away.

She was old, somewhere in her seventies, and thin as a rake. These cat's scraps must have been her only food for the whole day. But from her gait and manners, from her shyness and obvious reluctance to be noticed, it was plain that she was not an ordinary beggar (there were lots of them in Moscow that autumn, sitting in the streets or warming themselves in Metro passageways). She was clearly ashamed to steal and obviously had to do so for survival only.

We could not offer her food: it was obvious she would refuse it. Instead, we started putting some bread and sausage or an occasional piece of meat on the old tin plate shortly before her usual 'collection time'. And you should have seen how happy she looked having picked up these 'heaven-sent' gifts, though more than once quick and greedy local cats beat her to it and she was left holding her empty bag.

Who was she? Most likely just another lonely pensioner who had worked all her life, but now couldn't keep body and soul together on her token pension of seventy roubles a month, one of the forty-one million Soviet citizens living below the official poverty line.[1] And for me she was also an incarnation of Russia herself.

It was October 1989, the end of the fifth year of Gorbachev's reforms. The whole country was starving. Of 1200 basic consumer items only fifty were on sale,[2] but even they could be acquired only after hours of queuing. Verbal exchanges, abuse and even scuffles became normal in these never-ending lines.

At the very same time the hungry and frustrated country was shocked to learn that members of the elite, the Party and Soviet officials, issued a secret decree sharply increasing their salaries. Monthly wages of a District Executive Committee Chairman grew from 340 to 500 roubles. His Deputy would get 500 roubles instead of 270. The pay for instructors at a Regional Communist Party Committee was raised from 250 roubles to 400, that of a Department head from 380 to 600, that of a Regional Committee Secretary from 450 to 750, and that of a First Secretary from 550 to 850.[3] The same levels of increase applied to KGB officials, where the most minor functionaries were now entitled to a minimum of 400 roubles a month.

For comparison I must add that as a leading journalist on the top Soviet magazine *Krokodil*, which sold more than five million copies of each issue, I earned 160 roubles a month.

I hope these figures don't seem dry to you. To me they look eloquent enough. They illustrate that the communist rulers had betrayed their poor people for the umpteenth time, widening the gulf between themselves and their slaves, between the haves and the have-nots, paving the way to civil war.

Only this time the betrayal was slightly different. It was done covertly, overnight, at a time when the biggest issue on the agenda at the newly-elected Congress of People's Deputies was where to find extra money to feed the homeless and the poor.

This shameful act of high treason towards the people was committed with Gorbachev's tacit approval. The architect of perestroika's own salary also suffered a more than two-fold increase, and by June 1990[4] had reached 2500 roubles a month. It was a devastating blow to me as a pro-perestroika journalist. My already failing hopes and aspirations were shattered beyond repair.

The spiritual atmosphere in Moscow in autumn 1989 was quite exciting, despite the impending chaos. Glasnost, no matter how limited and incomplete, was bringing its first fruits. It made a tremendous impact on my daily journalistic routine. I kept writing regularly for *Krokodil*, but was also doing a lot for the Western media. Not a single day passed without one or two telephone interviews which I used to give straight from my tiny Moscow flat. I was also appearing regularly on the *Saturday Night Clive* show. It was broadcast from Ostankino TV studios in Moscow by satellite.

Usually the technicians on both sides had lots of problems with sound which was pretty off-putting for me as a contributor. Also the producers of the show were rather naughty in the beginning. When they first called me in Moscow and suggested that I should appear on the programme, I had a rather vague idea of what kind of show it was. They told me it was going to be a serious political interview, so I put on a suit and tie and a sombre Soviet look and went to the studio. But after the first questions, I smelt a rat: they didn't sound serious. I changed my attitude and went back to my usual ironic self.

As a presenter Clive James was very helpful. He was always trying to reassure me before the actual interview started. It was uncomfortable to realise that they could see me in London on their monitor whereas I was sitting alone in the studio facing the camera and could only hear Clive in the earphone – not very clearly at that. When Clive asked me once whether it was true that people were constantly watched in Russia, my answer was that I was not so sure about Russia but dead sure that I was being watched in Britain at the moment. Saying that, I didn't touch wood (there were no wooden objects in the studio), and pretty soon had to regret it.

One evening in September I had a call from the BBC in London. We were talking for about three minutes about a possible interview later that day, when my interlocutor was distracted by someone and asked me to hold on. While I was waiting for him to come back I suddenly heard the whole of our conversation – his questions and my answers – on a very low level in the receiver. When my would-be interviewer came back on the line, I asked him whether he was recording our conversation. He said 'No, why?' 'Never mind, just asking,' I answered.

A couple of months later when the KGB started harassing me in the open and the experience was repeated, I recalled that small incident as a first sobering signal for someone who had been intoxicated by glasnost and lost his sense of reality.

Indeed, the reality was misleading enough to make one drunk (though spirits as well as most of the basic foodstuffs were unavailable). Pro-democracy meetings and rallies were held in Moscow practically every day. The people in Pushkin Square and in Arbat – the new Soviet Speakers' Corner – were heatedly (sometimes even too heatedly) discussing recent political events: the session of the Congress of People's Deputies, the tension between Gorbachev and Yeltsin, the latest statement of academician Sakharov and the never-ending privileges of the elite.

Moscow was swarming with Western journalists and TV crews filming prostitutes, gangsters, neo-fascists and other newly-acknowledged Soviet realities. At one stage, I was working as a consultant with an Australian Channel 9 crew filming prostitutes at Leningradski railway terminal. We were in Komsomolski Square setting our cameras and microphones when all of a sudden a minibus halted next to us and another Australian TV crew climbed out with their cameras ready. The two crews were unaware of each other's presence in Moscow.

'What are you doing here, mates?' our cameraman enquired. 'Filming prostitutes,' his opposite number replied. 'And you?' 'Filming prostitutes as well.' My friend Alexander Kabakov very aptly called this and similar developments the 'crazy turns of perestroika'. By the way, his own rise to fame as a writer could also be treated as one of these crazy turns.

After seventeen years of writing for himself, Alexander Kabakov became famous overnight in June last year with the publication of his short novel *The Man Who Wouldn't Return* in a small circulation magazine called *Iskusstvo Kino* (*The Art of Cinema*). The scenario was one of bloody civil war in Moscow in 1993 where neither food nor money was available. There is rationing, though the ration cards can buy practically nothing. The newly-established dictator, General Panayev (something of a Ligachev figure), who had come to power after a rightwing coup in 1992, travels around Moscow in an armoured personnel carrier escorted by horsemen, since there is no longer enough petrol for cars.

At the time the manuscript first started circulating in Moscow there was more cause for optimism about the future of the USSR. His friends asked him sceptically if he really believed that these things would come to pass.

'Yes, it is all very likely,' he said. 'There is going to be bloodshed. Gorbachev has let go the reins and now the huge bulky cart of so-called Socialism is rolling down the slope, gaining speed uncontrollably and disintegrating on the way.'

Developments since then have confirmed his futuristic insights and led to comparisons with Orwell. You have only to read Kabakov's projection of a 1993 Moscow Radio broadcast.

> Yesterday in the Kremlin the First Founding Congress of the Russian Union of Democratic Parties began work. Delegates from all political parties of Russia are participating: the Christian Democratic Party of Transcaucasia, the Social-Fundamentalists of Turkestan, the Constitutional Party of the United Bukhara and Samarkand Emirates, the Catholic Radicals of the Baltic Federation and the Leftist Communists of Siberia (Irkutsk).

This was written long before the First Congress of People's Deputies, when the Nationalist Movements in the country were still rather tame and unformed.

4

The novel's other striking prophecy was its vision of former Afghanistan soldiers killing people in the streets with sappers' shovels. After the tragic events in Tbilisi in April 1989, where twenty demonstrators were killed by the soldiers in exactly this manner, many were inclined to think that Kabakov had added the sappers' shovels *post factum*.

The Man Who Wouldn't Return was the first anti-Utopian novel to appear since the limited licence afforded by glasnost. Its publication perfectly caught the mood of apathy and fear – and growing disenchantment with Gorbachev. It also articulated the conviction that the KGB still held ultimate power in the USSR, and would continue to do so for the foreseeable future. The main problem has been getting hold of copies, even though distribution has been aided by the large number of treasured photocopied versions in circulation. The British Ambassador had to rely on such a copy when he read the book that autumn.

For Kabakov public acclaim has been a long time coming. For almost fifteen years he worked on the railway newspaper *Gudok* (*The Whistle*), as editor of the satirical Page 4, writing fiction in his tiny cubicle of an office after working hours. These novels were then read aloud to a handful of friends in Kabakov's hospitable flat in Ostankino, his friends drinking tea or vodka, while Kabakov read to the assembled audience his latest piece of futurology.

After these reading sessions the manuscripts were taken to the gloomy *Gudok* office and safely locked in one of the drawers of his desk. They were unpublishable. Why? Because they were the writings of a free man without complexes. We – his friends – were all suffering from complexes, deeply rooted in us by the system. We were either frightened or inhibited, or both. Kabakov's main quality was complete spiritual freedom and utter integrity.

How did he manage to acquire this freedom? His life was in no sense special or unusual. His father was an army officer and Kabakov's family was constantly moving from one military town to another until finally they settled in Dnepropetrovsk. This southern Ukranian city with a tongue-twister of a name had a big influence on Kabakov's writing.

He graduated and became an engineer, a job he never enjoyed. After a period working at a secret military factory, he had a one-night stand with a Swedish beauty in Rossiya Hotel in Moscow – an indiscretion which became known to his bosses in Dnepropetrovsk the following day. He was sacked.

Soon after he went to live in Moscow and was effectively jobless for several years. He was attracted to jazz and quickly became one of the country's leading connoisseurs. Jazz was special at the time – it was something which united young people and was frowned upon by the authorities. Jazz fans travelled all over the country to watch the performances of popular groups. These concerts were usually held in small seedy halls and Kabakov was always the Master of Ceremonies. It was through jazz that he befriended Vassily Aksyonov, the brilliant Russian writer now living in America. It was through jazz that he started writing seriously. *Youth Café*, with its subtitle *Jazz Legend*, reveals a lot about his early years in Dnepropetrovsk.

He started writing journalism, but no Moscow newspaper wanted to employ him because of two serious drawbacks: he was both a Jew and a non-Party member. Finally he was lucky enough to be taken on on the staff of *Gudok*.

It was there that I first met Kabakov in 1981. I was a tyro journalist and, just like Kabakov had been at the end of the sixties, was practically jobless. I was in desperate need of money.

He greeted me as a friend and immediately offered me a job writing a column for his page. Though he doesn't like me to mention it now, he practically saved me at the time. And not only me. It's hard to name all the people whom he helped while working at *Gudok*. His tiny office was more like a club. People were always crowding in there and no-one left without friendly advice.

To increase its circulation, *Gudok* used to send a team of Page 4 contributors to different parts of the country for public appearances and comic recitals. It was during these trips that Kabakov and I became especially friendly. Once, in Gorky, where for some reason we were performing in the local circus, we had a three-hour break between the shows. 'Come, I shall read you something,' he said. We went to a nearby park, sat on a bench and Kabakov produced pieces of paper covered with his tiny handwriting. In his low, guttural voice he started reading.

Kristapovich's Approach was a thriller, but there was much more to it than that. It was the story of a man whose sole aim in life was to fight the secret police. The novel was a real cliffhanger and I was sure it would have become a best-seller if published in the West. As for Russia, in 1984 there was still no chance; it was essentially an anti-KGB novel.

The Man Who Wouldn't Return, however, became the Russian novel of the year. You can often hear in Moscow streets today a popular phrase: 'Oh, it's exactly like in Kabakov's novel.' People say that on learning of yet another wave of national unrest or renewed food shortages.

The long-awaited fame came to Kabakov, but he is not going to be spoiled by it. His only regret is that the main message of the novel – its anti-KGB stance – had been overlooked by most critics. Briefly, the plot concerns a Moscow engineer who invents the means of travelling into the future. He is immediately approached by KGB men who want to send him to 1993 to spy on what's going on there. Despite a terrible ordeal in the Moscow Civil War he prefers to defect to the future, to the terrible bloodbath, rather than return to 1988 where the KGB are still in power. 'Here [in 1993] I was not afraid of them [the KGB]. I've got used to the feeling of danger. Here I could always lie down and tightly press my body to the ground.'

'There is a terrible dilemma now facing every person of renown,' Kabakov said in one of his 1989 interviews. 'At some point you must choose whether to become an informer or leave the country.'

Yes, in the past Kabakov had also had his share of KGB harassment. But despite all this he is trying to be optimistic: 'My aim was to frighten people, to warn them. It's much better than to reap the terrible fruits of disaster. Who knows maybe if someone had warned us of the impending danger of Stalinism fifty-five years ago – the Terror itself could have been avoided.' *The Man Who Wouldn't Return* is more than mere fiction. Shortly before my departure from Moscow I asked Sasha what he would change in the novel if he were to write it now in 1990.

'I would have changed the time of the Civil War from 1993 to 1991,' he said.

I could not help noticing how the ignominious privileges of the elite against which I had been fighting for many years were coming to life again. In the autumn of 1989 many special shops for the elite closed several years before under pressure from the progressive press, were reopening their doors for the executive bureaucrats. As for the hated hospitals, clinics and sanatoriums of the Fourth Department of the Health Ministry, catering exclusively for the rulers, they didn't even bother to close them temporarily. Overnight (most of the mean things in the Soviet Union still happen overnight, just like under Stalin) they were transferred from the Fourth Department of the Health Ministry to the newly-formed Medical-Sanitation Association of the USSR Council of Ministers (MSA) and the former head of the Fourth Department became Director-General of MSA.[5] The signs on the doors were changed, but all the rest remained as it was, though the rulers hurried to claim that the Fourth Department had been liquidated.

This was clearly the end of the process of social renovation which had been started several years before. What initially was widely perceived as a revolution was proving to be no more than a meagre attempt to save the system.

The opening of the new five-star hotel smack in the centre of Moscow that autumn was another example of the elite's all-pervading hypocrisy. In fact it was not a new hotel, the Savoy's modern interior was simply stuffed into the time-beaten walls of the old Berlin Hotel. It was luxurious even by Western standards: marble, gilt, wood panels etc. The hotel had a very plush restaurant with a mirrored ceiling and a great fountain with golden fish in the middle. It could also boast a real English-style pub and the first and only casino in the Soviet Union. Gambling was – and is still – illegal and constituted a major criminal offence in Russia, but the Savoy's foreign guests were exempt from Soviet laws. This casino has quickly become a star attraction for members of the Moscow underworld and one can observe them losing hundreds of dollars there in a matter of minutes.

For normal Soviet citizens, of course, the Savoy was as inaccessible as the Moon. And not only because it was guarded day and night by the burly, Cerberus-like KGB 'doormen', but also because roubles were not accepted. And that was probably for the best, since the contrast between the hotel and coming out into a Moscow street with its ubiquitous lines for food snaking in all directions and with the stinking 'ordinary' canteen just opposite, was hair raising. Some of my Western friends who visited the Savoy assured me that nowhere else in the world had they come across such a striking disparity.

The canteen in question was called Pelmennaya. It was always crowded, extremely dirty and emitted unbearable smells. The distance from the plush main entrance of the Savoy was just five metres across the road.

While on an inspection tour of the Savoy (for an article I was preparing which has never seen the light in Russia) I met there, in the bar, a curious pair – two young guys one of whom was no-one else but the grandson of Leonid Ilyich Brezhnev, Andrei, and the other no-one else but the son of academician Sakharov, Dima. They were friends.

We got talking and they told me a number of moving stories. When academician Sakharov was exiled by Brezhnev to Gorky, Dima (naturally!) was thrown out of the University and publicly ostracised. The only person who offered him help was . . . Brezhnev's grandson Andrei. Now – in 1989 – the situation was reversed: it was Andrei who was jobless and booed as the scion of 'the creator of stagnation'. But Dima Sakharov who was 'on the horse', as we say in Russia, didn't leave his friend in trouble. For me it sounded like a good human story.

Several days later Andrei Brezhnev invited me to his flat which was still full of mementoes of his grandfather, from a shiny Mercedes (grandpa's gift) in the garage to the collection of old wines and cognacs, some of which dated back to the last century. Sipping wine, Andrei told me how he and Dima had grown up together in Zhukovka, a village not far from Moscow where both the Sakharovs and the Brezhnevs had their dachas. The summer cottage of Mstislav Rostropovich, where Solzhenitsyn lived for several years, was just round the corner. One evening Andrei, having run out of matches, went out into the village street to ask for a light. In the dark alley, not far from Rostropovich's dacha, he saw a black Volga with three smoking men sitting in it. He went over, bent down to the car's window and asked for a light and at that very moment he clearly heard Solzhenitsyn's voice, saying something to Rostropovich, coming out of the car's radio. I thought the story was fascinating, though I couldn't know then how topical it would prove for me in the very near future.

The big portrait of Andrei's grandfather in hunting apparel was hanging on the wall. Brezhnev the elder was smiling magnanimously from the photo looking very harmless and homely. It was difficult to imagine that this was the same man who had led the country to catastrophe, who had stamped his iron foot on Czechoslovakia in 1968 and had invaded Afghanistan in 1979.

'I hate Gorbachev', Andrei said after a pause. 'He has ruined this country.'

'But was your granddad better?' I asked.

'At least there was food in the shops under him.' He shrugged his shoulders and downed his glass in one quick gulp.

Another event which occurred that same autumn and left a deep imprint on my soul was a trip to the Moscow suburban town where I spent the first three years of my life. I went there with my mother on a gloomy rainy day in September.

This was the place where my parents were sent to work shortly after they got married in 1952. My father was a nuclear physicist and was involved in developing the first Soviet atomic bomb. There was a secret factory in that very town where he was conducting his research and my mother worked as a chemical engineer. Times were tough. Stalin wanted to develop nuclear weapons by hook or by crook to achieve military parity with the West and then, ultimately, superiority over it. My parents had to work for twelve hours a day and there was practically no protection against the excessive radiation. My mother told me how skin peeled off her palms while she was pregnant with me (so I must have got my tiny share of the stuff too). She also told me about the people who literally died before her eyes from overdoses. My father was particularly affected, since he had to deal directly with radioactive substances. He died at the early age of fifty-six.

Regardless of the ever-present danger, the people who worked at the factory had their lives to live. They were all young and cheerful, they fell in love, they cried bitterly when Stalin died. Also they were scientists and the job was interesting. They couldn't possibly perceive what a deadly weapon they were creating. Of course, I don't remember much from these distant years; I was too young. But strangely enough I could recall some smells, feelings and vague images when I came there after thirty-three years of absence.

The factory was still there and the whole town was still surrounded by the thick concrete wall with barbed wire on top. You could get in only through a couple of checkpoints, provided you had an invitation from someone living inside. We were invited by a woman who worked with my parents many years ago and still remembered them.

At the checkpoint, a young military guard, having carefully scrutinised our invitation and credentials, gave us a one-day pass and let us in. 'It hasn't changed a bit in thirty-three years,' my mother noted sadly.

Things inside the town remained equally unchanged. The factory itself was still located in the grounds of the old monastery. Some church buildings, which many years ago used to belong to the monastery, still dominated the landscape. Only instead of crosses, they had red metallic stars mounted on their domes – just like on the Moscow Kremlin. What sacrilege to use churches (even deconsecrated ones) for the production of such weapons.

My mother recognised the house where we used to live. Yes, it was still there, though the people who inhabited it thirty-three years ago were for the most part no longer listed among the living.

This truth we learnt from the lady who had invited us. She was the only one still alive of those who had worked with my father. The treacherous effects of radiation, dormant for many years, finally came to the surface and destroyed them. Very few lived to his or her sixtieth birthday. And the lady herself? Yes, she was alive, but she looked eighty years old, no more than a skeleton covered with skin. Her hands were trembling incessantly and her skull was practically bald. She was a far cry from the smiling plump young girl on the old, yellowish photo my mother had once shown me. And, God, what a miserable life she led. Alone in the whole world, without any relatives or friends, she was dwelling in a tiny, one-room kitchenette. Books were piled everywhere: on the shelves, on the bedstead and under the table. There was not a single romance or thriller, nothing which could pass as pulp or easy reading. It was almost exclusively art, history or philosophy – very esoteric stuff.

She offered us tea and produced a small packet from the drawer saying

10

that it was her monthly ration. Having wasted all her youth and strength for the sake of the system, what did she get in return? A seventy-five rouble pension, a tiny hole of a flat, a kilogram of greyish sausage and one bloody packet of tea a month!

But nevertheless she said she was happy. 'I have lots of books and lots of memories – what else do I need?'

I was ready to kneel before this old Russian woman, who was not so very old at all. Yes, then I suddenly saw that she was genuinely beautiful despite her ugly looks. Her beauty came from within, from a curious, intangible and indescribable thing which is sometimes called Russian soul. How lucky our rulers must be to have such kind and patient people as their underlings. How inhumanly cruel they must be to abuse this unparalleled patience for so many years. But even Russian patience has its limits. How long will it be before it finally runs out?

You should have seen how the woman's eyes brightened up when I promised to send her two volumes of the collected works of ancient philosophers of which I had a spare copy. I couldn't help feeling that I was looking into the eyes of the same old lady who picked up the cat's scraps from the plate under my window. There was a deep reproach somewhere at the bottom of those eyes as if they were yelling: 'What have they done to us?'

As I continued to gather bits and pieces of information about all those frightening occurrences that were starting to permeate our lives, I couldn't help noticing how tragi-comic everyday life was becoming. Russian humour has always been distinctive, but during 1990 there was a growing sense of the absurd, of people laughing now through tears. There was little – if anything – to really laugh about, but laughter in Russia is the only way to outlive the sombre reality.

But isn't it a bitter irony that by the end of 1990 – forty-five years after the end of the War – defeated Germany was helping one of the victorious Allies to avoid famine by sending over to the Soviet Union the Berlin strategic reserves, put together in 1948 in case of . . . a Soviet blockade!

When in September 1990 tens of thousands of troops in combat gear appeared around Moscow, the absurd official explanation, published in the Soviet press, was that they were helping with the potato harvest. Potato pickers in flak jackets![6]

On returning from his trip to the Soviet Far East and being genuinely appalled by the slums, desolation and empty shops he saw there, Boris Yeltsin, the President of the Russian Federation, declared that the solution was 'to create a special committee on Far Eastern affairs under the auspices of the Council of Ministers'![7] The Russian President was sure that by creating another bureaucratic body he would resolve all the pressing problems of the region. Or maybe he simply needed someone who could eventually be blamed for failing to resolve them? What a wonderful example of an apparatchik's mentality!

When food shortages in Moscow reached their peak in summer 1990, the city council decided to issue a special cardboard visiting card to every Muscovite over fourteen years of age. Such a card, with the bearer's photo, would serve as proof of Moscow registration and give the right to acquire scarce foodstuffs in the shops. The cards have never come into being. And do you know why? They couldn't find enough cardboard to make them![8]

In January 1990 'the most shameful scandal in the economic life of the country' (as the then Prime Minister Rizhkov put it) broke in Moscow. It was connected with the ANT cooperative, set up by the government to conduct barter trade with foreign countries. After investigation into its activities, it was discovered that the cooperative had been involved in the illegal export of diamonds, precious metals and tanks.[9]

Indeed, the Soviet reality sometimes supersedes the wildest satirical fantasies. I remember going on a journalistic mission to a town in western Ukraine in the mid-eighties. There, in a restaurant, I got talking with a chap who happened to be the local Agricultural Machinery Factory Director. His factory produced combine harvesters. In accordance with the finicky procedures of the planned economy, they were receiving spare parts from different plants all over the country. One small component was especially difficult to procure. Even the hardened factory tolkachi (pushers), whose task was to roam the country in search of supplies, could not provide it. Somehow they found out that this detail was part of mini-tractors, assembled at a factory in the Urals. So the factory started ordering big consignments of these tractors, dismantling them, taking out the necessary component and throwing away all the rest. They have been working like that for years. Mind you, the mini-tractors were a very hard-to-get item in many parts of the country and were in big demand.

When I offered the Director to write a story on the absurdity of the whole procedure, he changed countenance and whined: 'No, don't, please don't! After such a story, they will stop sending us tractors and we won't be able to meet the plan targets in producing the bloody combines!'

In yet another instance, this time in Rostov-na-Donu, I was shown two factories standing side by side. One of them produced metallic hoops for wooden barrels, and the other wooden carcasses for the same barrels. You might think they would be cooperating. Nothing of the kind! The first factory sent its hoops to the Far East and the second received the same hoops from yet another factory in Moscow!

I found a similar, tragi-comic attitude when interviewing the Moscow Chief Narcologist (the doctor treating alcoholics) in 1986. After spending the whole day in his office listening to the visitors (mainly women) pleading with him to cure their husbands and sons of alcoholism, I was rather taken aback when the narcologist offered me a drink with him after work. When I refused he started drinking himself in his office and after a while got rather pissed. 'I . . . I am in ex . . . experiment . . .) he was babbling drunkenly. But my main surprise came when, on my way home through the grounds of his narcologic hospital, with many alcoholics in in-patient treatment, I found a working liquor shop where patients were buying spirits on their way back from work (they worked at a neighbouring factory as part of their treatment).

Next morning I telephoned the narcologist and shared my surprise with him saying that I would like to write about this outrageous contradiction. 'Please don't!' he pronounced quite coherently (he must have sobered up after yesterday's bout), 'the shop belongs to the District Council, and I don't want to spoil relations with them!'

I did write about the shop, and also a separate piece about the drinking narcologist. The latter was not published: the drunkard proved to be a member of the city's Party Committee . . .

There was an even funnier case in Kirov where, in 1981, I visited the local sobering station. The chief of the station, a chunky ruddy-faced militia colonel, told me lots of interesting things like, say, the fact that the sobering station worked on a self-accounting principle: the more drunks were picked up, the bigger the salaries of the personnel.

In the evening I had an unexpected visitor at my hotel. It was the colonel from the sobering station. He brought two bottles of vodka 'to maintain closer contacts'. I didn't want to be inhospitable. We sat down and had a couple of drinks. After his second glass his eyes suddenly grew hazy, he collapsed on to my unmade bed and started snoring loudly. I was in the stupidest situation: here in my hotel room I had the chief of the local sobering station drunk as a lord and sleeping on my bed in his uniform. What could I do? In the end, I simply phoned his colleagues at the station who picked up their chief and carried him, like a log, to the militia car. They were not in the least surprised by his condition.

In September 1990 it was announced by TASS news agency that medical data on 500,000 people exposed to radiation in the 1986 Chernobyl nuclear accident had been destroyed by teenage computer thieves who had burst into the Radiation Treatment Research Institute in

Minsk and erased the information from computer discs.[10] With computers (and hence computer thieves) practically unknown in the USSR, it was hard to imagine teenagers breaking into an Institute simply to erase computer files. Even if they did know how to do this, it wouldn't be simple to achieve. But now the authorities have a good (though implausible) excuse not to treat the contaminated people and spend money and rare drugs on them.

On 12 October 1990 the Reuters news agency claimed that a little-known government department in the USSR specialises in supplying blue films to the country's elite. The films were supplied to government and Communist Party leaders, whereas for the public, sex still remained a taboo subject.[11] I recollected this on 5 December 1990 when on the Soviet TV news programme *Vremia*, which is broadcast via satellite to Australia, I heard about President Gorbachev's latest decree calling for the launch of an implacable struggle against pornography, eroticism and the low morals which had permeated the country of late.

The salespeople of the liquor store N1 in Nighni Novgorod (formerly Gorky) were about to lose their jobs in November 1990: not a single bottle of liquor (or even of beer) had been delivered to their shop for a long while. The ingenious vendors kept their heads and started selling funeral accessories instead.[12] Now, I reckon they don't have queues as long as they used to have when selling vodka.

The following story is so zany that I myself would have never taken it at face value, had it not been published in the most respected and reliable Soviet newspaper.

In the early hours of the morning of 1 November 1990, unknown wrongdoers sneaked into an ordinary-looking shed in Yaroslavl. They broke the lock and stole a ram and a bagful of rabbits. The thieves were probably hungry for there was absolutely nothing on sale in Yaroslavl food shops. Next day a local newspaper carried an announcement which read: 'The regional clinic of skin and venereal diseases informs the population that experimental animals – a ram and two dozen rabbits – have been stolen from our vivarium. The meat of these animals is inedible and can cause serious infections, if consumed.' As it appeared, the rabbits were used by venerologists in laboratory experiments and for these purposes were infected with syphilis. The Deputy Chief of the Yaroslavl militia commented that thefts of foodstuffs and domestic animals had become quite common in Yaroslavl since supplies had disappeared from the shops.[13]

In March 1991 new merchandise appeared at flea markets throughout the country: burnt-out electric bulbs (three roubles each) and empty vodka bottles (one rouble for a bottle). Since new electric bulbs were not available in shops, the only way to light a flat was to steal a bulb from one's work, replacing it with a burnt-out one to conceal the theft. As to the empty bottles, they had to be handed over when buying a full one on a ration card (one bottle a month per person), otherwise – no vodka. The trade in these two crucial items was flourishing.[14]

Spontaneous fluctuations of this antediluvian 'market' were matched by no less primitive moves of the country's leadership. At the end of January 1991 Gorbachev issued a decree withdrawing all fifty and one hundred rouble banknotes from circulation within three days, and virtually putting the banks under direct KGB control. The aim, as stated by the newly-appointed Prime Minister Pavlov, was to penalise speculators and the mafia allegedly dealing in high-denomination banknotes.[15] Well, what can I say? It's enough to make a cat laugh! As an expert in Soviet organized crime, I can assert with a full sense of responsibility: the mafia and the racketeers were never dealing in fifty or one hundred rouble notes (they were probably expecting such a move), preferring good old 'chervontsi', ten rouble notes, instead. Besides, miraculously, the underworld had managed to find out about the impending withdrawal several weeks before it was announced and had hastily changed the few big banknotes they had. The main blow fell on poor Russian babushkas, who had been saving some money for a rainy day or their own funerals, keeping the notes under their mattresses. Overnight they found themselves robbed of all their modest savings since it was inconceivable for them to try and change the money in three days with unimaginably long lines, scuffles and fights outside the few banks doing the exchange.

Enough to make a cat laugh indeed, but also quite enough to make millions cry.

The brave fighter against old babushkas, Prime Minister Pavlov, went even further. Confronted with world-wide condemnation, he claimed in an interview with *Trud* newspaper a week later that confiscation of high-denomination banknotes was aimed at foiling a western plot to overthrow Mikhail Gorbachev! No more, no less . . . Certain unnamed Canadian, Austrian and Swiss banks supposedly wanted to flood the Soviet market with billions of fifty and one hundred rouble banknotes to undermine the country's non-existing 'economic stability', so to eventually oust Gorbachev from his unelected presidency.[16] How about the insidious mafia? It was well forgotten. 'The claim would be laughable if it did not have such dire consequences', *The Economist* editorial stated bitterly. 'The

Soviet Union does not need devious western plotters to provide it with financial disaster. It has been doing a fine job on its own.'[17]

Pavlov's insane pronouncement was echoed by the KGB Lieutenant-General Savinkov, the head of the counter-espionage sixth directorate, saying in a newspaper interview on 12 March 1991, that the Western Intelligence Services were falling over themselves to steal Soviet technological secrets and know-how on a scale previously unseen.[18] One may wonder: what for? To drive the West to the same state of anarchy and collapse?

Indeed, all this might have sounded funny, had it not been so sad, had it not signified the return to the half-forgotten ways and rhetoric of the Cold War. Following recent events in the Soviet Union, one can't help feeling that one is watching the final agony of a dying body: hence the unpredictable twists in foreign and internal politics; hence the delirium of crazy allegations of Western conspiracies. It is amusing sometimes to watch how the Western media tries to analyse seriously these chaotic actions and random statements. Agony is beyond analysis. It is equally impossible to predict the movements of an agonizing giant: whether his right or left arm will twitch first before he dies . . .

Agony of a social monster, stuffed with nuclear weapons, is also very dangerous. I felt it was a bad sign when I heard of the sudden resignation of the Soviet Foreign Minister, Shevardnadze, at the end of December 1990. In his resignation speech Shevardnadze warned of impending dictatorship. 'We must be prepared for the worst now', I wrote in the *Guardian* on 22 December. 'Shevardnadze's resignation is bad enough in itself, but something much more sinister is about to happen.'[19]

In a couple of weeks the Soviet military intervention in the Baltics occurred. Tanks were crushing the singing crowds of unarmed Lithuanians in Vilnius. The black berets were shooting Latvian militiamen in Riga. Tracer-bullets were piercing brownish cognac-coloured sky and snow was heavily spotted with blood.

The timing for the bloody suppression of independence could not have been better chosen, coinciding as it did with the start of hostilities in the Gulf. Naturally, the brutal action in the Baltics caused much less attention and condemnation that it would do under normal circumstances.

Yes, the timing was devilishly clever, but not unprecedented. Remember the initial occupation of the Baltic republics in 1940, when the world's attention was distracted by the Nazi invasion of France? And the onslaught in Hungary at the moment of the Suez crisis in 1956? The killings started only days after Gorbachev's solemn promise not to use force in the Baltic (just as in the case with the blockade of Lithuania in spring 1990). The civilized world can contain only one bloody dictator at a time . . .

Had the Western politicians listened to the few voices of reason trying to warn them against deifying Gorbachev, against giving him the Nobel Peace Prize, the bloodshed in the Baltics, as well as the Gulf War, may well have been avoided. Yes, my deep conviction is that the Gulf crisis started not with the Iraqi invasion of Kuwait, but in spring 1990 with the Soviet blockade of Lithuania. By turning a deaf ear to the cries of help from the tiny Baltic country, the West unwittingly encouraged Saddam to proceed with his plans of invasion. Indeed, Hussein's line of thought could have been: if the Soviets can get away with the blockade, why can't I get away with the invasion? Freedom is a global concept. It cannot exist within the boundaries of this or that state only. If the ideal of freedom is sacrificed in one country, a chain reaction will follow. And there is not much difference between Iraq's proclaiming Kuwait its nineteenth province and the Soviets claiming their right to own republics which they forcibly annexed as a direct result of the ignominious Molotov–Ribbentrop pact or, in plain words, Stalin–Hitler collusion.

The use of Soviet troops against the peaceful civilians in the Baltics, as well as earlier in Tbilisi and Baku, cannot be justified by any human considerations. As to the political ones . . . well, when politics ceases to be human-oriented, it loses its essence and becomes nothing but a 'general line' of a dictator as opposed to the expression of popular will.

This brings me to the role of Gorbachev, who found himself unable to interrupt his lunch when Lithuanian President Landsbergis called him with the plea to stop the bloodshed. Bon appetit! Gorbachev publicly claimed he did not know about the attack in Vilnius and was asleep when his troops were murdering unarmed people.[20] The question arises: If that was so, what kind of president is he?

But the truth is simpler: the Shchit (Shield) military group investigation, conducted in February, proved that Gorbachev knew about the action in advance.[21] So I was not surprised to learn that the members of the investigation team were arrested by the KGB in Vilnius shortly after completion of their report.

But even without Shchit it was plain that Gorbachev was responsible. He neither punished, nor even publicly reprimanded the generals directly involved in the bloodshed. (He didn't do it after events in Tbilisi and Baku either, by the way.) On the contrary, on 4 February 1991 – only twenty days after the killings – he promoted Boris Pugo, ex-KGB general and his new Interior Minister, who had exercised direct command over the invading troops in Vilnius and Riga, to the rank of the colonel-general.

This was clearly a worthy presidential reward for the black cardinal behind the massacre.[22]

Reading about Pugo's promotion, I remembered the story of Loreta Asanaviciute, the twenty-four-year-old Lithuanian woman and one of the many victims of the bloodbath near Vilnius TV tower, a woman who will never turn twenty-five. The story was reported by the *Independent Magazine*:

> Shouting 'Fascistas' and 'Lietuva' (Lithuania), Loreta ran towards an armoured personnel vehicle, even as it spewed out tear gas. The commander, the eyes of a chanting crowd fixed steadfastly upon him, halted the vehicle. He disappeared inside, and it started to roll back. Everyone cheered. But then the wheels spun round and it lunged forward again. The wheels turned slowly, crushing Loreta's body little by little. Before she died she managed to throw a handful of flowers into the driver's viewfinder gap. She was the first of the 15 people who died that night.[23] Good on you, general . . .

Two days after Loreta's murder, Gorbachev, irritated by the criticism of the crackdown in the liberal Soviet press, tried to force Parliament to suspend the recently-passed press law and return to unyielding censorship 'to ensure the objectivity of news.'[24] He appointed Leonid Kravchenko, an inveterate hard-liner, as chief of the Soviet TV and Radio State Committee. One of Kravchenko's first actions was to ban *Vzgliad*, by far the most popular and liberal programme on Soviet TV, and to evict from the State Committee premises the independent Interfax news agency. The main news programme *Vremia* returned to its old Brezhnev-style pattern featuring heroic tractor drivers, enthusiastic workers and occasional petty criticisms of minor inefficiencies. *Moscow News* and *Ogonyok* were practically banned too: their many subscribers haven't received a single issue since the end of January 1991.

This was clearly not just the end of glasnost, but also the end of the five-year-old propaganda campaign ironically called 'perestroika'. As the prominent members of Moscow intelligentsia wrote in the open letter to their fellow-citizens, 'all our hopes are shattered. Now we see that perestroika, initiated in Moscow in April 1985, was shot in Vilnius on the night of 13 January 1991.'[25]

On 13 January 1991, Elena Bonner, academician Sakharov's widow, wrote a letter to the Chairman of the Nobel Committee. The letter was published in *Moskovskiye Novosti* (Moscow News):

> In 1975 Andrei Sakharov was awarded the Nobel Peace Prize. The government of the country, whose citizen Sakharov was, did not allow him to go to Oslo. In accordance with his will and under the high power of his attorney, I took part in the ceremony instead. Sakharov's volition is also

18

expressed in his testament, according to which I am the only heiress to his copyright, ie the right to publish all his works and to use his name.

Supported by his will and his certified trust, I am asking you to remove the name of Andrei Sakharov from the list of the Nobel Peace Prize Laureats. I deem it unacceptable for his name to stand in the same rank with the name of the CPSU General Secretary Mikhail Gorbachev, who as a head of state bears full responsibility for the bloodshed in his country (Karabakh, Tbilisi, Baku, Fergana, Uzen, Osh) and for today's events in Lithuania, staged to the scenario of Berlin in 1953, Budapest in 1956, Prague in 1968 and Kabul in 1979. Their tragic similarity completely excludes the existence of any ideology of 'new thinking'. I am ready to come to Oslo and return the medal and the Prize.[26]

Gorbachev's record in late 1990/early 1991 is that of uninterrupted movement to the extreme right. He nipped in the bud the so-called '500 Day Plan' of economic reform and transition to the market economy, a plan which was timid and mild in itself. He got rid of all of his reformist supporters and advisors: Shatalin, Petrakov, Yakovlev, Shevardnadze, Bakatin and many others – and instead appointed Yanayev and Pavlov, two notorious hard-liners, as his Vice-President and Prime Minister respectively, and two former high-ranking KGB officers Pugo and Bessmertnykh as his Interior and Foreign Ministers.

Yes, Alexander Bessmertnykh too has a long KGB career behind him. Let's open John Barron's well-argued and respected monograph *KGB Today. The Hidden Hand.* Among other things it describes the story of the famous KGB defector Stanislav Levchenko and tells how, after defecting to Washington in 1979, Levchenko was confronted with the local KGB resident who sought to talk him out of his decision. 'Instead of a heavy-handed operative from line KR, the KGB sent a suave colonel, Alexander Bessmertnykh, minister counsellor of the Soviet embassy.'[27]

Isn't it amazing that no-one in the West has noticed this so far? Or maybe people simply don't want to notice, preferring pleasant illusions to sad reality, when both internal and foreign policies of the world's biggest nuclear superpower are now in the hands of former KGB chieftains?

The people inside the Soviet Union are not as blind as some Western politicians, though. There were widespread protests following Gorbachev's decree to give the KGB sweeping powers, issued at the end of January 1991. This decree gives the KGB the right to enter premises without hindrance, if they deem it necessary for the investigation of 'economic crimes'.[28] By another decree, joint army and police patrols were sent onto the streets of the main cities and towns with the hidden aim of restricting the activities of political opposition and curbing antigovernment demonstrations.[29] Armed personnel carriers in Moscow streets. *Pace* my friend, Alexander Kabakov.

'Gorbachev, resign! No-one Believes You Any Longer!'; 'Gorbachev Is Our Saddam!'; 'Dictatorship Won't Win!'; 'You Will Never Wash Lithuanian Blood Off Your Hands!' Such were the banners carried by the participants of the 300,000 strong rally in the centre of Moscow at the end of January 1991. Similar – and even bigger – rallies swept over the country in February and March.

Miners all over the Soviet Union launched a political strike calling for Gorbachev's resignation in March 1991. 'Michail Sergeyevich! The crisis from which our country can't find its way out of,' the Workers' Committees Council of Kuzbass, the biggest mining region of the USSR, stated in its address to Gorbachev on 7 March 1991.

For almost six years already you have been at the helm of our state and here are the results: political and social tension within society, national discord, plummeting living standards, onslaught of crime, empty counters in shops. You, as the head of state, are personally responsible for all this. You have fallen behind all reasonable time limits in implementing your politics. You have exhausted the credit of people's trust. The working collectives of the majority of Kuzbass mines are demanding your resignation. They have decided not to stop striking until their main demand – your resignation – is answered. We urge you to rescind your powers as the President of the USSR. In case you choose to ignore our demands, we'll continue our strike and will call the citizens of the USSR for the acts of civilian disobedience.[30]

An opinion poll of 1,050 Russians aged eighteen to twenty-five, commissioned by *Readers' Digest* in early March 1991, gave Gorbachev the support of only 6 per cent of those questioned.[31]

The world chess champion, Gary Kasparov, called Gorbachev 'the master of Stalin's lessons'.[32] And here's the opinion of a Soviet Army major serving in East Germany:

The gunfire in Vilnius showed Gorbachev's true face. I trusted him and pinned my hopes on him, but what he did was all play-acting. The West made him powerful, gave him money and grain, and now the Nobel Peace Prize – what for? He should now be stripped of this honour after allowing people to be killed in the Baltics. He is a puppet of the KGB.[33]

As you see, all layers of society: intellectuals, workers, young people and even some of the military are opposed to Gorbachev's rule. The understanding is gradually coming to the West too. As it was put by William Safire in the *International Herald Tribune*, 'After five years of talk about restructuring, Gorbachev has built only a new edifice of power for himself, the KGB and the Red Army generals, making the Soviet Union safe for dictatorship.'[34]

It is very painful for me to watch all these sinister developments from a distance, without being able to go onto the streets to join the ranks of protesters. But I can't do anything about it. At the end of 1990 I was visited in Melbourne by a former Moscow colleague of mine. 'It's good for you not to be in the Soviet Union now,' he told me. 'They would have killed you . . .'

I don't want to be a passive observer though. My battleground is the clean sheet of paper. My combat mission is writing the truth. My dateline is Freedom.

I try not to be overwhelmed by gloom and doom and to always see a funny side of things: after all I am a former satirist! Laughter and tears have always been inseparable.

I couldn't help smiling, say, while watching Boris Yeltsin's interview on Soviet TV on 19 February 1991. When confronted with the presenter's sarcastic question: 'What has the government of the Russian Federation, headed by you, done for its seven months in power?', he answered: 'We have done a lot. We have adopted one hundred and forty laws!'

I couldn't help laughing when to commemorate Gorbachev's sixtieth birthday in March 1991 the Soviet television released a documentary where Gorbachev was lauded as a 'hard-driving man of the people on whom the outside world placed its hopes for peace'. Interviews with his mother and childhood friends portrayed the young Gorbachev as 'determined to dedicate his talents to working for the prosperity of his homeland'. 'He stood out among the other children as an organiser – always thinking up competitions or other ideas,' a Komsomol (Young Communist League) leader of Gorbachev's home village said in the film. As Robert Evans of Reuters reported from Moscow, 'In providing a totally positive view of the Kremlin chief, it [the film] was strongly reminiscent of past films on Soviet leaders, later denounced for creating their own personality cult. An anonymous commentator said at one point: 'So many hopes for peace are placed by the people's of the world on the Soviet President', a remark which strongly echoed similar claims made of Nikita Khrushchev and Leonid Brezhnev.

Somehow I was reminded of the poster which one could see all over the country in the late 1970s/early 1980s: the huge bulk of Brezhnev towering over the crowd of ant-like smallish underdogs underneath, and the inscription in big red letters: ALWAYS AMONG THE PEOPLE.

It evoked analogies with the childhood stories of Lenin and, strangely, with colourful descriptions of the exploits of Kim Il Sung, 'the sun of the nation', we were so fond of reading in the Russian-language *North Korea Magazine*, distributed in the Soviet Union. It was reassuring to realize that somewhere else in the world they had an even bigger personality cult of their leader. Sadly, history seems to repeat itself over and over again.

Personality cults are disgusting, but don't you think that they are also somehow funny, with their pompous, meaningless epithets, ardent cheers and applause at pistol's point? Only for this sort of laughter one might pay with one's life.

Even so, there's no way to stop people laughing at their dictators.

And I am laughing, laughing through tears. And my country, a hungry miserable pauper – with a plastic bag for cat food in her trembling hand – is laughing with me.

2

The Squall

By a sad irony of fate, my final Russian journalistic 'trophy', the long awaited Ilf and Petrov Prize for satirical journalism, was awarded to me on my last day in the Soviet Union.

Ilya Ilf and Yevgeni Petrov are among my favourite writers. Their brilliant satirical tandem became world famous in the twenties and thirties for its shrewd and hilarious exposés of Soviet reality. Both of them were lucky enough to avoid Stalin's purges: Ilf died of TB in 1938 and Petrov perished in an air crash four years later. The book containing their two best novels – *Twelve Chairs* and *The Golden Calf* – is with me in Australia now. I keep reading and re-reading it and know it practically by heart.

The Prize was awarded for my exposure of organised crime in the Soviet Union. Back in 1987 I was the first Soviet reporter to use the phrase 'Soviet Mafia' in print, and after my four big stories on the Dnepropetrovsk-based criminal organisation, 138 mafiosi were put behind bars. I received the Journalist of the Year Honorary Diploma for that investigation. Now looking back at all these awards I can see that they never meant much to the authorities. Otherwise they wouldn't have forced me out of the country.

Many unsolved mysteries were associated with my story of the Dnepropetrovsk mafia, whose leaders for the most part had managed to escape responsibility. (I described the investigation in detail in *Special Correspondent.*) During my last year in Russia rumours that Matross, the Sailor, the gang's leader, had been freed from prison reached me periodically. Luckily they proved to be nothing but rumours.

In January 1990 *Literaturnaya Gazeta* reported the sudden demotion of Nivalov, First Secretary of the Chernovtsy (a city in the Western Ukraine) Regional Party Committee, for 'seriously breaching the norms of the Party's ethics'. This small piece of information was hardly noticed by anyone. But I rejoiced. Nivalov, the former Second Secretary of the Dnepropetrovsk Regional Party Committee and the Sailor's closest friend, was one of those mafia protectors whose names I knew but had been unable to disclose either in my Dnepropetrovsk stories or in the book. The corrupt Party apparatchik used to play billiards with the leader of the city's gangsters almost every day and provided cover for many of his operations. After the crackdown on the Dnepropetrovsk mafia, Nivalov was safely transferred to Chernovtsy and promoted to the First Secretary. Judging from the information in *Literaturnaya Gazeta*, he didn't change his ways. Old habits die hard, especially mafia ones . . .

It is curious that until now – just as it was under Brezhnev – Dnepropetrovsk has remained a sort of breeding ground for power-hungry Party officials. Some time ago I was dismayed to learn that Vladimir Ivashko, the Dnepropetrovsk Party Committee First Secretary had been appointed Party leader for the whole Ukraine and then President of the Ukrainian republic; and in 1990, he was made the Deputy General Secretary of the CPSU, second only to Gorbachev himself. And though I had no proof of Ivashko's direct involvement in the Dnepropetrovsk criminal network, I did feel suspicious: the old promotion pattern, Dnepropetrovsk–Kiev–Moscow, seems to be still in operation. This was the road taken by Brezhnev, Chernenko, Shcherbitski (the former Ukraine Party boss and Politburo member), Chebrikov (the former KGB head and Politburo member) and many others. If some restructuring was really implied by perestroika, then immediately it should have got rid of this suspicious power pattern. But it didn't, which shows that old mafia ties are still at work. As Vassili Seliunin, a leading Soviet economist, put it: the structure of the Communist Party apparatus was (and still is) very similar to that of an organised criminal group.[1]

By 1989 organised crime in the Soviet Union was on the rise and has turned into one of the main threats to the very existence of the country, no less dangerous than the crumbling economy and persistent national conflicts. It was like a squall ready to sweep away what little law and order remained.

A total 2,461,692 crimes were registered in 1989, an increase of 31.8 per cent on the previous year.[2] Data for the first eight months of 1990 show a further 20 per cent increase.[3] These were the official figures. Research conducted by two Leningrad journalists who visited every single militia precinct in the city and compared their own murder figures with the official ones, revealed that the real figures were three and a half times greater.[4] So much for glasnost.

As for organised crime, even rigged information was much more difficult to obtain: the press didn't carry it. At an Interior Ministry briefing I attended in autumn 1989, they told us that for the last three years more than 3000 organised criminal groups were exposed by the militia, of which 1200 were 'liquidated' in 1988. One can only imagine how many more remain unexposed, and hence 'unliquidated'.

Figures, no matter how large and impressive, fail to illustrate the atmosphere of fear and panic which paralysed Moscow and other major cities at the end of 1989. People (especially women) were afraid of coming out into the streets after dark. Gang fights with gunshots became a common phenomenon. The cost of a guard dog has increased sharply. Many people were keen to buy firearms themselves in order to protect their families. It was not impossible. On the Moscow black market a pistol could be acquired for 800 roubles and a Kalashnikov machine gun with ammunition for between 1000 and 1500.[5] Most of these arms came from Afghanistan or were stolen from the army and the militia. There was a case of two soldiers who stole a tank machine gun from their unit and sold it for 380 roubles, four bottles of homebrew and ten bottles of beer.[6]

The precarious situation became quite obvious to the foreign journalists too, despite their relatively privileged and protected existence. The number of robberies and assaults on foreigners was growing. Gangs of taxi drivers blocked the roads from Sheremetiyevo airport, intercepting visitors on their way to the city and robbing them.

'Life in Moscow is increasingly dangerous as it becomes dominated by people who are living beyond the law,' Helen Womack wrote in the *Independent* magazine in October 1989. 'A severe shortage of consumer goods in the shops is matched by a flourishing black economy. If you know where to go, almost anything from moonshine vodka to personal computers is available or can be obtained for a price. Foreigners are especially at risk because they have much-wanted foreign currency and goods, as are Soviet citizens who enter Moscow's underworld.'[7]

No wonder that under such circumstances the militia themselves, being severely underpaid and confused by the flow of press criticism, more and more often became directly involved in crime. David Smith, the Channel 4 correspondent in Moscow, wrote about an American friend who was stopped by the police without any plausible reason three times in one night. 'First he paid in dollars, then cigarettes, finally roubles.'[8]

The newly-formed cooperative (read: private) enterprises became easy prey for the extortionists and racketeers. The information I got from the militia puts the number of cooperatives regularly paying protection money to organised criminal groups at a huge 90 per cent of the overall figure.

The progressive *Ogonyok* ran an interview with such a destitute cooperator:

From what I've heard, gangsters have got their hands on almost every cooperative cafe and restaurant in Moscow, as well as a number of shops and

25

clothing cooperatives. Soon they'll control the whole cooperative movement. You only have to go to the Riga market and see some of the odd-looking types prowling around. Every single trader there is paying them protection money.[9]

Indeed the Riga market, which was not so far from where I lived in Moscow, has become a real hotbed of organised crime. Profiteers, pimps and other underworld creatures were swarming all over the place. No-one seemed to buy the goods displayed on the numerous stalls. They were simply a cover-up for the 'real' trade which was conducted under the counter. There you could buy western cigarettes (a single packet cost three days' average salary), condoms (one for one day's salary), spirits, clothes, drugs, small arms and even sex. Racketeers patrolled the market openly, sporting their 'uniforms' – black leather jackets – as a sort of psychological pressure on obstinate traders: you see, we are the real masters here, and no-one can stand in our way. And it was true. The militia were rare guests at the Riga market, and even if they came, they pretended not to see or to hear anything – just made a quick tour of the market square and left. True, there was once a militia raid, but everyone at the market knew about it three days in advance. And you know why? The date and time of the operation were announced on the Moscow radio!

It was a real vicious circle: to be able to pay the racketeers, cooperators, even the honest ones, had to steal and cheat their customers, and this made them more and more vulnerable both for the militia and the extortionists. Only one case of successful resistance to gangsters was reported in Moscow. It occurred at Vnukovo airport, when the bandits tried to racketeer a cooperative of private taxi drivers. They were making good money by driving wealthy Caucasians from Vnukovo airport to Moscow and back. One day the guys in leather jackets turned up at the parking lot near to the airport and said 'Pay up'. They wanted the drivers to pay them on a daily basis just to be able to use the parking facilities. The next day more than a thousand drivers with spanners in their hands gathered at Vnukovo. 'You know our cars and we know yours,' they said to the gangsters. 'You burn one of ours and we'll burn one of yours. You smash one of our skulls and we'll smash one of yours.' The racketeers had to withdraw.[10]

One of the main reasons for this proliferation of crime was the persisting economic catastrophe into which the country had been led under 'the wise guidance of the Party'. Another reason was the great disillusionment brought about by the failure of democratic reforms and the hypocritical stand of our leaders who were talking democracy, but meanwhile clinging desperately to their privileges. Through the press, the extent of this hypocrisy became widely known and in this no-win situation people could not help becoming pessimistic and cynical. Society was seriously, even fatally ill. And large-scale crime became one of the most ominous symptoms of this disease. When beliefs and ideals are shattered, malice thrives.

It was in this atmosphere that I began my investigation into organised crime in Leningrad, the second largest city in the country: 'The fish starts rotting from its head,' as the Russian proverb goes. The investigation was prompted by my readers at one of my public appearances in Leningrad. I was speaking about my exposures of mafia, neo-fascism and high-level corruption at the Leningrad Palace of Youth in a hall which accommodated about 2000 people. It was full. As usual, after I'd finished there came lots of questions scribbled on odd pieces of paper. 'You've written the *Amur Wars**,' one message ran, 'now why don't you investigate the Leningrad mafia and write *Leningrad Wars*? Organised crime in our city has become a major problem.' This was in April 1989 and in July I started my inquest.

The sceptic who thinks that the press deliberately overestimates the scale of Soviet prostitution is advised to go one evening to the Moscow Hotel in Leningrad. Here his scepticism will evaporate like a glass of vodka spilt on a starchy restaurant table cloth.

The hotel is awash with hundreds of prostitutes, hard-currency peddlers and profiteers. The former are so conspicuous that they resemble the heroines of bad Soviet movies about the decaying West: they possess the whole gamut of provocative habits from the turn-of-the-century Odessa brothels. Without a hint of fear or shyness they openly accost 'chukhontsi' (the Finns), 'shtatniki' (the Americans) and other foreign tourists. In different, but inevitably broken, languages they pronounce sacramental addresses of the type 'Man, why don't you treat a lady to a good cigarette/drink/meal etc?' After quick bargaining, the newly-formed couples disappear inside the hotel past the seemingly-impregnable bouncers who hospitably open the doors for them.

The prostitutes are anything from eleven to fifty-five years old.

Here one can also see swarms of profiteers with their ubiquitous shoulder bags. They adroitly intercept foreigners going to the Metro and the buses. Smiling charmingly, they blurt out their ingenious lexical minimum, acquired from teach-yourself books and supported by practical studies outside the hotel.

*This was the title of my novel published in *Krokodil*. The full investigation was published in *Special Correspondent*.

This underworld idyll is quietly watched by the flock of militia patrolmen. From time to time they approach the prostitutes and exchange a couple of half-whispered kind-hearted words. I was told by the Leningrad CID that practically all the militiamen guarding the Intourist hotels are on the payroll of both the prostitutes and the spivs to whom they give *carte blanche*.

However, the real masters here are neither the militia nor the spivs but the racketeers. I had the privilege of observing the latter in action in the Moscow Hotel restaurant. The huge hall was fuming and bubbling, fuming with champagne and bubbling with passions. The restaurant variety show girls were dancing on the brightly-lit stage throwing their long legs up in the air. The Russian folk band was thrumming the balalaikas. The 'ladies of a certain behaviour' could be seen at almost every table, sipping champagne and smoking languorously. The multi-lingual hubbub drowned the sounds of music.

I was so carried away by what was going on that I didn't notice how a flock of young guys dressed in T-shirts and sports trousers rushed into the hall, swiftly dispersed and dashed to where the prostitutes were sitting. Running past their tables, they lingered for a moment or two exchanging half-words, half-glances with the whores. The women groped in their purses and quickly shoved something over to the guys with their clenched little fists with sharp, heavily-manicured claws. This something went down into the racketeers' shoulderbags before you could say Jack Robinson. It was all happening with such speed and dexterity that a detached on-looker was unlikely to notice anything at all.

The guys were the 'shestiorki', the errand boys, members of the gang's lower echelons. By the unwritten rules of the criminal hierarchy, they were supposed to be directed by the team leaders. And here they were too, swaggering into the restaurant, two more sportively-clad guys with muscles bulging under the sleeves of their T-shirts. Having ascended the steps leading to the restaurant's second tier, the team leaders started coordinating the movements of their troops. One after another the errand boys ran up the stairs for quick consultations with the two. It all resembled an Australian football match when messengers run across the field to convey the coach's instructions to the players. I later found out that both team leaders were Masters of Sport* in boxing.

The punishment for a prostitute who refuses to pay over her earnings is severe: torture – burning the face with a cigarette butt or cutting off an ear, gang rape or even murder. Sometimes though, the gangsters make

*One of the highest sportsmen's titles in the Soviet Union.

mistakes and start extorting women who came to the restaurant simply to have a meal.

In June 1989, the racketeers mistook one such lady for an evasive prostitute. She was dragged out into the street, beaten and raped in a car parked near to the hotel. Her screams attracted two militiamen on the beat but on seeing that the attackers were 'friends' (ie those who regularly paid them) the guardians of law and order decided not to interfere and retired.

This rape was one of the many horrors perpetrated by N. Almiashev's gang, team leader and World and European classic wrestling champion in 1986 and 1987. His group was liquidated by the Leningrad anti-mafia squad in spring 1989. It included the bronze medallist from the European classic wrestling championship, R. Ibragimov, Master of Sport International Class (boxing) I. Smirnov, and Masters of Sport O. Gunyashin and V. Ulibov (boxing and wrestling respectively).

People often ask me why so many prominent sportsmen end up as gangsters. The point is that in the Soviet Union for many years sport has been treated as an industry rather than a leisure activity. The aim was to produce records, records and more records at any price; winning took precedence over any legal or moral qualms. But as soon as the record-breakers were exhausted as sportsmen, they were simply thrown out of the competitive arena. Being still physically fit but morally crippled by that incessant drive for sporting achievement, they couldn't find a place in their new life. They had no assets but bulging muscles and were already well schooled in the practice of turning a blind eye to the law and placing themselves well above mere mortals. Most of them were also used to taking drugs before important competitions. It has become systematic within Soviet sport, but was strictly taboo for the press. I remember a colleague of mine offering an article on this subject to *Krokodil* in 1989. It was ardently refused by the editorial board: glasnost, such as it was, had its limits.

The crackdown on Almiashev's gang was prompted by a letter sent to the militia by the staff of the Moscow Hotel restaurant. 'Recently the racketeers' visits to our restaurant have become more and more frequent,' the letter ran. 'At first they only extorted prostitutes, but now they have started fleecing the restaurant staff as well. We are absolutely helpless against them and we demand extreme measures be taken to restore order in the restaurant. If such measures are not carried out, if the safety of waiters and clients is not guaranteed, we will refuse to work late hours and will go on strike.' There were twenty-five signatures under the letter.

The threat of a strike made the militia act swiftly. The bandits were 'realised' (in militia jargon that means 'arrested') with the help of an OMON-militia special-purpose unit, a sort of commando outfit. Despite the gangsters' impressive sports records, they were quickly overwhelmed by the militiamen. The whole operation took no more than five minutes.

You should have seen how bitterly Almiashev cried during the interrogation, claiming that he had just dropped in to the restaurant to have his normal non-alcoholic supper. But the pistol, the truncheon and several thousand roubles which he carried with him didn't really fit with this version. Arrest was like a bolt out of the blue for him and for his cronies: they were dead sure that their glorious sportsmen's past and their bosses' connections were solid guarantees against any unpleasant surprises.

Yes, they had bosses. With all their medals and titles they were still no more than low- or middle-level extortioners. The upper-echelon, so-called leaders, were still well out of reach of the militia.

There are three main underworld leaders in Leningrad at present. Each runs an organisation of between 200 and 300 members. The whole city is divided between these three gangs, all with strong ties to the authorities. Not only are these gangs involved in extorting money from speculators and prostitutes, they also organise artificial shortages of goods in the city's shops by bribing the officials responsible. They vie for superiority, killing each other in the streets and arranging road accidents for their rivlas. As well as being well-armed and mobile, the gangs also possess the latest Western electronic equipment, allowing them to maintain contact with each other and to eavesdrop on the militia's radio communications.

Recently there was a case when during interrogation a gangster managed to hide a bug under the investigator's desk. For a whole month his criminal colleagues were able to hear every word uttered at CID headquarters.

The leaders' names are known to the militia, but they are powerless against them: the Soviet Criminal Code is not competent to deal with a criminal organisation because until recently organised crime did not officially exist in the Soviet Union and the Criminal Code as an official document couldn't possibly reflect something which was not officially recognised.

From the point of view of the existing law, the leaders are innocent and guiltless, though the lion's share of a criminal group's income goes straight to the leader's pocket. The one in charge of Almiashev's group, say, was getting between 40,000 and 50,000 roubles a month from racketeering at the Moscow Hotel alone! Of course, he had never come close to the hotel himself.

An interesting detail: the salary of a militia detective in the Leningrad anti-mafia squad is 200 roubles a month. Something for you to think about . . .

By now you must feel pretty confused by all these leaders, team leaders and errand boys, so it's high time to throw some light on a typical gang's structure. Not surprisingly, the Soviet legislation lacks a definition for organised crime as such, although an anti-organised crime department has been recently formed within the Interior Ministry. The closest shot at definition so far was made by the deputy head of this department, Colonel G. Chebotaryov, at a press briefing at the Ministry held on 13 June 1989: in his words, organised crime is 'a relatively wide functioning of controlled associations with hierarchical structures involved in criminal activities as a business and creating by way of corruption their own protection systems'.

So what is the enigmatic 'hierarchical structure' in plain words? It is the scheme according to which the money travels up the ladder – from the lower echelons (racketeers), led by the team leaders (former sportsmen), to mafia bosses (leaders) protected by corrupt officials. Here is how it looks graphically:

BOSS or ELITE   ←PROTECTION GROUP
↑   (corrupt lawyers, militiamen and Party officials)

TEAM LEADERS
(former sportsmen)
↑

GANGSTERS or GUARDS
↑

ERRAND BOYS
(low-level extortioners and scouts)
↑

THE SWAMP
(speculators, prostitutes, pimps, pick-pockets and other underworld deni-zens serving as a source of money for the whole organisation)

As a matter of fact, one of the leaders of the Leningrad underworld, whose name I can't mention for obvious reasons, gave me a slightly different scheme which, despite being drafted on the other side of the tracks, so to speak, was very similar.

31

What becomes clear is that in their everyday 'official' lives the leaders, as a rule, pose as pretty unimportant people: waiters, public-bath attendants, hairdressers, taxi drivers or petty clerks. These occupations allow them to have unnoticed contacts with many people and also, being of a shift character, leave plenty of time for planning and managing criminal operations.

The protection group is the most confidential link in the whole organisation. If the names of the leaders themselves are known to the team leaders and some of the racketeers, the protection group is thoroughly camouflaged and is connected directly only to 'the elite'. Not only does it protect mafiosi from the sword of Themis, but also points out potential wealthy 'clients' with the help of the bribed militiamen. In Leningrad I was told that with every 'realised' criminal group, two or three corrupt militiamen usually go to prison. As to the more high-standing members of protection groups, their names are well hidden by the clouds resting on the peaks of power. Getting to them with the poor mountaineering equipment which the militia have at their disposal, is like storming Everest in a wheelchair.

Each working morning the Leningrad anti-mafia squad starts with one and the same problem: where to get petrol for their three elderly and half-ruined jalopies. Even for the dangerous crimes department (of which the anti-mafia squad is a part) petrol is strictly limited by numerous bureaucratic instructions. So what do they do? They send a messenger to one of the local militia precincts. To be more exact, he is not a messenger but rather a beggar, since his mission is to beg for petrol for his colleagues who may have to start chasing the gangsters at any moment.

Those three cars are the squad's main grief. Apart from having to beg for petrol, the detectives have to repair them with their own money since the city's militia department refuses to maintain them. On 200 roubles a month, as you may well imagine, you can't be too extravagant.

By an irony of fate, or rather of the system, the shabby militia garage is situated next door to the huge Regional Party Committee garage. On the way to their jalopies the detectives cannot help observing dozens of brand-new black Volgas with their powerful engines idling day and night. The yawning drivers in white shirts keep the engines running in case some important bureaucrat suddenly wants to rush to a meeting or simply home for lunch.

Cars and petrol are far from being the militia's only concerns. They have big problems with the simplest tape recorders: in fact there's only one for the whole department. Their pistols are also in short supply and virtually obsolete. There was also the case of a prosperous cooperative which, well aware of the militia's poverty and eager to get some protection from them, offered to buy a bus for the squad members. The accounts department resisted: we don't have a credit item just for a bus, they said . . .

It is not only the Leningrad militia, by the way, which leads such a squalid existence. In Moscow, in the Interior Ministry – the headquarters of the whole Soviet militia force – I was shown a pair of special 'retention handcuffs' used by police all over the world. In the Ministry they had only one pair – a souvenir from a visiting Swedish policeman. The Ministry official who demonstrated the handcuffs to me was in a bad mood. 'For the militia to get to grips with reality, we have to buy at least thirty million dollars' worth of equipment, but there is no chance whatsoever that the government would give us the money.'

Yes, this is the sad reality: the state which has enough money to regularly increase the bureaucrats' salaries, which can afford to launch spacecraft and artificial Earth satellites almost every other day, which manages to maintain by far the world's largest army and to waste billions of dollars annually on foreign machinery only to leave it to rot under rain and snow in the littered yards of plants and factories – this country cannot find any money to re-equip its own militia – the only force potentially able to stop the squall of organised crime, the ever-growing threat to its very existence.

As for the Leningrad anti-mafia squad, I could see that it functioned solely on the devotion, enthusiasm and, if you wish, fanaticism of its members. I couldn't help admiring them – these underpaid, neglected, exhausted people, working selflessly without leave or days off, without normal family evenings and weekends, but at constant personal risk.

Of the very recent cases, the rounding up of Sidiuk's group is well worth mentioning. They operated in Leningrad for many years and were very well equipped. They had many cars – Volvos and Saabs among them – and also walkie-talkies and numerous arms. They spread their influence outside Leningrad and had connections with the Riga market in Moscow, with the flower traders from Baku and with the Sverdlovsk underworld. Understandably, operating on such a scale, they needed good protection. This came from the Interior Ministry and the KGB.

The Sidiuks' methods were fairly traditional, only unusually ruthless. They made their victims dig their own graves and tortured them with scorching soldering irons. Torture by electric shock, when the electrodes were applied to the victim's head and genitals, was especially popular with them. This was not fatal and left no traces, but caused harrowing pain which no-one could endure. Naturally, faced with such tortures the 'clients' were quick to cough up.

The nucleus of the group was formed of strong men, mostly Masters of Sport. Sidiuk himself was one of the best karate fighters in Leningrad and was even nicknamed Kolya the Karate. The gang also included the boxer with the tongue-breaking name Meftehundinov-Mikatadze and the 130-kilogram monster Gevorkian. The group could boast a real (and quite well-known) film and theatre actor, A. Shalolashvili, who had managed to combine the roles of a Leningrad Theatrical Society director and a racketeer with a long criminal record. He was also a bulk of a man capable of killing with his bare hands.

Since Sidiuk's arrest the position of supreme leader of the Leningrad underworld has remained vacant. The leaders of the three main gangs are fighting for it using all possible means: blackmail, threats, beatings and pre-arranged killings. In the space of a couple of months several team leaders from the vying clans perished in suspicious car accidents. The boys from the anti-mafia squad (there are only sixteen of them for the whole Leningrad area) told me how once they were chasing four bandits in a car. After a long pursuit (luckily the squad car didn't run out of petrol on the way) they pressed the gangsters' Lada to the curb, pointed pistols at them through the windows and ordered: 'Come out! Militia!' To their surprise the bandits obeyed eagerly. 'Thank God!' they said, climbing out of the car with their hands up, 'It's the militia. That means we shall not be killed . . . We thought it might be Talishev's guys . . .' (Talishev is the name I have given to one of the leaders. I have not used their real names for obvious reasons.)

An incident at Deviatkino market also serves as a fine example of the unceasing and deadly power struggle in the Leningrad underworld. This flea market appeared spontaneously on the edge of the city in the region of Deviatkino village in 1987. Everything could be acquired there – from a bottle of Czech beer to a car or even (by some unconfirmed data) to a small nuclear bomb. Naturally the market attracted profiteers as a lonely street lamp attracts nightly midges. And of course the racketeers were quick to catch these speculating midges in their webs. The market was divided into spheres of influence between two gangs. Let's call them provisionally the Petrovtsi and the Ivanovtsi.

In the beginning the two groups coexisted quite peacefully. They introduced common 'income tax' for different types of profiteers. From those who traded in clothes they took ten roubles a day, from beer traders, five roubles. Another potential source of income for them was the thimble game (a favourite one in the Soviet underworld) which was very popular there.

The rules of the game are more than simple. A chap sits on the ground with three thimbles on a flat piece of plywood in front of him. Next to the thimbles he puts a small fluffy ball made of paper or of thick wool. Lifting the thimbles quickly with both hands he covers the ball with one of them and moves them around several times. Then he stops and asks: 'Where is the ball?' The on-lookers have a very misleading feeling that they can easily tell under which of the three thimbles the ball is hidden. And usually their first guess is correct. The person who gave the right answer wins say, ten roubles which are readily provided by the crook who then suggests another go for twenty-five, fifty or a hundred roubles. The lucky on-looker being very pleased with how easily he duped the simpleton out of 'chervonets' (ten-rouble notes) hurries to accept the challenge. And here something strange occurs: no matter how attentively he follows the swift movements of the chap's hands, the ball inevitably turns up under the wrong thimble. The gullible on-looker can thus loose hundreds of roubles in a matter of minutes. As soon as a militia patrol appears the crook picks up his simple gear and quickly – as a rat up a drain – disappears into the crowd.

'Napiorstochniki' – that's what thimblers are called – never work alone. They usually employ one or two stooges to dupe passers-by into having a try. The stooges win, and all the rest eventually loose.

This thimble game is very profitable and both the Petrovtsi and the Ivanovtsi maintained their own 'thimble tools' (another gangster's expression) in Deviatkino market. Each thimble tool brought its operators up to 2000 roubles a day. Alas, gullible people are not rare in a Russian crowd.

The confrontation between the two gangs started over a trifling incident. One speculator was robbed of some clothes and complained to the Ivanovtsi team leader to whom he was paying protection money. The team leader's name was Sergei Miskaryov, nicknamed Broiler, and he was a former militia officer, a graduate of the Militia Higher Political School. Before becoming a gangster he had worked for several years as the chief political officer at a labour camp.

Broiler was quick to find the robbers, who were part of the Petrovtsi gang, and restored the status quo by beating the stolen clothes out of them. The Ivanovtsi bore him a grudge and the following day, when Broiler was busy squatting and counting the money from the previous day's take, he was attacked by seven Petrovtsi led by their team leader, Fedia the Crimean. Broiler's fitness acquired at the militia school didn't help this time: he was flattened by the prevailing force of the attackers. When he came round, Broiler complained to his leader who decided that the Petrovtsi must be taught a lesson. 'Razborka' (the fight to settle accounts) was fixed for the following Saturday. Both gangs appeared at full strength on the grass next to the market. The Ivanovtsi arrived well armed: their leader had a pistol and his bodyguard, nicknamed the Elephant, was brandishing a PPS machine gun. The Petrovtsi, rather taken aback by this arsenal (they were prepared for a scuffle, not a shooting), sent forward Fedia the Crimean as a negotiator. He was waving his white handkerchief in the air but the Ivanovtsi mistook his advance for the start of combat actions. The Broiler, who hadn't fully recovered after the beating, without further ado finished Fedia off with a knife. A terrible brawl ensued and several gangsters from both sides were seriously hurt.

The Crimean's murder was the official pretext for the militia to start rounding up both gangs. Both the Ivanovtsi and the Petrovtsi hurried to make peace with each other in the face of the militia threat. They agreed not to squeal in case of arrest and would claim that they had seen nothing. As for the Broiler himself, it was decided that he should be sent into hiding and then killed. Neither leaders trusted their gang members to keep their mouths shut, so they gradually got rid of the main witnesses in pre-arranged road accidents. But the militia did manage to trace the Broiler, who didn't particularly resist arrest, realising that prison would be the safest place for him. Valera the Duke, Dima the Midget and Vasya the Chelentano were also captured. The others, like Kolya the Maradona, managed to escape. For the first time in many months the Deviatkino market traders could enjoy some quiet.

It is still relatively quiet there now, but the silence is misleading: the place is too lucrative for the criminals to stay away for long. The market itself is situated on the hill, from where one has a clear view of all the neighbourhood. This makes sudden militia raids ineffectual: the criminals observe them at a distance and disperse. Many times the militia have approached the city authorities with pleas for the market to be transferred to some other place less suited to the gangsters' needs, but without result. Again, one has the feeling that the authorities are not very eager to create hardships for the criminals.

The apparatchiks and the militia in Leningrad remain at loggerheads. Formally the city militia headquarters still remains one of the city council's departments. The instruction under which the militia can't arrest any employee of a city's or a district's council – no matter what the crime – is still in force. They can't even detain a night guard or a caretaker if he or she is employed by the apparat.

Another tradition in Leningrad has always been to appoint the demoted big Party officials as heads of the militia department. The Party bosses who brought havoc to the city's trade and communal services find refuge as militia commanders after being sacked from their Party posts. These people are as a rule very quickly promoted to the ranks of militia generals where they are empowered to launch or to stop any militia operation and can warn their old mafia friends of the impending raids well in advance. Clearly, such a system can only undermine the activities of the militia.

But the rank-and-file militiamen now are much less meek than before. Confronted with aloofness and maltreatment from the authorities, they conducted a protest rally in Palace Square at the beginning of 1989, the first militia demonstration in Leningrad (or indeed the whole country) since 1917. The authorities turned a deaf ear to the meeting and punished the ringleaders. Among other things, the demonstrators demanded protection from the growing underworld, since more and more militiamen were becoming victims of the well-armed and well-organised criminals. They demanded better arms, higher pay and more rights. The demonstration was triggered by a blood-chilling incident, when a seventeen-year-old juvenile delinquent had brutally murdered a militia woman, inflicting seventeen knife wounds. Her name was Valentina Zaitseva. She was an inspector of adolescent crime with two children. She was murdered during office hours, in the early afternoon, at her unguarded office in the basement of a residential house. No-one came to help her, no-one reacted to her screams. The assault seems to have been provoked by her trying to persuade the boy into taking a job as a factory worker. When I was having lunch with my new friends from the anti-mafia squad in the militia department's dirty and stinking canteen, I saw on one of the walls the hand-written petition to the Supreme Soviet, demanding Zaitseva's murderer be executed (persons under eighteen are not liable for capital punishment in the Soviet Union). The petition had hundreds of signatures.

The canteen itself deserves a separate description, awful as it is. It is open for four hours a day and is a good ten minute walk away. It is also too small and always crowded: it usually takes no less than an hour of queueing to reach the counter and be served a frugal meal. It is noteworthy that the huge oblong building housing the militia department also accommodates the city's KGB headquarters (the building in Liteini Prospect is popularly known as 'The Big House'). Researching a story on Leningrad neo-nazis I had to visit the KGB headquarters a couple of times and was very impressed by their excellent canteen, the round-the-clock buffets on each floor and the fleet of sparkling black Volgas at the entrance. Isn't it disgraceful that, working in the same building, the militia were treated like a neglected child, having to go a long way to have a lousy meal at a stuffy, stinking canteen. And somehow I had grounds to believe that the militia detectives had much more on their hands than the KGB agents . . .

'A cheap militia costs the state dear' the Leningrad operatives kept telling me. How true this is. Faced with all the militia drawbacks of technical backwardness, lack of legal rights and so forth, the criminal world grows more daring and starts acting almost in the open. Being well aware of the militiamen's low salaries, the criminals often try to force bribes upon them. One must be very stoic to refuse the sum of 100,000 or 150,000 roubles, the money they would have no chance of earning in three lifetimes of honest militia duty. And the underworld leaders thrive. There were several cases in Leningrad where the mafia leaders were able to jump the housing waiting lists and receive good flats, whereas for an ordinary family the wait may take anything from ten to twenty-five years (Leningrad is hugely overpopulated and suffers from a major housing crisis).

The gangsters coordinate their activities in regular meetings. Every afternoon at about three or four o'clock in some of the downtown restaurants, the leaders conduct conclaves with their underlings, the so-called 'skhodniaks'. They meet quite openly to plan future criminal operations, receive visitors, issue orders to the team leaders and collect 'taxes'. On a tip-off from the militia, I became a witness to one such daily meetings.

A cavalcade of four cars came to a halt at the restaurant's entrance. Half a dozen errand boys jumped out and quickly ran around the building. Having made sure that everything was quiet, they took up positions as lookouts near the doors. Then the gangsters appeared. Disdainfully, they entered the restaurant paying no heed to the sacramental 'No Seats' sign on the door. Having entered the lobby, they pushed the ordinary clients aside and formed a cordon on the staircase. Finally, accompanied by two team leaders, the leader himself emerged. He was a little podgy man with a tiny moustache under a long hooked nose. He passed the cordon of bodyguards going directly to his separate room where some of the most trusted prostitutes and some of the oldest cognacs await him. Sipping cognac and gently fondling the women, he set about his work, listening to the team leaders' reports and also receiving some of the errand boys who briefed him about which prostitutes, pickpockets and profiteers were doing business today on his territory. The leader takes note of all of them. If by tomorrow they don't pay 'tax' he will have to send some of the racketeers to reason with them. I was told by one of the elusive prostitutes: 'They approached me in the restaurant and said that I owed payment for going out with some Finns. I refused. Then they stopped me in the lobby, one gave me a kick in the stomach – they knew that I was pregnant – the other started punching me on the collarbone with a knuckle-duster.' And an obstinate hard-currency dealer recounted: 'They came in a Zhiguli 9 car and let out a small lad, no more than twelve years old. The rest were watching from the car. The stripling ordered me to take off my T-shirt, then lit a cigarette and jabbed it into my skin demanding money.' Using young boys to attack the 'debtors' is a particular kind of humiliation.

At the restaurant conclaves the leader also skips through lists of officials willing to be corrupt in order to select potential protectors, decides whom to bribe and with how much money, and pinpoints possible objects for racketeering (shops, restaurants, cooperatives etc).

What is the most likely course of future events? My militia friends' forecasts are as follows: since all the cooperatives are already 'taxed', the next stage for the growing mafia will be fleecing ordinary people – those who own a car or simply come to spend an evening in a restaurant. This is actually happening already. Many Leningrad restaurants have become risky places. And not only because there you can easily bump into a leader with his retinue. There were cases where racketeers demanded 200 roubles simply to let people out of a restaurant, or threatened to abduct the patrons' wives and girlfriends if the men didn't pay. But there is another much more dangerous trend: the pressure the mafia has started applying to the country's dying economy. Crime thrives on shortages so the bigger the shortages, the barer the counters, the better for the mafia. In Moscow in 1989 there were cases of mafia people coming to railway cargo stations and paying the loaders their monthly salary for NOT unloading perishable goods from the vans. These cases were reported in the press but no-one was caught. And when I hear for the umpteenth time that 70 per cent of the whole tomato crop didn't reach the shops, I can see the ugly face of the mafia behind it. The face which has become indistinguishable from that of the system itself.

Investigating in Leningrad, I obtained numerous proofs of the mafia's tightening grip on the economy's throat. There were cases where factory managers were paid not to send their products to the shops for several days. It could be anything – from toothpaste to tea-bags. For several days the army of profiteers, selling these goods for trebled and quadrupled prices, managed to make thousands for themselves and millions for their mafia protectors. As for official Soviet trade, two-thirds of it was part of the shadow economy.[11]

Leningrad was caught in paroxysms of panic buying: no-one knew what item would disappear next. It was very painful to watch people in the glorious city of Peter the Great, the cultural capital of the country, running around with their 'perhaps' string bags, frantically purchasing salt, sugar, cereals – whatever there was on the shelves. I remember taking loads of washing powder to my friends in Leningrad (washing powder was not available there) and bringing back several irons which had become scarce in Moscow. This was all happening in the fifth year of perestroika.

There in Leningrad I conducted a small investigation into the mechanism of deficit (that's how the goods in short supply are referred to in Russia). On the 6, 7 and 8 July 1989 not a single bottle of spirits was delivered to the city's shops. I visited dozens and everywhere the puzzled saleswomen were shrugging their fat shoulders saying that they had no idea why. The shops were beseiged by suffering alcoholics, but the counters remained empty.

At the same time Nekrasovski market was rife with speculators peddling cheap wine for five roubles a bottle (the state price was one rouble sixty kopeks a bottle). Vodka and champagne were peddled round the clock from the doors of restaurants for twenty and fifteen roubles a bottle respectively (state prices were nine and six roubles).

Three days passed and spirits reappeared.

'Cui bono?' the Romans used to ask. Who benefits? Mafia and the apparat. Only these two categories do not suffer from the vicissitudes of Soviet trade. They have similar structures, methods and interests, isn't it natural that they should collaborate and gradually merge. Who can guarantee today that decisions to create artificial shortages of spirits, cigarettes, soap, tea, sugar, toothpaste, audiotapes – whatever – were not taken at their joint sessions in some cosy restaurant and washed down with fine old cognac?

At the beginning of this chapter I mentioned my meeting with one of the leaders of the Leningrad mafia. Naturally, he agreed to talk to me only on the condition that neither his name nor the place of the meeting itself would be disclosed. Obviously, I had to acquiesce.

But why did he agree to see me? Partly out of curiosity and partly, I believe, to parade his own courage and inviolability. And strangely enough, he impressed me rather favourably: pleasant features, impeccably literate speech, the ability to back up his opinion. My militia friends explained that he was a typical representative of the new brand of criminal – an intellectual gangster. Indeed, he didn't correspond to the general stereotype of an underworld creature – a foul-mouthed tatooed rogue with a low forehead and pinched face overgrown with week-old bristle. So now let the leader speak for himself:

Our appearance at a given period in time is normal and unavoidable. Where do criminals come from? It never happens that a boy as good as gold suddenly becomes a racketeer. He is forced to become one by the natural desire to lead a normal life and a feeling of flouted justice. I for myself can't imagine how one can survive in our country on 200 or 300 roubles a month. I like to smoke good Western cigarettes which go for five roubles a packet on the black market. [In 1991 the price of Western cigarettes jumped to 30 or 50 roubles a pack – VV.] I smoke a lot – two cartons every week. That's 400 roubles on cigarettes alone. I also have to use taxis. For many reasons I prefer cabs to private cars. On that I spend another twenty-five to forty roubles a day. I like eating in restaurants – three times a day . . .

Is this prohibited? Why do they have restaurants then? I don't need all these Mercedes, but I do want a normal flat with a normal bedroom. I want to make good tea. Do you know how much a pack of Indian tea costs now? Bought from a speculator of course: you know as well as I do that there is no tea in the shops. Fifty roubles! Who is to blame for that? Who creates shortages? The state with its rationing system! Do you know how much the so-called radio-amateurs earn? They speculate in audio heads, those small things used in tape recorders. They have profits of more than 200 roubles a day. That is more than even I have sometimes. That's what I would call real organised crime. Do you agree that someone must control all those profiteers who have no notion of decency? The militia do not touch them. They fight those who are trying to prevent the crooks from filling their purses, us. The speculators grow fatter and fatter and burn rubber in their cars. I am not saying that I live honestly, but I have been brought up with a sense of decency and responsibility towards my friends. The profiteers lack these qualities, they have no sacred feelings in their souls. You know, I've been mixing a lot with Westerners. There are no speculators among them. And do you know why? Because they have no shortages in the West. They have unemployment benefits and one can buy a video on these allowances. When we have social security like that, there won't be any speculators left. And meanwhile . . .

We are keeping an eye on the so-called cooperative movement. Co-operators are legalised profiteers and spivs. Our group acts on the principle: better less, but regularly. We are guided by democratic principles, all viewpoints are taken into consideration. There is a great feeling of camaraderie among our members. [Here I recalled how they kill each other – VV.]

The Americans say: 'Money makes money.' Do you see what I mean? As to the sportsmen whom you have mentioned, of course the organisation needs them, but frankly it's an obsolete principle. We've crossed that Rubicon. Bullets are much more effective than muscles, even those of a world champion. So now our groups throughout the country are mastering only one sport – shooting. The Moscow Hotel wrestlers were stupid. They wanted to kill too many birds with one stone and failed as a result. One should act in a more subtle way, like we do. We pay certain people who can create the

41

appropriate atmosphere in a restaurant to enable the prostitutes, say, to enter the hall without a hitch and to work in an unfettered manner. This increases their earnings and then we appear.

We have strict discipline in our organisation. The main law is omerta*. When it is necessary to lose someone, we never do it ourselves but try to hire an assassin, preferably from another city. How much does a human life cost? It depends. Usually we pay from 5000 to 20,000 roubles, but there are specimens for whom even 100,000 wouldn't be too much. We have a mutual aid fund, so to speak, to buy each other out of trouble. And the protection, of course. I will never denounce my comrades, not because I am afraid, but simply because this is my main principle. How much do we earn? Not an easy question to answer. One thimble tool, say, can bring in up to 8000 roubles on a lucky day. The tools have to be protected by the guards, of course. Prostitutes generally pay us 500 roubles a month – those who work for hard currency. Rouble prostitutes pay less. Kidalshchiki† pay 10,000 roubles monthly. Certainly we have to pay guards and errand boys ourselves – 250 roubles a day for standing on lookout, say.

You and I are on different sides of the barricade, but I can tell you that in today's circumstances organised crime is inevitable. We get caught sometimes, but each captured soldier is quickly replaced by two newcomers. What else can I say? I feel very sorry for our great country. What have we come to? What have they done to us?! I am convinced that I haven't done any harm to Russia. Someone has to ransack the spivs. If I don't do this, do you think they will stop swindling? Never! That leads me to think that at this stage our activities benefit the country.

Listening to this bizarre anti-speculators diatribe, I couldn't help remembering numerous cases of the mafia's attacks on normal, honest people. There was an incident in the restaurant of the Pulkovskaya Hotel, where the Leningrad underworld leaders were celebrating the termination of Feoktistov's (the supreme leader of the underworld in the seventies) prison stretch. Alexander Rosenbaum, the famous Leningrad bard, poet and singer, was among the restaurant's clients on that day. The drunken mafiosi dragged him to their table and tried to make him sing for them. Rosenbaum refused. The thugs put a gun to his temple: 'Will you sing now?' The end could have been tragic were it not for Feoktistov himself who took pity on the singer and ordered his boys to leave him alone. When I told this story to my mafia interlocutor, he shrugged his shoulders: 'To err is human' he said. 'Sometimes we make mistakes, but who doesn't?'

The present-day situation with organised crime in the Soviet Union

* Omerta: a conspiracy of silence in the Mafia.
† Kidalshchiki: speculators in cars.

was shrewdly summed up by Yuris Blaumanis, the editor of the new *Strictly Confidential* monthly: 'The economy is stuck in a deep swamp. The widespread strikes went out of control. State trade and distribution are virtually controlled by the mafia. Blood is being shed in many republics. Civil war is here. Anti-semitic hysteria occurs right on Red Square testifying to the impending pogroms. But the country's leadership doesn't seem to be worried by all this. They are troubled – of all things – by the peaceful parliamentary revolution in the Baltic republics. God forbid that these Baltic "separatists" introduce some kind of order – what will occur to us then? That's where the force of the mafia is hidden. That's where it begins and ends.'[12]

In August 1990, *Moscow News* published an interview with the newly-elected President of Armenia, the outspoken 'Karabakh' Committee member Levon Ter-Petrosyan. Among other things he said: 'For two and a half years the mafia has been conducting its dirty, provocative activities against our movement [the Armenian National Liberation Movement – VV]. And I can state officially that it was – and it is – supported by certain forces from the centre [Moscow – VV].'[13]

It was put even more succinctly by the famous Moscow cooperator Andrei Fyodorov, the director of the first Moscow cooperative restaurant Kropotkinskaya, 36. 'Look, it is very simple,' he said, talking to David Remnik, the *Washington Post*'s Moscow correspondent. 'The Mafia is the state itself.'[14]

The last thing to be said about the Soviet mafia is that the squall of organised crime is spreading beyond Soviet borders and starting to surface on the international scene. The Soviet-based criminals maintain close ties with their counterparts in Sweden, Finland and Japan and gangs of recent Soviet emigrants operate successfully out of Brighton Beach in New York, a newly-formed Russian district. The US police are having a hard time with this new group of criminals. As one New York police officer told me, it's much easier to deal with those who break the law than with those who do not know that the law exists.

An article published in the *Observer* in March 1990 put it like this:

Berisford International has claimed that in two years its American jewellery subsidiary lost $54 million worth of gold, diamonds, coloured stones and other stock as a result of systematic thefts by members of the so-called 'Russian mafia'. The thefts took place at NGI International Precious Metals between 1986 and 1988. Berisford bought NGI for $33 million in 1985. NGI claims in a civil action brought against its insurers that the thefts were conducted by employees who were members of or associated with organised crime groups active among Soviet immigrants in New York. The FBI estimates there are twelve organised crime groups among the sizeable Russian community there. These have surfaced in a number of frauds and the infiltration of legitimate business.[15]

A short article appeared in the *Sunday Times* in January 1991, some of which I'd like to reproduce:

> They are more shabbily dressed than their United States counterparts and their Zhiguli cars have little of the glamour of Cadillacs but there is no mistaking the sinister intent of the men who now rule the streets of Leningrad.
>
> With the economy collapsing, food scarce and life becoming harder, crime is the only profitable business. It is perestroika's dark side, and the explosion of gangs involved in kidnapping, protection rackets and arms dealing has overwhelmed the authorities.
>
> An alarming feature is that gangsters are taking an increasing interest in Western tourism and businessmen . . . Police believe there are two or three main gangs in Leningrad. Members who break the rules are severely dealt with. One mafia 'soldier' who fled to Sweden with part of the proceeds of a protection racket was traced to Stockholm and beheaded.[16]

In July 1990 I spent a day at Brighton Beach. The whole place looked seedy. The nasty-looking Odessa types were standing in the doorways of restaurants and shops. Near the beach, in a big wooden shed with peeling stucco and a tattered 'Members Only' sign above the door, the burly, ruddy-faced men were playing cards.

I went to a barber's shop somewhere on Ocean Avenue. The old Jewish hairdresser, who had recently emigrated from Belorussia, was cutting my hair and telling me blood-chilling stories about local crime. 'They kill each other. They rob. Only last week at about midday they burst into the jewellery shop round the corner, killed the owner and took away everything. They are the masters of Brighton Beach and I wish I had never come here.'

The Soviet mafia maintains close links with emigrant criminal groups, forming international crime cartels dealing in drugs, jewellery, computers and art. It has ceased to be a purely Soviet concern. Will it grow into an international criminal organisation similar to the infamous Cosa Nostra? Whatever the scale, many mafia people with whom I spoke expressed their desire to migrate to the West.

3

Twenty-Nine

In September 1989 a short article in *Literaturnaya Gazeta* attracted my attention. It said that a French TV crew had been allowed into 'the last Gulag', labour camp thirty-five, for 'especially dangerous state criminals' – a euphemism for political prisoners – in the Perm region. I was surprised, since a year earlier it had been publicly claimed that all prisoners of conscience in the Soviet Union had been freed. Gorbachev made a big thing of this and the West had readily believed him.

Again I was confronted with the obvious contradiction between his words and his deeds.

As a journalist and as a human being I was eager to know the truth. I couldn't understand why the French journalists were allowed to visit the camp, whereas none of their Soviet colleagues was given such a chance. Besides it was hard to believe that the authorities have suddenly grown so magnanimous. We all knew of the arrest of Sergei Kuznetsov in 1988, a member of the Democratic Union and a correspondent for *Glasnost*, a Samizdat magazine. He had been charged with slander and sentenced to three years in a labour camp. While in prison waiting for trial he was humiliated and brutally beaten.[1] What was that if not a political case?

One of my Western friends showed me the issue of the bulletin *The Voice of the Martyrs* for February 1989 with the Reuters News Agency information on the revelations of Abraham Shifrin, a veteran of Soviet labour camps who had recently emigrated to Israel:

Glasnost is just a show. It's a performance for the West. Gorbachev has cheated the world. Life in Soviet concentration camps has become more strict. In Gorbachev's days the penal regime is even more severe. Prisoners now get less food, no food parcels from their families for the first half of their sentences and fewer meetings with relatives. In the past, after fifteen days in a punishment cell, a prisoner had to be let out for a while. Now the punishment can be renewed until death. Under Gorbachev they released approximately 170 well-known political prisoners including a few religious believers. But we count approximately one hundred thousand believers still in concentration

45

camps. In each camp there are hidden political prisoners; in special political camps in Moldavia, the Urals and elsewhere there are between 5000 and 6000 political prisoners.[2]

These revelations echoed one of the letters I received after my stories on the Leningrad mafia, from a prisoner in a Komi Republic labour camp in northeast Russia:

I beg on you journalists to do something about us prisoners. I realise that you are not God , but you help to form public opinion. I have been here since 1986. The degradation is almost complete. I am on the brink of going mad. When will there be a law defining our rights? We are not asking to be allowed to strike: we are slaves and slaves have always been shot when they express dissent. But what have they done? They have armed our warders with truncheons and now call this democracy. Funny? But not for us! Why is the word 'prison' in our society associated with black bread, rotten food, shouting and beatings? I have long forgotten how fresh vegetables and fruit look. Are we human beings or aren't we? For the time being we express our discontent rather meekly. But remember Newton's law: each force breeds a counter-force. I am not sure whether you will understand me or not. After all there's only one real intellectual left in the country – academician Sakharov. I am sealing the envelope now and keep thinking: why?

So I decided that I must go to labour camp thirty-five. If they let the French media in, I thought, how can they deny me access. But to get permission proved very difficult. I had to act through GUITU – the Chief Directorate of Corrective Labour Institutions of the Interior Ministry. Without their authorisation I couldn't even dream of getting close to a labour camp. The situation was made more complicated by the fact that there was another Directorate responsible for labour camps at the Interior Ministry – GLAVLES. It dealt with camps where inmates were involved in wood cutting and carpentry (*Les* in Russian means 'wood'). After a month of haunting the two Directorates' thresholds, I got permission on condition that in my future story I would refrain from using the words 'political prisoners', since officially they did not exist. So far, so good . . .

I was a little worried that my new KGB 'friends', who had started harassing me by that time, would intervene and prevent me from going, but for some reason this did not happen. Having arrived at my decision to emigrate, I realised that this investigation could easily become my last one in Russia, so I wanted to do a really good job. First of all, I refreshed my knowledge of the history of Soviet labour camps which was not an easy thing to do: the information available was more than scarce.

I was well aware of the fact that political dissent had always been treated as a major threat to Soviet power. From its very first days the Bolsheviks

46

mercilessly suppressed any kind of disagreement with the Party's general line. I think the first concentration camps for dissidents were created not by Hitler, but by Felix Dzerzhinski, the first chief of the Cheka (the KGB's predecessor) on Lenin's orders in 1918. The Nazis simply copied the Russian model twenty years later.

Under Stalin, labour camps became the main instrument of political repression. By some estimates, more than sixty million people were murdered there during his thirty-five-year rule. The very word 'Gulag', which stands for the Chief Directorate of Camps, has turned into the main symbol of the Soviet totalitarian regime. Under Khrushchev the name was changed into GUITU, but the message and the system remained the same, though of course the population of 'Gulag Archipelago' was considerably reduced. Under Brezhnev the labour camps thrived, but with détente in progress the authorities grew more cautious. They were falling over themselves to avoid purely political trials, instead charging dissidents with criminal offences: hooliganism, theft, speculation etc. Certainly the allegations were rigged, but this enabled the authorities to place dissenters into the same prisons as ordinary criminals. Dissident historian Vladimir Bukovsky, refusenik Natan Sharansky, physicist Yuri Olov, priest Gleb Yakunin and many others were treated like that.

When the notorious article seventy of the Criminal Code (anti-Soviet agitation and propaganda) was abolished in 1988 as a result of pressure from the West, the rulers became even more fastidious in making sure that every dissident was prosecuted for some other 'state crime' as well. If you look into the files of the present-day prisoners of conscience, you will see that all of them have a combination of charges. It is either article seventy plus article sixty-four (betrayal of the motherland or high treason, ie an attempt to emigrate without permission) or seventy plus sixty-six (Terrorism) or seventy plus seventy-six (divulging state secrets to foreigners) etc.

So how many Soviet labour camps are there? What's the present-day population of the 'Gulag Archipelago?' Naturally, there is no official record, but I know the exact figure!

At the beginning of 1989 I attended a press briefing at the Interior Ministry on Zhitnaya Street, Moscow. Such briefings had become regular, but as a rule they were just token tributes to glasnost with the participating militia officials as tight-lipped as ever before. In this case, though, it was different, largely due to the fact that the outgoing Interior Minister, General Vlasov himself, was presiding. Everyone knew that he was in for a big promotion to become Prime Minister of the Russian

Federation and that this briefing was probably his last public appearance as Interior Minister. We journalists tried to use the opportunity to drag something really important out of him, thinking he would prefer to leave his post with good face in the eyes of the press. By the end of the briefing, when there was just a handful of us left in the room, I asked: 'Comrade Minister, what's the overall number of prisoners in our country now?' Vlasov grew tense and wrinkled his nose in disapproval. 'Are there any foreign correspondents here?' he queried. 'No,' we cried out in chorus. 'I am not supposed to answer that question,' the Minister went on gravely. 'But I will answer it today. The number of accused criminals in different sorts of forced confinement is 1,000,300. This figure is by far the largest in the world. The United States of America, say, have two and a half times less prisoners – about 400,000.' A note of fiendish pride in the Minister's voice couldn't escape our ears. The figure was too big and too precise to be false.

But this was not a faux pas on Vlasov's part, as we were inclined to believe. When some of my colleagues tried to make this figure public, they were bitterly disappointed: the censors did not allow them to publish it. Vlasov knew what he was doing.

Just imagine: one million of our compatriots behind the barbed wire in the fifth year of 'democratic' reforms!

In the course of my journalistic career I had several opportunities to visit labour camps and prisons. So what is the difference between the two? Very often in the West one may hear that someone in Russia was tried and sent to prison. This is not entirely correct. The penal system in the Soviet Union is such that one usually goes to prison only before the trial. The correct name for most of the prisons in the USSR is 'the pre-trial isolation wards'. The accused stays there on remand during the investigation and then, if the court condemns him (which happens almost automatically), he goes to serve his term in a labour camp where he must work.

Before camp thirty-five I had visited only two others. Both were of the so-called 'strict regime'. The camps of such a regime stand in the middle of the simple Gulag hierarchy. The first stage is 'general regime camps', reserved for petty criminals, pregnant women and foreigners (only for those who commit crimes, don't worry). Discipline is not very strict, work is not too hard and the food is not as bad as elsewhere in Gulag. The strict regime labour camps are much tougher: the inmates are allowed to move around only in formation with their hands behind their backs, they are not supposed to sit down in the barracks during the day and so on. They are also involved in hard manual labour. The last and the most terrifying tier of the Gulag pyramid is occupied by the 'special regime camps' where murderers, rapists, bribe-takers and inveterate recidivists are kept. The conditions there are so awful that I will spare myself the pain of describing them.

The first strict regime camp I visited was in Latvia. The supervisor was a smiling young officer, a 'humanist' he said. To reassure the inmates he arranged a big flowerbed in the middle of the camp grounds. To work there pulling weeds or cutting grass was the biggest reward a prisoner could receive. 'I wish you could see,' the supervisor confided to me, 'how selflessly they work there. These murderers, burglars, drug addicts and other scum suddenly become human beings. If someone pulls out a flower – the others will give him a really hard time afterwards.'

'Flowerbeds? What nonsense!' the supervisor of another strict regime camp in Rostov-na-Donu exclaimed, when I told him the story of his Latvian counterpart. 'They deserve bullets – not flowers!' he fumed. 'Flowers! The very idea!'

And indeed the inmates of this second camp looked miserable. They didn't even have the room to stretch their legs after work. The barracks were unkempt and dirty. Iron bars were everywhere. It all looked like a big cage with watchtowers in the corners. The guards on top of these towers always had their machine-guns ready. The staff however had a swimming pool and a special musical room for meditation. These were also behind the barbed wire, though, so I didn't envy them their job.

It is important to see that even the conditions in labour camps were subject to a certain flexibility, depending on the human qualities (if any) of the supervisor.

On a gloomy morning, 23 October 1989, I flew to Perm from where I was to go to the labour camp, which was situated not far from Vsesviatskaya railway station, about 400 kilometres from Perm. Despite the fact that it was only the middle of autumn, the city was already covered with snow.

First of all, however, I had to visit the regional Department of Corrective Labour Institutions (part of GUITU) to get some transport. The Department was attached to the regional militia headquarters, but was located in a separate five-storey building in the centre of Perm. From this nondescript house Permlag – one of the biggest units of Gulag – was administered.

The mass-produced portrait of Gorbachev was looking down at me blankly from the wall of the office of the assistant chief of the Department. Khrebtov had told me on the way from the airport that he was the KGB supervisor of Permlag and actually the most important person there. He was dressed in civilian clothes, a dirty pink shirt and an old-fashioned sea-wide tie. He had cold, expressionless eyes which, as my experience showed, were a characteristic feature of most KGB people.

'Well, go to the camp,' he said reluctantly, scrutinising my press card and the authorisation. 'But remember: don't ask for the prisoners' files.' 'Why not?' I wondered. 'We have glasnost now and their files are not confidential.' Gorbachev on the portrait was watching me sternly in an obvious disapproval of my persistence. The KGB man was equally disapproving: 'They are especially dangerous state criminals. Their files constitute state secrets.' Some logic . . .

Anyway, I was given a car and a driver and we left Perm that very afternoon. For almost seven hours we drove in pitch darkness under unceasing snowfall. The road ran through taiga* and was very slippery. Visibility was practically nil. From time to time we were overtaken by heavy trucks and we perched behind them for protection. Passing through the miners' town of Chusovoi we stopped for food. It was only half-past eight in the evening but all the shops and canteens were already closed. The only place open was the railway station buffet. It had nothing but stale bread on display. We bought two iron-hard loaves and chewed on them stubbornly for the rest of the journey.

Dead tired, we arrived at Vsesviatskaya at half-past ten and were put up for the night at a small hotel which belonged to camp thirty-five and was used by the visiting officers and inspectors from Perm.

As soon as we settled down we had a visitor, Lieutenant-Colonel Bukin, the former regime chief of camp thirty-five. Several years before he had been promoted to supervisor of the neighbouring special regime labour camp, which housed not political but 'ordinary' criminals.

Bukin was very nostalgic about his camp thirty-five. There were less problems with 'politicians' (his word) than with murderers and burglars. He said that he remembered Natan Sharansky, Yuri Orlov, Lev Ginzburg and other 'famous' political prisoners very well. Now that they had been released he bore no grudge against them and spoke of them without spite, rather with a certain fascination. And guilt. 'Sharansky was not a bad fellow, but he did not want to work. No, we never beat him. He was quite healthy and we were just trying to make him work. That was no fault of mine. He was sentenced by the court, not by me. I was simply performing my duties.'

Bukin was an avid reader and an amateur bookbinder. He spoke sadly of his new position: 'At camp thirty-five they now have only twenty-nine inmates. At mine – camp ten – we have 1700. Every day there's some kind

* Coniferous forest bordering the northern tundra.

50

of emergency. The prisoners smuggle vodka into the camp, they make home brew in bowl lampshades, they get drunk on Pomorin – Bulgarian toothpaste. Always ready to hurl abuses at you or even to stab you with whatever comes to hand. We have to work twenty-five years before retiring, and of these we spend eight full years behind the barbed wire – a prison term, only without sentence. Voluntary confinement.'

I did pity Bukin, but didn't try to reassure him: render unto Caesar that which is Caesar's. No-one forced him to become a warder. Certainly, it is not very gratifying to realise that you will be known throughout the world as an oppressor, whereas your recent prisoners, the dissidents, have suddenly turned into heroes and martyrs. But again, the choice was his . . .

Next morning after a quick breakfast we started towards camp thirty-five (or Perm 35 as it is sometimes called) which was ten miles further away from Vsesviatskaya. I will never forget that trip. We were moving along a snow-carpeted corridor between the fences of labour camps. On both sides of the track were unending rows of barbed wire, watch towers with freezing fur-coated guards on top, dogs barking angrily from behind the concrete walls. One camp followed another; there were simply no other structures for miles. It looked as if the whole country and the whole earth were ensnared by some giant villain – shackled, chained and put in irons. And that was only a tiny part of Permlag. Here I could see very clearly that the figure given by General Vlasov was not an exaggeration. It took great effort to imprison one million people. And lots of space too. The Soviet state has never had enough space to provide adequate housing for its citizens, but it has always managed to find somewhere to accommodate its prisoners and dissenters.

How should I describe what I saw and heard in camp thirty-five? I have been thinking about it for a long time. 'You should not pass judgment on anyone,' the Bible says. It is especially difficult to try and judge your fellow humans. That's why I decided to refrain from judgments and let my readers draw their own conclusions. My role here will be purely descriptive, a character among other characters. I shall give the floor to the warders and to the prisoners who volunteered to speak to me. Each of them deserves his own say. Luckily the camp's KGB representative was on leave when I came (KGB men, like normal people, must also relax from time to time) and I gained access to the prisoners' files with their official sentences. This will enable me to let the system speak for itself too.

I shall also give you the testimonies of Natan Sharansky and Leonid Lubman, former prisoners of Perm 35. Leonid Lubman was released in April 1990 after almost thirteen years of incarceration.

51

The population of the camp at the time of my visit was just twenty-nine men. Just? Yes, if one remembers that only one year before there had been 105 of them. But twenty-nine men means twenty-nine souls, twenty-nine lives which will not be lived again. Who are they – these twenty-nine men, these zeks?*

Let's enter the camp (as guests, not as inmates – fingers crossed), let's look into the barracks, the infirmary, the canteen.

Metallic click. The iron-barred doors swing open with a squeak – a first door, a second, a third. The plate on the wall reads: 'Unescorted women are strictly prohibited from entering!' Muffled barking of dogs. Guards on watchtowers.

Lieutenant-Colonel N.M. Osin, camp supervisor: Our institution was set up in 1972 on the site of Skalninskaya corrective labour colony for female juvenile delinquents. The accommodation limit is 400 persons. Now, as you know, we have only twenty-nine. Those prisoners who had been convicted under article seventy of the Criminal Code alone (anti-Soviet agitation and propaganda) were freed in 1987–8. We used to have all kinds of people here. Sharansky, say. Apart from article seventy he also had article sixty-four (betrayal of the motherland). He was later exchanged for Louis Corvalan, Secretary General of the Chilean Communist Party, who had been imprisoned by Pinochet. Vladimir Bukovsky was a pure dissident with only one article – seventy. So at present he wouldn't have been even detained. Yuri Orlov, the physicist was also a pure 'seventynik'. His term was seven years. Now he lives in America and gets good coverage in our press. I also remember Gleb Yakunin, the priest. Now, as far as I know, he is working in the Church again. What do I think about them all? They had enough spite towards our system, I assure you. Those who were working diligently, who didn't break the camp's rules, were treated well. After all, we are neither judges nor legislators, we haven't convicted them. They were brought to us with their verdicts and we had to comply.

Today for twenty-six inmates we have three doctors: our staff remains unchanged since the time when the camp was full. Food is OK. We taste it every day, you will see for yourself. Who are the present-day prisoners? Thirteen spies, nine defectors who wanted to escape to the West – some of them attempted to hijack planes – seven war criminals who collaborated with German fascists during the war. We sometimes call those last 'chastisers' . . .

* Russian slang for prisoners.

The atmosphere in the camp is quiet. Not a single crime has been committed here since its foundation. By the end of this year we plan to release three more prisoners, so we'll have only twenty-six altogether. We wouldn't mind if they were all released and can only hope that in the course of time there will be no defectors, spies or chastisers, even if it means that we ourselves are left jobless.

Natan Sharansky: Osin was an enormous flabby man of around fifty, with small eyes and puffy eyelids, who seemed to have long ago lost interest in everything but food. But he was a master of intrigue who had successfully overtaken many of his colleagues on the road to advancement. During my brief time in the camp he weathered several scandals and always managed to pass the buck to his subordinates. I could see that he enjoyed his power over zeks and liked to see them suffer. But he never forgot that the zeks were, above all, a means for advancing his career and he knew how to back off in a crisis.[3]

VV: It is quiet here indeed. As quiet as it can only be in a labour camp or a cemetery. Along the pathway powdered with snow, past a little stadium with football and volleyball pitches, I walk to the barracks, a two-storey low-built house with small curtains at the windows. The barracks are empty: the prisoners are at work. Only the man on duty is sitting on a chair by his bedstand in a large spacious room. He is using his bedstand as a table to write one of his recurrent appeals to the USSR Supreme Soviet to strip him of his Soviet citizenship. This prisoner's name is Pavlov. He was convicted for spying for the US and Canada (at least, that's what his verdict says). He is planning to emigrate to the West immediately after his release. 'One can achieve nothing here,' he explains.

According to the regime two prisoners must share one bedstand, though in Perm 35 due to the small number of inmates the administration decided to waive the rule and gave a bedstand to each. This piece of furniture is very important to a zek: it's here and here alone that he can store his few personal belongings: a toothbrush, a pen, books, paper.

The dormitory is quite spacious: fifteen square metres for each inmate, whereas in Moscow, say, the limit of 'living space' considered normal is five square metres per person. On the wall one can see posters with daily routine regulations – reveille at six-thirty am, retreat at ten-thirty pm, models of bed-making and lists of clothes and footwear each prisoner is entitled to have: a fur hat, a summer cap, a half-length overcoat, a hat with earflaps, a padded jacket, cotton overalls, a pair of rubber boots, wide trousers, felt boots, two singlets, two pairs of underpants. On the neatly-covered bunks there lie some newspapers – *Komsomolskaya Pravda*,

Rahva Hääl (in Estonian) – and a Hebrew textbook. On a little shelf there stands an alarm clock – one for all. In the corner there's a special closet with the record-player, called 'our discotheque' by the zeks. In the adjoining sports room weights, dumb bells and a guitar (?) are stored. In these unpretentious surroundings twenty-nine adult men spend long years of their one and only life. The thought gave me the creeps. The radio was playing and the call-sign of Mayak ('The Beacon') radio station. It sounded too loud and out of place – like a military march in a crematorium.

Natan Sharansky: 'Perm 35 was no more than a small clearing in the woods, approximately 500 metres square and surrounded by numerous fences, rows of barbed wire and electronic warning devices. Rising above it was the 'birdhouse', a booth where the duty officer sat with a unit of noncommissioned officers. Unlike the criminal camps, the political zones were quite small. Whereas Perm 10, only a few hundred metres away, contained about 3000 zeks, Perm 35 held between seventy and eighty. After prison, however, this seemed like an entire country. We all slept in the same barracks, stood for roll-call in the morning, went to work together and took our meals in the same dining room. In the evening you could spend your free hour or two over a cup of tea, talking or strolling.

At six each morning a siren rang and you woke up to the call 'Get up'. In a few minutes the guard passed through the barracks and anyone still in bed would be reprimanded or punished. Then you washed, dressed, made your bed and went outside for roll-call. After that it was off to the dining room to gulp down the morning swill. Still, camp food was better than prison food and there was more of it too. Here at least you could see the meat, and whenever a zek returned from the punishment cell, his friends made sure there was extra food for him.

After breakfast we had half an hour free before work. Some people dozed, some read (there was a modest camp library) and some drank tea with their friends. At seven-thirty we went to work. Officially we were working for the Sverdlovsk instrument factory. In addition to the lathe shops there was also a sewing shop where old men sewed sleeves from morning to evening, as well as a workshop that produced special souvenir chess sets with inlaid pictures and chiselled pieces.

In the evening after work there was another inspection. Then, after supper, you could read a book, look at newspapers or read letters from home if you were fortunate enough to receive any. You could also play chess, billiards or table tennis. Twice a week there were political instruction classes but, like most of the 'anti-Soviet' prisoners, I refused to attend.

Sunday was a holiday with a cutlet at dinner, followed by a film. Sometimes they showed foreign films. Once a year there was a special dinner for the best workers, who then received two cutlets and got to watch an additional film.

Another enormous difference between camp and prison was that here you were entitled to an annual private meeting of up to three days with your family. During the entire period of the visit you actually lived with your family in a special room with a kitchen. Naturally, you could always be denied a meeting for 'poor behaviour'.[4]

Prisoner V.I. Ostapenko, born in 1922: I was convicted for war crimes in the Belgorod region during World War Two. Yes, I did serve in the German police, but against my will, you understand? If I'd refused, I would have been shot, I think. I was a rank-and-file policeman. I didn't participate in punitive actions against Soviet citizens. I was only brought to trial in 1979: my colleagues denounced me. Prior to that I worked honestly and had the honorary title of Labour Veteran. That's how it was. What did I do as a policeman? All kinds of things: stood at my post guarding German positions, escorted the arrested to interrogations. Yes, you are right: not 'the arrested', but 'the Soviet prisoners of war'. At the end of the war the Germans took us abroad with them – first to Romania, then to Italy. We were building fortifications at the German-American front. In April 1945 we voluntarily surrendered to the Americans and found ourselves in Pisa, Italy. The Americans treated us well, gave us good clothes and kept saying that we shouldn't go back to Russia. But I decided to return all the same and worked quietly ever since. If it were not for my colleagues who denounced me . . . I can't say that I am totally innocent. I bear some guilt, but I never took part in repression and I joined the police against my will.

The System, from the verdict on V.I. Ostapenko: Residing on temporarily occupied Soviet territory, betrayed his motherland by going over to the enemy. In July 1942 voluntarily joined the occupants and was enrolled in Group 725 of the Secret Field Police which was part of the 213th Security Division. Underwent a short-term military training course, took an oath of loyalty to fascist Germany and was given a gun and a rifle. Was fitted out with the uniform of a German soldier and was put down for all allowances. Carrying out the orders of the German officers, escorted arrested Soviet citizens to prison and to interrogation, took part in punitive operations against partisans and personally shot Soviet patriots. As part of a team of volunteers took twelve arrested Soviet citizens from the position of his unit to Dalni park in Belgorod for execution. There each of the policemen (Ostapenko included), at the command of a

German officer, fired one or two shots into the doomed people. Took part in the punitive operation near the village of Solomino in Belgorod region: armed with carbine searched a wood firing at unarmed people suspected of belonging to partisans. As a result of this operation ten Soviet citizens were killed and the same number arrested. Together with other policemen also escorted thirty Soviet citizens from Belgorod prison to their place of execution near the former monastery. Before being shot, the doomed people were stripped to their underwear whereupon the policemen cordoned off the grounds and took the arrested one by one to where Willy Schwartz, the German officer, shot them in the back of the head. Also, among other policemen, escorted the column of the prisoners of war from the town of Sumi. Five partisans and seven prisoners of war were shot by policemen on the way. Also guarded the place of execution of two girls suspected of having connections with partisans. The girls were shot dead.

VV: I was talking to Ostapenko near the two-storey workshop building. Downstairs there's a small lathe shop producing cutting and mortising tools, upstairs – a little sewing shop where zeks sew dust-covers for Druzhba ('Friendship') motorsaws. The annual value of the workshop's output is one million roubles. The working hours are from eight in the morning to six at night with one holiday – Sunday.

Prisoner Y.A. Steiblis, born in 1923: I am Lithuanian and was condemned for having served in the Lithuanian battalion of the German army when I was seventeen. I was convicted in 1982. Before that I worked as a construction manager, had a good reputation and was trusted with large sums of money. Then I retired – and suddenly became an enemy! You can't prove anything to the Soviet authorities. They have their truth and I have mine. What has the Soviet army done to Lithuania? We greeted Soviet soldiers with flowers in 1940, but we were seeing them off with bullets. What have they done? They have killed thousands of Lithuanians and now they tell me that I am a war criminal. It's not me who is the war criminal, it's them. If the Soviet soldiers hadn't been shooting our civilians, if they hadn't exterminated or exiled them, then the Lithuanian battalion where I served would never have been formed.

The System, from the verdict on Y.A. Steiblis: In June 1941 betrayed his motherland, went over to the enemy and voluntarily joined the so-called Battalion for the Protection of the Peaceful Labour of the People, the Second Auxiliary Police Service, in Kaunas. On 28 October 1941 was personally involved in shooting Soviet citizens in the town of Slutsk in the Minsk region. Several thousand people altogether were executed there by the soldiers of the Lithuanian battalion. After the war was tried several times for embezzlement.

VV: The camp canteen is located in a big log cabin. At the entrance there's a tiny food shop where the choice is several times better than that in the ordinary shops in Perm. It has three brands of cheap soap, tea (both soap and tea were being rationed throughout the country at that time), honeycakes, butter, several sorts of sweets and even filter cigarettes which cannot be got for love nor money outside the camp. Milk is delivered daily. What else? Jam, pickled onions, canned fish, sunflower oil. A prisoner can spend up to twenty-five roubles a month here, which are then deducted from his salary.

Prisoner Y.V. Pavlov, born in 1935: I was laboratory head on board a research ship and was convicted of espionage. They published a whole novel about me in *Pravda* in 1985. It was just a pack of lies. Certainly I am not sinless, but that *Pravda* story was 99 per cent fantasy. I was told by one KGB man that some points in the article had been deliberately stretched for the sake of propaganda to put others off spying. But how can they feed lies to the people? My case is full of unclear and vague points about which I keep writing to different bodies. The answers usually take many months to arrive and there hasn't been a single concrete one yet! I don't think I am guilty of spying. Yes, talking to foreigners I divulged a state secret, I agree to that. I considered myself hurt since my inventions were shelved in the Soviet Union. I even went to see Romanov, First Secretary of the Leningrad Party Committee, but was shooed away from his office: don't meddle in our affairs, we are busy compiling the guidelines for the Leningraders to lead them through the next five-year plan, they said. And I decided to tell the foreigners about my innovations. I think that a spy is someone who consciously collects data and analyses it and I did not collect anything. I simply told them about something that I myself had discovered. What sort of a spy am I? I have ten more years to serve with five years' exile to follow. Who will help me? I am sick and tired of writing, of appealing for reconsideration of my case.

The System, from the verdict on Y.V. Pavlov: Worked as the chief of a radio-chemical unit on the ships of the Arctic and Antarctic Expedition of the State Environment and Meteorology Committee. In 1981–3 for mercenary motives established and maintained contacts with the US and West German intelligence services and passed over military and state secrets to them for material remuneration. On 17 October 1981 in the port of Alesund (Norway), on his own initiative sent a letter to the West German

Consulate with offers of collaboration and promised to provide information on the Soviet navy in exchange for substantial payments. In this
letter also described his distinctive marks, specified time and places of
meetings, and gave some information on the active zones of the atomic
energy installations on board Soviet ships and on research into locating
nuclear submarines with non-acoustic methods thus divulging a state
secret. In August 1982 in the port of Hamburg met a BND (West
German intelligence) agent to confirm the authenticity of the information. Also disclosed his sources and received the remuneration: 800
Deutschemarks. In May 1982 in the town of Santa Cruz de Tenerife
(Canary Islands) again met a BND representative and submitted his
ship's research programme and received the fee of 4000 Spanish pesetas,
300 Deutschemarks and 150 Dutch guilders for the information he had
supplied before. In November the same year in Copenhagen and Rio de
Janeiro supplied West German intelligence with the characteristics of
Soviet nuclear submarines and was given another assignment: to collect
data on Soviet navy warships. In February 1983 in Montevideo
(Uruguay) was instructed on the contact procedure for US security
agencies and received 100 US dollars and 1000 Spanish pesetas. Also
had meetings with US intelligence representatives in the town of Port
Louis (Mauritius). In July 1984 made an attempt to establish connections
with the US security services through the US Consulate General in
Leningrad by letter. Was detained near the Consulate entrance.

Leonid Lubman, former Perm 35 prisoner: Yuri Pavlov is fifty-four. His term
is fifteen years plus five years' exile. He was arrested in 1984 and was tried
by military tribunal in Leningrad. He is a nuclear physicist and has visited
many countries in about twenty years working on Soviet research ships.
The discovery which he failed to introduce in the Soviet Union, despite
his many appeals to Soviet and Party bodies, concerns turning graphite
into diamond crystals with the help of a nuclear explosion. Having lost all
hope of interesting anyone in the USSR, he passed it over to the West.
Pavlov maintains that apart from his own invention he hasn't given any
secret information to the West. At present Pavlov is very unwell, he suffers
from constant head and heart pains and his blood pressure is unstable.
This man requires serious medical attention of which he is practically
devoid in the camp.[5]

VV: The library is one of the most interesting places in the camp. It stores
4500 books. The librarian is prisoner F.* He used to work for the Soviet

---

* F asked me not to disclose his name.

military mission in one of the African countries, combining this with spying for the US. The library subscribes to four national newspapers at the camp's expense. Besides, each prisoner can subscribe to any Soviet publication at his own expense. 'We subscribe to everything,' the prisoner-librarian says. 'To *Literaturnaya Gazeta, Znamia* (The Banner), *Oktiabr* (October), *Druzhba Narodov* (Friendship of the Nations) [all progressive magazines – VV], and even to the yellow *Ogonyok*. Why yellow? Because it's trashy and time-serving . . .'

It was intriguing to learn that the prisoners can now read *Gulag Archipelago* by Solzhenitsyn, published by *Novy Mir* magazine to which the library also subscribes.

'All twenty-nine inmates have library cards,' the librarian continues, 'though less than half read actively. It's like a kindergarten here – peaceful and quiet. We never use foul language and never fight.'

Prisoner A.V. Sherbakov, born in 1947: Does my name ring any bells for you? No? That's strange: the press has written a lot about me. My popularity was self-imposed, due both to my statements and my deeds. I used to work as chairman of the Voluntary Fire Brigades Society in the Brezhnevski district of Moscow. Now, as far as I know, it has been renamed Cheriomushkinski again. I wish Leningrad – the glorious city of Peter the Great would revert to its old name, St Petersburg, too. Well, I have always opposed Soviet power. I think the Russian people lost their motherland in October 1917. Those who took power then used barbaric methods: they pointed their machine guns at the Constituent Assembly [Russian parliament – VV]. Then they brought down their axe on the White Movement – and now you can see what we've ended up with. In short, I wanted to leave the country of triumphant socialism. I wanted to live in Paris and work for the emigrant press there – to conduct ideological sabotage against the USSR, as they used to say. But how could I leave? You probably know that in 1913 nine million exit visas were issued in Russia for a population of ninety million. In 1985, when I was trying to flee, there were only several thousand issued for 270 million people. I had no choice but to hijack an aeroplane. If you ask me, hijacking a plane is no worse than dispersing the Constituent Assembly, the more so that I didn't use any arms. It was more a political demonstration against the closed borders. Let's open the borders and see whether planes are hijacked then. Pardon me, what did you say? Ah, the passengers. No, I don't think I was jeopardising their lives. I announced immediately that I didn't want to kill anyone, but would have to blow up the plane if it didn't land in Stockholm. The passengers got me right. I remember telling my wife jokingly that if the plane did land in Stockholm, half of them would stay in the West with us. It landed not in Stockholm but on the military airfield in Estonia. I started helping the passengers to disembark. So you see: I was caring for them even then. An escape from slavery has never been a crime, and there was no other way out for an honest man at that time. Well, theoretically there existed another possibility: to officially give up my citizenship – and to go straight to psikhushka, the lunatic asylum. So let's talk about the aim, not the means.

You are willing to treat the realisation of my right to emigrate as a terrorist act. But this right is supported by the Universal Declaration of Human Rights, clause thirteen. I was guilty before the people only to the extent that the borders were closed. You keep talking about mothers and children on the plane, but you don't want to understand how I felt living in the Soviet Union. Whatever you may think, you must write in your article that I am a political emigrant.

The System, from the verdict on A.V. Sherbakov: Having married Malisheva, started sytematically blackening Soviet reality in her eyes. On 16 November 1985, arrived with Malisheva by train in Tallinn with two passports, two shoulderbags, an atlas and a knife. Bought two tickets for flight 8082 Tallinn-Riga-Vilnius with the intention of hijacking the aircraft to Sweden. For self-orientation in flight, acquired a compass. Established the distance between Tallinn and Stockholm and planned the route for crossing the border. Speaking to Malisheva, informed her about his intentions to use the knife as a weapon against those who would create obstacles to hijacking and instructed her to notify the passengers that he possessed an explosive device. Shortly after takeoff of the AN-24 aircraft, through the stewardess Tumasene, ordered the crew to change course and proceed to the USSR state frontier. In the event of any disobedience, threatened to blow up the plane with thirty-one passengers and four crew members on board. To imitate possession of an explosive device, partly opened the zipper of his bag, thrust his left hand inside and held it there. Since the crew took these threats seriously, to prevent the passengers from perishing and after consulting with the ground services, they decided to change course and, under the guise of landing in the foreign airport, land the plane on the military airfield near Haapsalu, Estonia. After landing at 13-22 while threatening to blow up the aircraft, forcibly kept the stewardess and passengers on board using them as hostages and thus inflicting psychological damage on them. Failed to carry out his intentions of fleeing the USSR owing to circumstances over which he had no control, and was arrested.

Leonid Lubman, former Perm 35 prisoner: Alexei Sherbakov is forty-one years old. His term is fifteen years plus five years' exile. He is a Muscovite and was condemned in 1986. Together with his wife he tried to imitate possession of demolition explosives and hijack a plane. His wife was sentenced to five years and has already been freed. Sherbakov was convicted on two articles of the Criminal Code: betrayal of the motherland (article sixty-four) and hijacking of an aircraft (article 213). Curiously enough, he got ten years for hijacking and fifteen years for high treason (ie for the attempt to leave the country). It is also noteworthy that Sherbakov never indulged in political activities.

VV: The mouth-watering smell of freshly cooked shchi – Russian cabbage soup – was spreading all over the camp canteen. I sit down at one of the tables and take a wooden spoon. A deep metallic plate of steaming soup appears before me to be followed by an iron bowl of mashed potatoes. Pieces of meat are placed into a big basin in the middle of the table. The meat is for everyone to share, but there is quite enough of it. On each table there are boxes of spices – salt and pepper, and also onion heads and raw onions. Under the tables, two well-nourished gleaming cats dart around the prisoners' boots. I can't say that my lunch at this canteen was a gourmet delight, but at the Moscow café where I used to have a snack from time to time the quality of food was much worse. As to the cleanliness of the place, there can simply be no comparison: both the canteen and the kitchen at Perm 35 were spotlessly clean.

As you may understand, I am far from trying to create a sort of labour camp idyll. My aim is to describe what I saw there with the utmost precision. I may assume that they have made some special preparations for my visit. Or perhaps (and more likely) Perm 35 is simply on the way to becoming a GUITU showcase for foreign correspondents. I really don't know. But everything there was exactly as I decribe it. In any case, they could have tidied the place up, put curtains on the windows and things like that, but they could not possibly window-dress the inmates. And to tell you the truth, after that lunch at the camp canteen I had severe heartburn for almost twenty-four hours.

Prisoner V.V. Potashov, born in 1949: I have ten years more to go in this camp. My health leaves much to be desired, and I have no hopes of surviving my sentence. I never refuse to work, though under the labour camp conditions such a refusal is a prisoner's last opportunity of preserving his ego. The main thing here is not to lose one's identity, to resist mental and moral degradation. I would like to thank the camp administration for allowing me to carry out creative work. At present I am

61

researching a TV project which would allow viewers to appear on a TV screen and become direct participants in a programme or a film. What for? For the sake of transformation. Which of us hasn't dreamt of changing himself into a hero? Or into a villain? I have undergone such a transformation myself, only not on TV, but in real life.

I used to work at the Institute of the USA and Canada, had a PhD in history and worked on the problems of disarmament. My articles appeared in many Soviet publications, including *Krokodil*. I often went on missions abroad, mainly to the US. At some point I suffered a personal drama: my wife gave birth to a child, but it was not mine, you understand? I had just returned from America. When I learnt about it, I was ready to kill myself, then went on a long drinking bout. When I went on my next mission, I was recruited by the CIA. They provoked me first. With a woman, you understand? It was all so primitive and disgusting. I was made to sign something, then they tested me with a lie detector on a train and kept threatening to throw me out of the window if I lied. It was only then that I realised what a huge force was confronting me. At first they demanded information on my father-in-law who was a prominent Soviet diplomat. I refused. So they changed their tactics and said: 'You are an expert on disarmament. Could you give us your considerations as to Reagan's zero option?' I agreed and returned to Moscow where I divorced my wife, despite my in-laws' objections: they were afraid it might spoil their records and careers. In my messages to America I tried not to harm our country. Yes, I was critical of Brezhnev's approach to the zero option as non-constructive, and this message went to them. But 95 per cent of it was not secret. Now you can easily read the same stuff in *Pravda*. How did I transmit the information? First I would receive an inquiry over the radio – just like in spy thrillers: figures, figures . . . It would take me five or six hours each time to decypher. Then, when I got hold of the information, I would send letters – encoded ones, of course – to the specified address. They paid me for that. I have $92,000 in an American bank account. After the earthquake in Armenia I wrote asking to transfer this money to the victims' fund.

Two and a half years before the arrest I stopped sending messages altogether and kept refusing trips abroad in order not to maintain contacts. They kept threatening me, even tried to arrange a car accident, but I remained firm. I don't know why the investigators who dealt with my case didn't take this into account. No, I didn't give myself up. The Americans told me that if I did, they would arrange for me to be shot. I didn't have any anti-Soviet feelings, my motives were purely personal: I wanted to revenge myself on my wife and in-laws, on the whole bloody family. The Americans kept offering me political asylum – I refused. I am very sorry for my father. He was director of a big factory, had an Order of Lenin. When I was arrested he was forced to retire of course. Yes, I've let him down. Could you do me a favour and find out whether my last book, *War and Peace by the Year 2000*, has come out? It was to be published in Helsinki. If it did happen, could you ask them to send all my royalties to the Peace Fund?

The System, from the verdict on V.V. Potashov: Being on a long business mission in Washington DC, for mercenary motives established criminal relations with American intelligence. During secret meetings divulged highly confidential information and state secrets. Promised to collect and transmit further information for the remuneration of $1500 a month. In 1982–6 used to withdraw espionage materials from special hiding-places equipped for him in Moscow. Received eleven encoded messages with secret instructions and posted eight coded dispatches containing military secrets. In October and November 1981 underwent a special training course in secret service communications. Also possessed espionage equipment: Panasonic radio receiver with headphones to receive and decypher coded messages with secret instructions from US intelligence headquarters. Also sent espionage information by post using coded letters as a cover-up. Was detained on 1 July 1986.

Leonid Lubman, former Perm 35 prisoner: Vladimir Potashov is forty-one years old. His term is thirteen years. He was convicted in Moscow in 1986. Potashov is a Muscovite, a Candidate of Science. He worked in the USA and Canada Institute and was involved in the preparation of the medium-range missile limitation treaty (the treaty has been concluded). Potashov confesses that he had contacts with the American special services, but maintains that he did not possess any secret information. The data he sent to the West, in his opinion, was designed to foster the speedy conclusion of the disarmament treaty.

In *War and Peace by the Year 2000* Potashov analyses the problems of nuclear disarmament. Only recently, already in the camp, was he officially recognised as the book's author. He has transferred the royalties due to him for the book (11,500 roubles) to the Soviet Peace Fund.

Potashov's health is bad. He has constant heart pains and headaches.

VV: There is a small movie hall in the camp club adjoining the canteen. One day before my arrival *The Woman from the Moon* was shown but only an elderly war criminal dozing in his chair remained to the end. The rest did not like the film and went to watch TV instead.

In the club there is a ping-pong table and a billiards table with the English inscription 'Lucky hit' on all its sides. This was done by Ivanov, the former American spy who had been freed shortly before my visit.

Among other 'sights' in the zone (slang for labour camp) one must mention the bath. At its entrance the administration has put up some posters: 'Socialism means peace', 'Stop the war!' They also show some intricate diagrams supposed to represent 'the economic strategy of the Party'. This was probably done in order to brainwash the prisoners' minds before they wash their bodies. I won't comment on the possible effects of such 'visual agitation': it has none.

Inside the bath there's a steady smell of kitchen soap. The prisoners' slippers (for some reason, they are called 'vietnamki' – Vietnamese women) stand under the wooden bench like soldiers on parade. On the table in the corner there's a stack of *Ogonyok* magazines. The prisoners may not only wash themselves and read the 'yellow' press while cooling down after the steam room, but also do their laundry. For that purpose they have a couple of big washing machines in the dressing room.

Prisoner A.O. Udachin, born in 1965: In the Soviet press one can now hear it said that we no longer have pure political prisoners, that is people convicted on article seventy only. For instance, Professor Nazarov, a lawyer, claimed in the magazine *Smena* that those condemned on article seventy plus another one were simply rapists, bandits and murderers who had been shouting 'Down with Soviet Power!' at the time of their arrest. At this camp there are only three inmates on article seventy – Klimchak, Goldovich and myself. None of us has either killed or robbed anyone. Please tell Professor Nazarov that we are outraged at his slander.

You must have heard of the Jackson-Vanik* amendment. The very existence of our labour camp stands in the way of its abolition by the US Congress. Something must be done about it: the Soviet Union is not wealthy enough to deal with the present situation. After all, who is left here? Defectors? But under the laws of any civilised country, fleeing abroad is not a crime. Chastisers or war criminals? But look at them: they are all little old men now, and during the war they were adolescents. There is a talk of humanism now in the press and elsewhere. These old men worked for their Soviet motherland for many years after the war. And after all these years, despite the fact that they had voluntarily returned from abroad, the forgiving motherland put them in a labour camp.

I am still very young. From the age of sixteen I was under covert KGB

* Whereby economic aid to the USSR was made dependent on Soviet emigration and our human rights record.

surveillance. I was living in Moscow and even before I was drafted I received several official warnings. What did they warn me against? Against reading and disseminating books by Solzhenitsyn, which I did. Then I learnt that my father, who was a top Soviet intelligence person in Britain, had defected and blown the whole Soviet espionage network in that country. He was tried in his absence in Moscow and sentenced to death. Out of naivety I nevertheless attempted to enter a higher educational establishment. I remember how at the Foreign Relations Institute [the most prestigious Soviet college mostly for the sons and daughters of the elite – VV] they looked at my record and said: 'My dear boy, even if you were as wise as Solomon, we would never accept you!' Well, I couldn't think of anything better than joining the army. And where do you think I was sent to serve? To East Germany! This time I simply didn't mention my father in the questionnaire – and no-one checked! A couple of years later, after I was arrested, half of the military registration and enlistment office where I had been recruited simply disappeared together with the district chief enlistment officer himself. Do you know what the most chaotic and inefficient organisation in the Soviet Union is? The army, of course. There I started having ideological arguments with our company's zampolit [a commissioned officer responsible for the correct political orientation of the personnel – VV]. At first he trusted me and had me nominated as the company's Komsomol [Young Communist League – VV] leader. The trouble was I told the truth at Komsomol meetings. In particular, I told the soldiers that the American Sixth Fleet posed no threat to the security of the German Democratic Republic, that the intrigues of Western imperialism simply did not exist, apart from the normal intelligence activities conducted by both the US and the USSR. Indeed, what's the use of intriguing against our country – she is eating herself up! You don't even have to push her – she will collapse anyway. Of course, the zampolit didn't like this. Tell me, have you ever tried not to sleep for twenty-eight days in a row? In the army I had twenty-eight extra night duties in succession. In the end, there was nothing else left for me but either machine gun half of the unit or . . . Eventually I simply beat the shit out of the zampolit. Yes, I know that was not a proper thing to do – not very pedagogical – but there's no other way to teach a stupid scoundrel . . . After that, our osobist [the KGB representative in an army unit – VV] explained to me that I had only a couple of months of freedom left: prison was waiting for me in the long run. So what was I supposed to do? I simply left the company positions and went away. Where did I go? Wherever my feet carried me. 'My Mother Russia, why are you so cruel to your sons? And do I need the Motherland which doesn't need me?' I repeated like a prayer. I didn't notice how I reached the border, the Berlin Wall to be more exact. I looked at the guards, spotlights and barbed wire and realised it was impossible to cross. I sat for a while on a bench in Alexanderplatz and then stood up and started walking back. Six hours later I was arrested by the East German police. I was already ten kilometres away from the border. Why on earth have I been convicted on article sixty-four (high treason, refusal to return from abroad)? Yes, I am guilty of leaving my unit without permission, but it has nothing to do with betraying one's motherland or high treason. They also imposed article seventy-two (participation in an anti-Soviet organisation) on me. Have you ever seen an organisation consisting of only one member? Take a good look at me: I am the organisation. No-one was detained or interrogated as my accomplice. I tried to appeal against such verdicts, and I did get a reply signed by General Marov who recently presided at Churbanov's trial, who is Brezhnev's son-in-law. The reply was just a retyped copy of my verdict. I was condemned in 1984, on my birthday, and started serving my stretch in Mordovia. Then I was transported from one place to another four times. Eventually in 1988 I came here. I must say, this place is blessed. Here I am able to study languages, physics, mathematics. Where else could I have found teachers with the degrees of Candidates and Doctors of Science? Here they had lots of them: mathematicians, sociologists, journalists – fascinating people! We have long talks, discuss philosophical problems. My main task now is to learn to think in English – not just to speak. I became fluent in that language after spending four years in London with my parents. We lived in Highgate, where my father worked at the Soviet Trade Representation – a disguise for the KGB station. I am also learning Japanese. What next? I want to emigrate to the West, to have children. And I don't want them to write in their questionnaires that their grandfather was a famous spy and their father a political prisoner. I am absolutely sure that I am here only because of my father. I have no complaints as to the camp's regime. The only thing I don't understand is why they make us wear crew-cuts all the time. Do we have typhus here or what? And why did they stop selling skin moisturiser at the shop?

The System, from the verdict on A. O. Udachin: Lived, before being called up, in Moscow and systematically mixed with various dissenting elements. At home listened to foreign radio broadcasts on the BBC and Voice of America using radio receivers. Under the impact of these, formed a negative attitude towards the Soviet state. Told his friends that the USSR lacked constitutional freedoms of speech, press, meetings and demonstrations. Being on active service in a group of Soviet troops in East Germany, made preparations for flight: drafted route of escape along highway 101 to the border with West Berlin, prepared civilian clothes hiding them away in a specially equipped secret place. On 22 August 1983 at about one o'clock in the afternoon changed into plain clothes and, intentionally acting to the detriment of the military might of the USSR, left his unit's positions with the aim of fleeing to the capitalist state. Having covered about thirty kilometres on foot, took a taxi to the centre of Berlin and waited for darkness to fall in order to cross the border unnoticeably. Failed to achieve his criminal intentions owing to circumstances outside his control: was detained by the GDR police. A manuscript found in his bag contained hand-written text on the programme of a new political party. In this document wrote of class distinctions in socialist society, the absence of democracy in our country and the backwardness of the Soviet economy.

Leonid Lubman, former Perm 35 prisoner: Alexander Udachin is twenty-four. His term is ten years. He served in the army in the GDR, approached the West German border (Berlin Wall) then came back of his own will. Apart from the attempts to cross the border, he is charged with participation in some obscure anti-Soviet party. Udachin himself thinks that a party cannot consist of only one man.[8]

VV: 'Institution 389/35 Central Hospital' – I saw this proud sign at the entrance to the camp infirmary. In fact it's more like a small hospital than an infirmary. Three doctors work here: two therapists and a dental surgeon, a young lieutenant who recently graduated from the Perm Medical Institute. The hospital has electrocardiographic, orthopaedic and physiotherapeutic consulting rooms, a general treatment room, a small operating theatre and a dental surgery where a half-polished set of artificial teeth, designed for one of the war criminals, was lying on the table. Valentina Mikhailova, the chief camp physician, is a fragile diminutive woman with exquisite features. 'Aren't you afraid working here?' I ask her. She smiles: 'Not at all. The prisoners treat me well.'

This idyllic picture is slightly marred by the fact that the isolation cell, the most ominous part of the camp, is also located in the hospital building.

Prisoner Igor Mogilnikov, born in 1963, is one of the most tragic figures in the camp. He was very hard to talk to. I had to drag answers out of him. It took me at least five minutes to get an answer for each question. He's got a fixed look and his eyes are so full of pain and suffering that it is plain this chap has seen something really awful, something that an average person of his age cannot even imagine. This is the only instance when our labour camp drama will switch to dialogue.

VV: Tell me about yourself, Igor.

IM: (*pause*) What can I tell you? I was born in a village in Perm region. Finished secondary school and was called up. Spent six months in Termez, Uzbekistan, at the sergeants' training centre, and was sent to Afghanistan.

VV: What military profession did you have?

IM: Truck driver. But my licence for some reason did not arrive from Termez: they must have lost it somewhere. Our platoon commander didn't believe me. He kept saying that I had hidden the licence deliberately to avoid working as a driver. They used to taunt me at my unit, beat me up every day.

VV: The treatment they usually give to new recruits.

IM: Exactly! I didn't know where to hide.

VV: How did you become a prisoner of war?

IM: I don't want to talk about it.

VV: OK. What did you do after surrendering to the rebels then?

IM: Nothing special. Just what everyone else in the gang did.

VV: So you think it was a gang in the true sense of this word?

IM: (*long pause*) Of course not. It's just what everyone calls them. In reality they were ordinary Afghan peasants defending their land against the occupiers.

VV: Were you a prisoner or rather a member of this – gang?

IM: I don't want to talk about that either.

VV: How did you come to return to the Soviet Union?

IM: Easy. I was simply taken away. The gang leader said someone had come and wanted to drive me away. They must have sold me or something.

VV: Did you know where they were taking you?

IM: Sure. Where could they? I knew they were going to shoot me.

VV: Did you take part in combat actions with that Afghan group?

IM: Not really. Well, there were cases when we had to return fire breaking out of encirclement.

VV: Are you hoping to be amnestied now?

IM: (*hesitation*) Yes. I want only one thing: to forget this nightmare as soon as possible, to forget, you understand?!

VV: What will you do if you are pardoned?

IM: I will go back to my village. All my folks are there: parents, brother, sister. She has just got married. I will work as a tractor driver.

The System, from the verdict on I.K. Mogilnikov: From June 1983 was on active service as a member of the limited contingent of Soviet troops in the Democratic Republic of Afghanistan. Due to low morale and political standards, service weighed heavily. Struck a don't-care attitude towards his military duties. This attitude caused a number of conflicts between Mogilnikov and his platoon comrades as a result of which some irregular methods of re-education were used against him. On the evening of 15 July 1983, after a recurrent conflict with his platoon comrade Brunko, decided to desert. Left his unit's positions and started for a region where gangs of mutineers were stationed. Having spent the night in a haystack met two local residents, who took him to Kutub, a kishlak [village in Central Asia], where the headquarters of the Afghan Islamic party gang led by Mamadadzhon were located. Told the chief that he had come to them voluntarily and wanted to stay in the gang, since he had been unwilling to serve in the Soviet army. Having obtained permission to stay, studied the local language and Islamic customs for about two months, converted to Islam and was renamed Islamuddin. During his thirteen months in the gang intentionally chose a course of high treason. Gave the gang's leader information on location, missions, combat and logistical support of his military unit, thus betraying military secrets. Later was appointed Mamadadzhon's bodyguard and, having received an AKM machine gun, guarded gang positions in the kishlak. For performing these duties received monthly payments of 1000 afghanis from the chief. Participated more than once in operations against the Afghan people and the Soviet army and also took part in gang raids against the activists of the People's Democratic Party of Afghanistan (PDPA). Took part in attacks on kishlaks, where villagers supported the people's power. In particular, was involved in a raid on the house of Khodja Ainulla, a PDPA activist who was captured and shot and his wife injured – all with his direct participation. Was dressed in Afghan national attire and wore a red turban. On 16 August 1985 was taken from the gang and driven to Soviet troop positions. In a letter to his parents, written from the gang, asserted that he was going to kill everyone he wanted, since there was war in Afghanistan. Never expressed any intention of returning home.

VV: On the wall of my tiny hotel room in Vsesviatskaya there hung an amateurish landscape painting depicting birch trees on a steep riverbank. It was painted by a prisoner and was called *'Freedom'*, though of course this pastoral scene was far from an ordinary Russian landscape as a prisoner's life is from normal human existence.

Vsesviatskaya is a curious village. It's population consists of guards, warders and other members of the two labour camps' administrations. That's why it's quite natural for the zeks from Perm 10 to be employed for construction, decoration and other work in the village. One often sees them around, looking like rooks on the snow in their black caps and overalls. But this is true only for the inmates of camp ten. Political prisoners – no matter how well-behaved – are never allowed outside their compounds.

Perm 35 has its own 'hotel' on the camp premises. They call it the 'rendezvous rooms'. It was here that Mogilnikov's parents stayed when they came to visit their son. It is here that the camp administration accommodates zeks' wives, the stoic and faithful women for whom their husband – prisoner or not – is always the best and the most desired one. Here the visitors can enjoy a tiny kitchen, a box with children's toys and narrow but clean and soft beds. The prisoners are sometimes allowed to stay with them for a night or two and to savour the well-forgotten simple joys of normal human life. This is the camp's highest reward for whose who work well.

In one of the rendezvous rooms I noticed a large coloured butterfly. It was beating itself desperately against the windowpanes. How did it get here, through barking dogs and barbed wire, through the biting frost of the early Urals winter? Or maybe it was the loving soul of a prisoner's sweetheart who turned into a butterfly not wishing to part from her loved one?

Don't think that the butterfly is just a literary metaphor. I did see it – so beautiful, bright and superfluous within those sad walls.

Prisoner V.A. Smirnov, born in 1945: I was tried by the closed court, both my case and my verdict are secret. I was convicted on article sixty-four on 23 April 1982 and six months previously I had voluntarily returned to the Soviet Union from the West. How did I find myself there? I was a senior research worker at the Moscow Institute of Electronic Computing Machinery and was in charge of the laboratory. Mind you, the Institute was not a secret one and I had no access to confidential information. This is very important. We were collaborating with Micron, a Norwegian company, on research in the field of computing machinery. I frequently visited Oslo to work with the Norwegians. During one such trip at the end of 1981 I made up my mind not to return to the Soviet Union and applied for political asylum which was granted, despite the fact that I hadn't been persecuted on political grounds in the USSR. After Norway I went to Munich and then to the US. Within five months I visited Florida, New York, Washington and then – I decided to return: I was desperately missing my family who at that time had no way of joining me. I kept torturing myself with the thought that I had practically left them hostages to the system. At the Soviet embassy in Washington they assured me that I could go back and that there wouldn't be any problems. Nevertheless I was arrested straight on arrival in Sheremetyevo airport, even before I underwent passport control. They drove me to Lefortovo KGB prison in a Volga equipped with carphone. There I was kept for six months in an isolation cell while the investigation was in progress. At the interrogations they kept asking where I had been, what had I seen, and in the end it turned out that I had supposedly divulged state secrets. There's an obvious contradiction here. As I've told you already, I didn't have access to secret work. If, as the KGB experts established, I had known some state secrets, then there appears a natural question: how come? How could someone without official authorisation become the bearer of such secrets? Where is the leak? Why hasn't it been found and stopped to prevent further drain? The funniest thing is that all these questions did not in the least worry the investigators. Now I can say with a full sense of responsibility that my verdict had a purely administrative nature and my case was concocted on instructions from someone powerful with political purposes which escape me. Who it was and why they needed me as political capital, I don't know. All the information about our work which I had at my disposal was equally known to my colleagues at the laboratory. Neither they nor I have ever made any signed statements to the effect that we shouldn't divulge it. And yet I have been here for eight years already.

The System, from the verdict on V.A. Smirnov: On 28 November 1981 went on a business mission to Norway where, induced by anti-soviet motives and personal mercenary interests, committed high treason by not returning to the USSR. On 7 December at meeting with Soviet embassy representatives announced his refusal to return to the Soviet Union and explained that he was driven by political considerations since he didn't like what was going on in our country. While in the West, was supported by the so-called Tolstoy Fund, subsidised by the USA special services. Divulged state secrets and also information on foreign firms' represent-atives in Moscow and their contacts. Gave detailed characteristics of the executive officials from Soviet government bodies he knew from his work. Received 1350 Deutschemarks and $280 in return.

Natan Sharansky: Smirnov was a software specialist who had defected during a trip to Norway and had settled in America. He found work in his field, but soon yearned for his wife and daughter. Living in a free society, he said, you quickly forget what the Soviet Union is really like. Incredibly,

Valery decided to go home and try and bring out his family. Despite assurances that he wouldn't be arrested, Valery was met at Moscow airport by a black Volga sedan. Without even seeing his wife and child, he was driven directly to Lefortovo and sentenced to ten years of strict camp regime.

Work in the prison camp was the same four years ago: sewing sacks with a quota of 345 units a day. If you made the quota on the following day you were fed according to norm 9A: otherwise, norm 9B. I hadn't become any more nimble over the past four years and I didn't even try to fulfil the quota. Valery, however, was amazingly fast on the sewing machine. He suggested that we divide up the work conveyor-belt style; he would undertake the more complicated operations while I would handle the simpler ones. As a result we both received a 9A diet. After work, Valery and I would practise our English.[9]

VV: Massive metallic locks clank, the heavy door slides open – and bright electric light nearly blinds me. Three prisoners in black robes with the word 'SHIZO' inscribed on their chests stand up from their tiny, almost toy-like stools to greet me. 'SHIZO' is the Russian abbreviation for a punishment (or isolation) cell. In camp thirty-five this is a pokey, clean room with barred windows. On one of the walls there are three plank beds which are now tucked up like sleeping berths in a train compartment: lying down during the day is strictly prohibited in SHIZO. There is no furniture apart from the three tiny stools. A lavatory pan stands in the corner. Some pieces of black and white bread are being 'toasted' on the radiators. And the bright piercing lamp on the ceiling burns all round the clock. A prison within a prison.

Only two of the punishment cell's three inmates agreed to talk to me. The third one, Kitenchiyev, a lean young fellow with a stern face and protruding cheekbones, refused to answer my questions.

Prisoner A.A. Goldovich, born in 1947: I was accused of fleeing abroad and helping foreign states conduct anti-Soviet activities. I do not fully understand what 'fleeing abroad' means and how it differs from simply crossing the border. The investigator failed to explain the difference to me. He kept asking whether under certain conditions, if I was tortured for example, I might divulge state secrets. I answered that I wouldn't, simply because I didn't know any. I was an engineer and wanted to emigrate. To do that legally was out of the question, it would simply mean ending up here anyway. The problem was that I did work at a secret factory in the end of the seventies, but of course in all these years the secrets I knew had obviously lost their topicality. In 1985 I was sentenced to fifteen years imprisonment and five years' exile. Why was I put in the isolation cell? Because I protest against slave labour. Yes, in the camp I had been a slave for four years. The labour here is servile. I am supposed to work against my will. What is this, but a form of slavery? I don't agree with the Soviet Constitution which urges every citizen to toil. I am dead sure that the whole slavish system will collapse soon. For that I am here. I have never been a dissident, but now I feel bound to become one: the camp administration keeps pushing me towards that. They understand only one language – the language of political action. By releasing some political prisoners they try to put a good face on the matter. I don't exclude the possibility of being used for that purpose myself in the future. I have already spent 150 days on end in SHIZO. It is freezing in here, the average temperature is ten or twelve degrees centigrade. It's impossible to sleep, to have normal rest. The only distraction is a daily five-minute walk outside. I spend my days in enforced idleness which for me is like torture. The letters I write to my mother are being confiscated under the ridiculous pretext that they contain confidential information. We have neither mattresses nor blankets. At least since September they have been giving us hot food. So far, so good. I've written three letters to the Interior Ministry to the effect that international laws are not being observed in this camp. They were confiscated as libellous.

The System, from the verdict of A.A. Goldovich: On 25 April 1985, was detained by a Black Sea frontier patrol boat about 12.2 miles away from the shore in the vicinity of Sochi. Was moving toward neutral waters in an inflatable rubber boat with his wife Sokolova. Worked as an engineer at the Construction Physics Research Institute. In April 1985 acquired $600 for 2100 roubles from an American citizen named Garrod, thus breaking the hard-currency operations rules. Systematically spread anti-Soviet insinuations among his friends and stored Western-published anti-Soviet books, illegally smuggled into the USSR. Divulged state secrets learnt during his previous job at the Aviation Automatics Research Institute to his wife and friends.

Leonid Lubman, former prisoner Perm 35: Alexander Goldovich is forty-two. His fifteen year term ends in 1998. Then – five years of exile. Together with his wife he tried to cross the Soviet–Turkish sea border in a rubber boat, but was captured by frontier guards. an audiotape with ostensibly secret data figured in his case. Had Goldovich really had it, he could have easily thrown it into the water before arrest.[10]

Prisoner B.S. Klimchak, born in 1937: I am a political prisoner. Why? This is something not to be discussed. On 14 September 1989 I declared a

73

political strike in the camp to protest against the confiscation of my letters. That's why I am not working. I was accused of crossing the border and writing eight essays which were branded anti-Soviet. That was in 1978. Now similar things, and even more iconoclastic ones, are being published by the hundred in the Soviet press, but I am still here. Mind you, I am in the camp now for my writings alone, since the maximum sentence for crossing the border is seven years. And I have been here for eleven years already. Not only do I refuse to work, but I also protest against morning roll-calls and marching in formation.

When they call me for re-education lectures here, I simply cover my ears with my hands. After five minutes they get bored and let me go. I act in the same manner when they try to persuade me to behave or to write an appeal to be pardoned. I am not guilty of anything, so there's nothing to pardon me for. I write a lot in the camp, but they take away everything, even my self-made vocabularies and notes from the world classics. I stand for the free, independent Ukraine – that's the main subject of my writings which are neither anti-Russian, nor anti-Soviet. I am not opposed to Soviet power in principle, but I am against the forms it took in the Russian empire, where it has become the system of the Party bureaucrats. I am the victim of this system, but I don't hate anyone . . . When they finally free me I'd like to spend some time in the West – to improve my health and learn more about Ukrainian history: I've heard that they have published a thirteen-volume Ukrainian encyclopedia in Paris. But then I'd like to come back and live in the Ukraine taking an active part in its national revival.

The System, from the verdict on B.S. Klimchak: Produced and stored a number of libellous anti-Soviet documents in the Ukranian language: 'The Problems of the Satellite', 'Letter to the Publisher', 'Tango Utal Ano', 'Memoirs of the Future', 'Amoral Code of the Builder of Communism', 'Twenty-four Hours in the Life of a Prisoner' and others. These documents propandise the principles of Ukrainian bourgeois nationalism, call for a struggle against Soviet power, for a so-called 'Independent Ukraine' . . . In spring 1976 decided to betray his mother-land and flee to England through Iran. Was planning to have his anti-Soviet works published in London. In the afternoon on 29 September 1978, having got off the Dushanbe-Ashkhabad train at the signal lights of Takir station, Turkmenia, walked over the railway bridge across the Kara-Kum Channel and, getting his bearings with the help of a compass, started towards the USSR state border. At 23-00 broke through the frontier hedges and committed high treason by fleeing to Iran. Was later extradited to the Soviet side by the Iranian government.

Natan Sharansky: Because the Shah didn't want to spoil relations with the Soviets, the police took Bogdan to the border and handed him over to the Soviet authorities. Bogdan couldn't believe it – Iran, the friend of America! The free world was betraying him? His simple peasant mind simply couldn't understand it and at the border he began screaming hysterically. He turned to the Iranian officer and spat in his face. 'Damn you,' he said in Ukrainian, 'damn your land, damn your people!'

At Perm 35 I found Bogdan Klimchak working as an orderly in the workshop where he moved with ferocity and determination. He would cut into the pile of metallic shavings with a sharp shovel as if he were fighting both the KGB and the Iranian police.[11]

Lieutenant-Colonel N.M. Osin, camp supervisor: Do you really think that after his release Klimchak will return to the Ukraine? As far as I know he plans to leave his motherland for good. From the West he will cry bloody murder about the Ukraine and will throw mud at us. The isolation cell is a means of punishment, but we do not restrict ourselves to that. We conduct lectures and political seminars for the prisoners. Klimchak refuses to attend them. We tried to make him change his mind, but in vain. He is consciously opposed to re-education. He claims that he is not allowed to write. According to the standing regulations, the prisoner may possess a copy of his verdict and his belongings mustn't weigh more than fifty kilograms. Klimchak has a pen and paper, so he may write whatever he wants, but naturally we have to confiscate all these later. We have our instructions which we must obey. Our role is minor: we are not legislators, we are executives.

Eleven months after my visit to Perm 35, when I was already living and working in Australia, I was sent by the *Age* newspaper on my first Australian journalistic mission to the small Victorian town of Leongatha. By a strange coincidence, the tape in my dictaphone, which I was using, still carried traces of my trip to camp thirty-five. So here they were, the voices of the inmates and the cheerful baritone of Lieutenant-Colonel Osin saying something to the effect that they were executives. Or executors? (The quality of the tape left much to be desired.) How alien and bizarre these half-forgotten voices sounded in the heat of Australia when I was testing my dictaphone before switching it into action! Distant voices in a new world.

'The finest quality of the human mind is the ability to forget,' Albert Einstein said. Yes, I may have well forgotten some of the voices, but the faces of the prisoners will remain with me forever. Yesterday there were twenty-nine of them. Today as I am writing these lines, there are twenty-six (Mogilnikov, Ostapenko and Lubman have been freed since my visit). And tomorrow?

My camp thirty-five story was published in the Soviet Union when I was already living in the West.[12] It was very badly edited and cut but nevertheless, I was told, it triggered a big response from the readers. I haven't seen their letters. As you know, the dialogue with my Soviet readers was disrupted.

'The Last Gulag' – that's what camp thirty-five has been called in several short and skin-deep Western publications about it. This is basically wrong. Whatever the name, Gulag or GUITU, the world's biggest network of prison camps, keeps growing. As you already know from former Interior Minister General Vlasov's casual remark, at present it accommodates more than one million people.

It is equally incorrect to think that Perm 35 is the last camp for political prisoners in Gorbachev's Soviet Union. There is proof that dissenters are still being kept in Chistopol, Lefortovo and Vladimir prisons, as well as in many special psychiatric asylums. Besides, many of them serve their terms in 'ordinary' labour camps like Perm 10.

Also, when you reread the verdicts on Sherbakov and Goldovich, who were arrested and convicted together with their wives, another question arises: where did the female political prisoners go after the trial? When I asked the camp thirty-five administration, I got an evasive answer: to some other place. So somewhere in Russia's vast expanses there must exist still another 'Gulag' – for women dissidents.

You see how careful one must be when saying something like 'the last Gulag'. As a journalist I fully understand the desire of my Western colleagues to be the first to report on the last Soviet camp for political prisoners, to coin a new cliché . . . But by hurrying to do so, they unwillingly play into the hands of those forces in the Soviet Union who now want to dupe the West again, apart from doing an ill-service to the prisoners themselves. From the several pieces on camp thirty-five published in the West and from the short French TV film (which was called, of course, 'The Last Gulag') it becomes plain that their authors never spoke to the prisoners alone and face to face, but only in the presence of someone from the administration. They have also confused many of the inmates' names and dates and so on. I can't help remembering the words of Alexandr Solzhenitsyn from his epic novel *Gulag Archipelago*:

Oh, those well-fed, carefree, short-sighted, irresponsible foreigners with notebooks and ballpens! – those correspondents who had been pestering zeks with questions in the presence of camp administrators still in Komi! – how much harm have you done to us in your vain passion to show off your understanding where in fact you haven't understood a single bloody thing.[13]

I am not going to comment further on what I saw and heard in camp thirty-five, this microcosm of Soviet life. I think that by giving the floor to both the prosecution and the accused I did the only right thing. Let them speak for themselves. And let's not hurry to judge them.

Finally I just want to pose one last question: what does 'to betray one's motherland' mean – the words to be found in almost every political prisoner's verdict? To betray someone or something one must first pledge allegiance to this someone or something. For how long will the natural desire of a human being to live and to go wherever he or she wants be treated as high treason in the Soviet Union? Despite all the talk about free emigration, the ominous article seventy of the Criminal Code is still in force. Under its provisions, contradicting all the norms of international law signed, among others, by the Soviet Union (the Universal Declaration of Human Rights, the Helsinki Accords etc), one can theoretically be sentenced to death for not returning to the Soviet Union from abroad. In the West you don't imprison people who want to go from England to America, say, without asking for the approval of the British establishment, do you? And in the Soviet Union one can still go to a labour camp for many years just for leaving the USSR without permission from the Soviet authorities.

I myself belong in this category. So while the present-day legislation remains in force, you may consider me honorary prisoner number thirty in Perm 35.

4

Churki and Yids

Among the readers' letters which I received after my stories on the Leningrad mafia was one from Vladivostok. The author, fifty-one-year-old V.A. Anashkin, is a factory worker and father of two. His wife is a maths teacher at a secondary school. An average, archetypal Russian. Here's his letter in full:

> Dear comrade Vitaliev, you've opened our eyes to the state of things in the criminal world. It is hard to believe that in the Soviet country, the best and the fairest in the world, there exists an underworld. We've got used to reading and watching movies about organised crime elsewhere, in the West, but now it appears it exists here as well. Believe me or not, this is not so bad. I want to express my own opinion, shared by many, and put in a word in favour of racketeers. We are literally plagued by speculators. These black visiting Caucasians – Georgians, Armenians, Azerbaidjanis and other churki* - are really getting us down. I don't want to give concrete examples of their behaviour towards Russian people and of how they rob us, I only want to express my passionate desire to clear our life of this stinking scum by hook or by crook. I don't need a kopek from them. The only thing I need is a good machine gun with endless ammunition belt and a comfortable firing position. You cannot even imagine the unparalleled bliss that I would derive from striking this riff-raff out of our life with a spurt of lead. They are worse than parasites, but no-one touches them – neither the law, nor the militia. They are thriving on our sweat. Is this just?

It gave me the creeps to reread this letter while translating it into English. But Anashkin is not to blame. He is one of many victims of a state policy of national hatred and intolerance, encouraged by the Soviet regime for many years. The corrupt and cruel system has always needed scapegoats to blame for its endless failures. Having forcibly united scores of different nations under its red, blood-stained banners, it has skilfully manipulated over-sensitive national feelings to its advantage. 'Divide and rule' – this Machiavellian dictum has become its main watchword. Indeed, if you

* A derogatory term denoting non-Russians with dark skins.

78

divide a nation into parts, if you set your opponents at loggerheads, you can easily have your own way.

Having proclaimed the ideals of equality and fraternity from the very beginning of its existence, the Soviet Union has quickly turned into the world's biggest chauvinistic empire, a real prison-house of nations. The authentic figures of genocide against many national minorities have been made public only recently. On Stalin's orders from 1941 to 1946 many small nations were rounded up, to the very last person, loaded into the cattle-cars of cargo trains and forcibly resettled in Kazakhstan, Central Asia, Siberia and the Urals. Among these were 400,478 Chechens and Ingushes, 60,139 Karachays, 81,673 Kalmiks, 193,959 Crimean Tartars, Bulgarians and Greeks, 774,178 Germans, 84,402 Turks and Kurds.[1] There's a human life behind each of these 1,594,829 statistics. These men, women and children were victimised by the system simply for belonging to this or that nationality. Thousands died en route, before even reaching their new places of settlement . . .

This is only one terrible page in the history of Soviet chauvinism. I am not going to delve into it here. Instead I shall tell you about my own encounters with Soviet nationalism and racism.

During our last four years in the Soviet Union, we used to spend the summer in a small village with the weird name of Zaveti Iliycha – meaning 'Lenin's Bequests' – not far from Moscow. Every evening, at about nine o'clock a tall, middle-aged black man would go past our house. He was probably returning from work in Moscow. The kids from the neighbouring dachas ran into the street to gape at him. He looked so alien in that Russian village among log cabins and wells with stray dogs barking at him angrily. His hands clutched string 'perhaps' bags heavily loaded with foodstuffs. He was tired and drops of sweat ran down his face. What was he doing there? Whom was he visiting? No-one knew. But in my imagination I can see him clearly even now – the son of Africa trudging the bumpy Russian cart-road in the dusk.

Racism in the Soviet Union is a totally uncovered subject. There is practically no mention of it either in the Soviet or in the Western press. It was also the subject of another of my unpublished investigations. 'Have you gone out of your mind?' the *Krokodil* executives asked me when in autumn 1989 I suggested the piece. 'We have enough internal national conflicts to solve!'

Many people are not even aware that there are people of colour in the USSR. Students from Asia, Africa and Latin America started coming under Khrushchev in the late fifties. Since then their number has grown steadily, attracted by a relatively low cost of study and rather lenient academic demands compared to Western countries.

Some of the students married Russians and settled in the Soviet Union rather than returning home. This foreign community is not a big one – no more than several hundred thousand in all. Recently it has been swelled by a sizeable number of Vietnamese workers, so it is less unusual nowadays to see different coloured faces in the streets of Moscow, Kharkov, Leningrad and other major cities.

Racism as a subject for me to write about was prompted by an acquaintance, Lena Hanga, who worked as a journalist on the *Moscow News*. She is black, and was born in the Soviet Union. Her father was a Tanzanian tribe chieftain, her mother was Russian. She is a cheerful, clever and very attractive woman. When she visited me once at our dacha in Zaveti Iliycha I told her about the mysterious African who passed our house each night.

'Yes, there's a handful of black people with Soviet passports living in Moscow,' she said. 'Our life is not easy. I think the Soviet Union is one of the most racist countries in the world.'

She started talking about what it meant to be black in Russia:

No one understands who I am. When I start speaking unaccented Russian, people get petrified. At parties they just gawp at me, as if I was some strange animal. Only because I am black. Terrible racism. I get so much abuse in the street. Do you know that I never go out alone after dark for fear of being assaulted? Everyone hates Africans, and this is the result of the official politics. Are you aware of the fact that not a single Soviet leader since Khrushchev has ever paid a state visit to Africa? Official propaganda has skilfully manipulated traditional Russian xenophobia. Yes, Jews are the main scapegoats, but Africans, Vietnamese and other 'churki' come next. The average Soviet is quite sure in his heart of hearts that African countries are fleecing money and resources out of Russia, whereas in reality it's the other way round. 'We are feeding them, these blacks,' they often say in the streets, 'and what do we get in return? AIDS!' It is also true that the Soviet Union has always supported the most cruel and opportunist African regimes, setting them against each other as with Ethiopia, Somalia and Eritrea all fighting one another with Soviet arms. Why don't you write about it? I tried myself, but no-one wanted to publish it. You are allowed a little more freedom in *Krokodil*. Just try to write about how awful it is to be black in the Soviet Union.

A popular children's anecdote: a small boy sees a negro on a train. 'Look, mummy, there's a monkey!' he cries out gleefully. 'No, I am not a monkey,' the black man intervenes. 'I am an African!' 'Look, mummy, the monkey is talking!' the boy exclaims . . .

There were lots of Chinese students in my native Kharkov at the end of the fifties. The boys in our street used to tease them. 'Narrow-eyes!' they cried. The Chinese only smiled. In the early sixties they disappeared, following the break in the Soviet–Chinese relations. Suddenly 'our Chinese brothers forever' became enemies. Chinese students were replaced by Vietnamese and Africans.

When I was at university, many Soviet students (especially girls) who went out with Africans or Asians became targets for ridicule, ostracism and even violence. Many times riots broke out in the hostels: the foreign students were protesting against the inhuman conditions under which they had to live. They were quickly subdued by the militia and all information about them was carefully silenced.

A friend of mine who was working with the foreign students at the Kharkov Politechnical Institute told me a shocking story of a Chilean student, the son of a Communist purged by Pinochet. He had Indian blood in his veins and was very dark-skinned. His other 'fault' was that he started going out with a Russian girl, whom he loved. This triggered an unprecedented hounding of both of them. The girl was expelled from the Institute and the chap was tormented not only by his Soviet fellow-students, but also by the teachers who invariably asked him impossible questions and gave him bad exam marks. 'I loved the Soviet Union so much before coming here,' he said to my friend. 'But now I see that you are worse than Pinochet.' He hanged himself in his room ... The Chilean embassy in Moscow demanded an investigation, but it came up with nothing.

As with anti-semitism, many ordinary Russians need someone to blame for their troubles and so pick on anyone of a different colour. I received a letter from an industrial city in the Ukraine in 1987 after my article on prostitution was published in *Krokodil*:

> Dear Comrade Vitaliev, if you come to our city of Zaporozhie, you will see our young girls with Komsomol cards in their handbags parading along Lenin avenue with negroes as their escorts. The negroes embrace them and the girls stick to them like lice to dirty clothes. I am no racist, but when I see such couples, or rather tandems, in the streets I feel like I am living in a nightmare. If you do come to Zaporozhie you could prevent the spreading of AIDS in our city. Your reader L-v.

When in 1988 I was coming back to Moscow by train from my first trip to the West, I shared the compartment with a strikingly beautiful black girl from Mali. She was an undergraduate at Krasnodar University and was returning from a holiday spent in Paris with her sister. There were lots of tiny cute plaits on her head and she kept showing me photos of her Malian husband, a policeman.

The attendant of our car, a middle-aged Russian man, was very sympathetic to me. 'How can you sit next to this black monster?' he would ask me whenever I went out for a smoke in the corridor. 'Would you like me to move you to another compartment?'

The girl had a difficult time at the border when the Soviet customs men entered our carriage in Brest. As if on command, they all dashed at her and started shouting: 'What are you carrying in your bags? Bibles? Pornography?' I tried in vain to intervene. They ransacked the poor girl's luggage and found nothing. To punish me for my intervention, they made me pay a heavy customs duty for the two videocassettes I was carrying. 'Next time think twice before you start protecting blacks!' one of them advised me as they left.

After that scene the girl told me of the life she led in Krasnodar. 'I have been there for four years already and I really don't know how I shall survive my fifth. It is like living in prison. I have no friends: Russian girls do not want to mix with me. The boys are even worse: they keep calling out to me in a vulgar manner. I have been attacked a couple of times in the street and now I simply do not go out after dark. The food is awful, but the worst thing is that everyone is lying – the teachers, the students, everyone. I am studying history, and the textbooks are full of lies too. I would have given it all up and come back home, but I want to get a degree. Besides, I have already endured four years, so it would be a shame to quit now.'

In Moscow I put her into a cab and she was driven away – back to her painful predicament.

In 1984 the Soviet Union started importing cheap labour from Vietnam. Driven by the poverty and devastation of their own country, the young Vietnamese were eager to come to the Soviet Union to earn money and buy the basic consumer goods which were still available at that time. In 1984 there were 5000 zan den ('black people' or 'underdogs' – that is what their compatriots in Vietnam who look down on them call them) in the USSR. By 1990 there were 90,000. A distressing account of their plight was given in *Ogonyok* at the end of 1989.

Vietnamese workers are employed by 350 Soviet plants and factories, doing the roughest, most unskilled and lowly-paid work; they get half as much as their Soviet counterparts. At the Moscow lorry factory, for instance, they are paid only seven kopeks for painting a whole truck. They have only one holiday every three years. Women are banned from having children at the peril of being sent back to Vietnam. They can't quit their job for a better one, since this is not allowed under their contract. They

EAST COPIES WEST As Macdonalds comes to Moscow, Russian women take part in
an American-style Beauty Contest, 1989.

ARMS AND THE MEN (*left*) Broiler, former militia officer turned Leningrad gangster with (*below left*) personal possessions; (*below*) Almiashev, twice world classical wrestling champion with (*foot*) some of his less sportive equipment; and (*opposite*) Stas, one of the young team leaders.

Brighton Beach in New York, also known as Little Odessa, stronghold of the Soviet mafia in exile, July 1990.

UNDER LENIN'S NOSE
Colonel Osin, Supervisor of Perm 35 in the Urals, officially the last remaining labour camp in the Soviet Union for political prisoners; (*below*) Vitali Vitaliev, honorary prisoner Number 30, lunching in the camp canteen.

Ленинградский областной комитет ВЛКСМ

ДВОРЕЦ МОЛОДЕЖИ

Большой концертный зал

Ул. Профессора Попова, 47

Транспорт: ст. метро „Петроградская", „Горьковская", „Черная речка"
Автобус: 25, 71, 134   Трамвай: 3, 21, 31, 37, 40   Троллейбус 9

21, 23 АПРЕЛЯ 1989 г.

ОСТРОСОЦИАЛЬНЫЙ
ШОКИНГ!

ВНИМАНИЕ! ВНИМАНИЕ!

НЕКОТОРЫЕ ПОДРОБНОСТИ О ЛЕНИНГРАДСКОЙ МАФИИ И НАЦИСТАХ, ДНЕПРОПЕТРОВСКОМ РЭКЕТЕ, СОЧИНСКОЙ ПРОСТИТУЦИИ, СУТЕНЕРСТВЕ, А ТАКЖЕ ПРОБЛЕМЫ СОЦИАЛЬНОЙ СПРАВЕДЛИВОСТИ В ПРОГРАММЕ

«ЖУРНАЛИСТ РАССЛЕДУЕТ»

рассказывает лауреат премии Союза журналистов СССР, четырежды лауреат премии журнала „Крокодил", лауреат премии „Золотого теленка" Литературной газеты, дважды лауреат премии Ильфа и Петрова, автор очерка „Амурские войны"

В. ВИТАЛЬЕВ

Редактор программы

А. АНДРЕЕВ

Начало в 19 час. 30 мин.   Билеты продаются в кассе Дворца.
Телефон кассы 234-10-26   Справки по телефону 234-52-29.

В. ВИТАЛЬЕВ The poster advertising my appearence at Leningrad's Concert Hall, April 1989.

VELVET GLOVE, IRON FIST
The difference between Gorbachev and Saddam
Hussein? Gorbachev has been awarded a Nobel
Peace Prize: a poster in the Baltic Republics makes
the point . . .

Tanks crush protesters at the television centre in
Vilnius in Lithuania, January 1991. Shades of
Budapest 1956 . . .

HU$$EIN PRIZE LAUREATE !

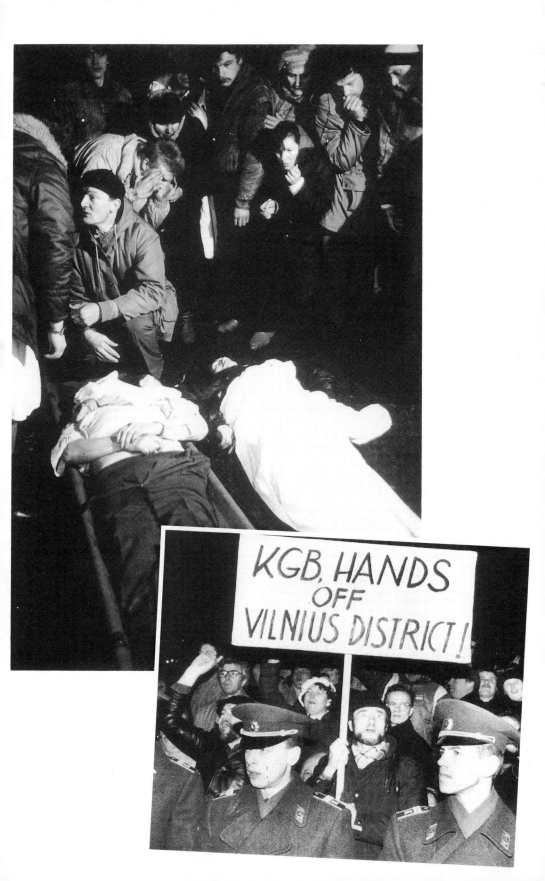

KGB, HANDS OFF VILNIUS DISTRICT!

DOWN UNDER
With Natasha and Mitya in Sydney, Australia, May 1990; (*left*) with my old friend Clive James at the Australian High Commission Party welcoming me to Australia, May 1990; and (*below*) with my new friend Peter Ustinov in Melbourne, September 1990.

are treated like prisoners, like slaves. And even worse. 'We cannot even go to a café or to a cinema,' one of the zan den said. 'Firstly we have no money, and second, the local hooligans are always ready to beat us.'

Not only to beat, it appears. In May 1989, Ngok, a Vietnamese worker, was found dead, with a bullet hole in his chest. The murderers were not found.

On 21 April in Kemerovo region, an unknown criminal hit Ngueng Hoang An, a twenty-eight-year-old bricklayer, on the head with a stone and nearly killed him. In September 1989 the twenty-two-year-old Le Khu Than was bashed to death by a bunch of unknown hoodlums.

More and more often zan den have to go on strike protesting against their inhuman treatment. In Ulianovsk the strikes were triggered by the severe beating of two Vietnamese workers in the street.[2] At the end of 1989, through my contacts in Belorussia, I learnt about a Vietnamese workers' strike in the Mogilev region. The reason was the insultingly low salaries which did not exceed 80 roubles a month, well below the official poverty line.

Anti-Vietnamese feelings reached their climax in Moscow in the autumn of 1989. These events became known as the 'shampoo riot'. At that time the country was suffering from terrible shortages of detergents – soap, shampoo, toothpaste and washing powder. One day a large consignment of imported shampoo was delivered to a Moscow department store in Orekhovo–Borisovo. A huge line immediately formed out of nowhere, long before the shampoo went on sale. A Vietnamese worker from a nearby hostel was standing in the queue, not far from the counter. He was soon joined by his Vietnamese room-mate, and the latter was in his turn joined by his friends. In no time it is claimed that about 300 zan den were standing in line instead of one. The Russian queuers got furious at such a breach of the unwritten code of behaviour. They started pushing the Vietnamese out of the line. The workers resisted. A scuffle broke out and soon turned into a real fight. Knives and knuckledusters were used by both sides. The Vietnamese poured out of the nearby hostels to help their comrades. They organised themselves into a huge crowd and started smashing shop windows and overturning cars. It was only with the intervention of the special militia riot squad OMON that they were stopped.

Instead of clean hair, hundreds of people – both Russian and Vietnamese – got wounds, cuts and bruises on their heads. This is what happens when people are hungry, frustrated and deprived of basic goods. And despite glasnost, neither the 'shampoo riot' nor the reasons behind it were covered in the media.

From our earliest years in school and even kindergarten, we were stuffed with fairy tales of the 'unbreakable Union of free nations, pulled together by the great Russia', lines from the Soviet national anthem which we used to sing. Russia was always referred to as 'the greatest', 'the best', 'the happiest', 'the most peace-loving' country. From the school history course we learnt that Russia had always conducted only 'fair' wars, that radio, the aeroplane, the electric lamp and the steam engine had been invented by Russians, that Russia was the eldest sister in a cheerful family of friendly Soviet nations.

Only the melody remains of the national anthem now. The words are being shamefully silenced. There is not much left of 'the unbreakable Union' either. The country is experiencing the unseen upsurge of national-liberation feelings, forcefully subdued for so many years. This is a major threat to the very existence of the system, and also a powerful tool in the hands of the rulers who go out of their way to retain their unearned power by keeping people apart. As a result of their disgraceful manoeuvering, thousands of all races have died in nationalist clashes throughout the country, and dozens more are still dying every day. The Soviet Union, which was artificially created by the ill-will of Lenin and Stalin, is coming apart. And no force in the world is able to stop its disintegration.

The most famous – or rather infamous – form of Soviet racism is anti-semitism. My parents were Jewish. I never fully realised this until at the age of sixteen I got my brand-new Soviet passport, where in section 5, the nationality column, it was written in black and white 'Yevrei' – 'Jew'. Did it mean that I was a follower of Judaism? Not in the least. No-one in my family, not my parents or grandparents, knew a single word of Yiddish or Hebrew or had ever been inside a synagogue. My parents were the products of two cultures: Russian and Ukrainian. I was also deeply influenced by English culture: I had started learning English when I was seven, and by sixteen could read and speak English quite easily. It was not our fault that we couldn't practise Judaism, even if we had wanted to. The only synagogue in Kharkov, where we lived, had been turned into a gym in the early forties. Besides, both my parents and myself were brought up in the spirit of communist ideals. My grandparents on both sides were old Bolsheviks and sincerely believed Karl Marx's premise that religion was the opium of the people.

As I proudly received my passport from the smiling militia officer, I could not possibly have realised that with this red hammer-and-sickled book I was acquiring a lifetime stigma. And there were numerous instances of that: 'nationality' in the Soviet Union is asked everywhere – in libraries, hospitals, schools etc.

It was not that I hadn't got occasional hints of being slightly 'unlike' other people earlier. When I was three I remember very clearly having a nanny, a young Ukrainian girl, who found pleasure in teasing me asking: 'Are you a Yid, Vitya? Tell me, are you a Yid?' Of course, I didn't know what this word meant, but since she repeated it often, I learnt it quickly and once, when my father was holding me on his shoulders, I cried out cheerfully: 'Are you a Yid, daddy? Tell me, are you a Yid?' He put me down on the floor immediately and looked steadily into my eyes. 'Where did you hear this word?'

She was sacked the following day.

When I was six, I liked to play with other kids in our courtyard. Once we decided 'to play nationality'. An older girl asked everyone what nationality he or she was. The kids of different nationalities were to flock together in the designated corner of the yard. We had small groups of Ukrainians, Russians, Jews. The older girl, who was the game leader, said she was Greek. We did not know at first which flock she was to join. Then someone said: 'Let her go to the Jews!' And she did happily. When my turn came and I was confronted with the question of nationality, I answered frankly that I didn't know. 'Go to your parents and ask what's written in their passports,' the experienced Greek girl advised. My parents were at first slightly bewildered by the question, but when I explained the game, they shrugged their shoulders and gave me the answer. 'I am Jewish! I am Jewish!' I cried happily on returning to the playground. I was very proud to be Jewish since it meant I belonged to the biggest gang of kids.

This new knowledge of mine cost me dear in a year or so, when my grandparents – grandpa Misha and granny Niura – took me to the country for the whole summer. We were holidaying in the village of Volniy near the town of Liubotin, about thirty kilometres from Kharkov, where my grandparents rented a room from a local collective farmer. I ran around the village barefoot and in a couple of days made friends with many of the village boys of my age. All went well until one day, remembering my Kharkov experience, I suggested to my new friends we 'play nationality'. To my surprise, they proved to be much more knowledgeable in this field than I had expected: they readily answered that they were Ukrainians. 'And I am a Jew!' I blurted out, expecting praise and envy. What followed this inadvertent confession is probably one of the saddest memories of my childhood. As if on command, the boys spat and went off leaving me alone in the village street with my toys. I could not understand what had happened: suddenly I had lost all my newly-acquired companions. Then after a couple of days the village boys started teasing me relentlessly. As soon as they saw me, they would begin chanting in chorus: 'Zhid, zhid!' Po veriovochke bez-hit!' – 'Kike, kike! Along the rope he runs!' It was a senseless stupid rhyme. Its gibberish nature, strangely, made it sound even more offensive and insulting. The vicious jeering grew every day. I had to stop coming out into the street and played alone inside the house. But even there I couldn't help hearing the mocking chanting sounds of the kids standing behind the window: 'Zhid, Zhid! . . .'

One day granny Niura gave me a small empty bucket and asked me to bring some water from the pump down the street. As soon as I went out of the gate, my tormentors appeared. One of them brought a younger brother who was no more than three years old. But, on seeing me, even this toddler started lisping nastily 'Zid, Zid!' He couldn't pronounce 'Zh' yet and saliva was running down his chin. I lost my temper, threw the bucket aside and rushed at them. I was quite strong for my age, but there were many of them. I got a good thrashing until a passing adult intervened and stopped the scuffle. I must have looked pitiful: my nose was bleeding and my shirt was torn. 'Bidniy khlopchik!' – 'Poor boy!' – he said in Ukrainian and patted me on the back. 'Why did they beat you?' The boys were standing around watching. 'He is a Jew!' one of them said pointing at me. The passer-by looked at me in utter disbelief, then, having scrutinised me for a moment, shook his head. 'No,' he said gravely. 'It can't be true. He is not a Jew, but a good boy!'

When we returned to Kharkov, I was not the same carefree boy as I had been before. My first inferiority complex had been implanted.

I must stress that apart from this one small episode I was never reminded of my stigma at school. We were quite a cosmopolitan company: among both pupils and teachers there were many Russians, Ukrainians, Jews, Greeks, Tartars and so-called 'polukrovki' – the children of mixed marriages. I started to like the Ukrainian language and literature. Studying them was not compulsory, but I attended all the lessons and was first in my class in these subjects. It's interesting to note that all Jewish kids attended the optional Ukrainian lessons, whereas many Ukrainian ones didn't. Some of the latter could not speak and read Ukrainian and did not want to. This showed again how conventional the very concept of 'nationality' was.

There was another occurrence during my school years connected not with me but with my mother. She was a highly-regarded engineer at a chemical plant and had many inventions to her credit. At some stage they decided to send her on a short mission to Britain together with the plant's chief engineer who was Armenian. My mother filled in all the necessary forms, submitted them to the Medical Industries Ministry in Moscow, which was in charge of her plant, and was told to wait. Since no-one knew how long the waiting would take, we decided to go to the Caucasus on holiday. After a couple of weeks in Zheleznovodsk, my mother was suddenly called back to Kharkov: the Ministry's decision was about to come through. We all disrupted our holiday and went back only to find that she was refused the trip. The refusal came with an angry telephone call to the plant's director. 'Have you all gone mad there or what?!' the official from the Ministry bawled. 'You must be crazy to suggest sending a Jewess and an Armenian to the West!'

The first serious trial for me, however, and for many of my Jewish and half-Jewish friends came when we finished school and were about to enter higher educational establishments – Institutes or the University. By that time, we knew that Jews and polukrovki were not accepted by some institutes and university departments. In the remaining higher educational establishments the number of Jewish students was not supposed to exceed 2 or 3 per cent of the total student body. We found this hard to believe. Igor Itskovich, a Jewish boy who lived in our house, was a brilliant mathematician. More than once he won All-Union schoolchildren's mathematical competitions. Nevertheless, when he tried to apply to the physics and mathematics department of Kharkov University they refused to let him take exams or even consider his application under the ridiculous pretext that he hadn't served in the army. Graduates from this department were usually sent to work for the Defence Ministry, and not a single Jew was among the students. No-one knows how many potential Einsteins were discarded on the grounds of the one word – Yevrei – written in the applicants' passports.

My best friend Sasha Kasjanov was a polukrovka: his mother was Jewish, his father Russian. He did enter the university biology faculty, but when taking an exam he accidentally got a glimpse of his own application form lying on the desk in front of the examiner. In the top right-hand corner it had two Russian letters written in red pencil. They stood for 'Mat' Yevreika' – 'Mother Jew'.

For me there was no question of where to apply. I was already fluent in English and knew some French, so my only choice was the interpreters' department of the foreign languages faculty of Kharkov University. My parents and friends tried to talk me out of it. 'You should know that they train military translators and interpreters to work abroad there, and it is next to impossible for a Jew to be enrolled.' But I didn't want to listen to them. When one month before the exams I brought my documents to the examining board, the lady clerk, who by the way, was Jewish herself, started trying to dissuade me from applying. Having looked at my school-leaving certificate with its excellent marks, having leafed through my many diplomas for winning regional linguistic competitions, she said in a half-whisper: 'Why don't you apply to the Pedagogical Department instead? You'll only waste time here and they will draft you into the army.' 'But I want to be an interpreter, not a teacher!' I declared firmly. 'Well, don't say I didn't warn you . . .' she shrugged.

The problem was that if I failed the exams I would be called up the following spring: I was to be eighteen next January, conscription age. I simply had to pass.

For the whole month I studied like hell – from morning till night. Then, three days before the exams and very run-down, I suddenly became ill. On the day of the first exam, I felt better, but still very weak. My parents, who under normal circumstances wouldn't have let me out of the house in such a state for love nor money, put a warm scarf round my neck although it was the middle of summer, and packed me off. I must have looked ridiculous.

I got the highest mark for the written essay. The only 'five' among all the applicants. I got the same mark in English and in Russian. There was only one more exam to go – history. And this was the most feared one. History, as it was taught at school, was a mixture of random facts and primitive indoctrination. One was supposed to know the exact dates of all twenty-five Communist Party Congresses, the main points of all Brezhnev's speeches (and he did like to make speeches!) and so on.

'They will almost certainly make you fail this exam!' my parents kept warning me. 'Try to get at least a three, and you'll still have a chance.' 'Three' was a satisfactory mark, which would leave me with eighteen points out of twenty. With four contenders for every place at the department, there would still be a slim possibility of being enrolled . . .

And they did try hard to make me fail. When I answered questions from my exam paper correctly, they started asking me additional ones which were well beyond the school curriculum. I was asked to name all the members of the Politburo and the leaders of the 'brotherly' Communist Parties of the Eastern European countries. Being an avid newspaper reader, I managed to cope with this. But then 'One last question before we let you go. Could you please name three ministers in Kerensky's Provisional Government?' The Provisional Government was formed in February 1917 and existed for only eight months before being over-thrown by the Bolsheviks. The names of these 'enemies of Soviet power' (with the exception of Prime Minister Kerensky) were not to be found in any accessible reference literature. But by an amazing stroke of luck I had just finished reading a collection of works by Sasha Chiorny, a Russian satirical poet of the beginning of our century, where he mocked and ridiculed some of the Provisional Government ministers. Yes, there were three of them with funny rhyming names. Hold on. Here they are! 'Lvov, Milyukov and Guchkov!' I blurted out. From the corner of my eye I could see the examiner writing a five on my matriculation card. 'Why didn't you try to enter the history department?' he asked. 'Congratulations!'

'Lvov, Milyukov and Guchkov!' I kept singing on the way home. 'Lvov, Milyukov and Guchkov!' What a wonderful bunch of people! Thanks to them I became a University student.

During my five years at the university I was reminded of my passport handicap only once. On my sophomore year I applied to go to Poland in summer with the students' construction team. Such teams are a good opportunity for students to earn some extra money during the summer vacations. As a rule, they work inside the country – in Siberia or Central Asia. That year they decided to send one to Poland. My application was turned down by the faculty Komsomol Committee. They didn't even consider it, just put it aside. I was told by a woman who was present at the Komsomol Committee gathering that one of the Committee members said that they were not going to send Jews abroad.

When I was a junior, (ie a third-year student) we had an unpleasant incident at the Faculty. Three second-year students were accused of 'Ukrainian bourgeois nationalism' and expelled from the University. Their 'nationalism' lay in the mere fact of speaking Ukrainian to each other. What was so nationalistic and bourgeois in speaking one's native language in one's native land, escapes me until now. But if you consider that in our Ukrainian city of Kharkov there was only one Ukrainian school, as compared to 200 Russian, and that at our university all subjects, even Ukrainian literature, were taught in Russian, the motive for their expulsion becomes clearer: 'Russification'.

At the end of my graduation year, I couldn't help feeling that some of my fellow students were looking down on me. They all knew that no matter how poorly they studied, they were in for good jobs abroad, whereas I, with all my fives, wasn't. They were proved right: four days before graduation I was suddenly left jobless, though I had a contract to work as an interpreter on fishing ships visiting foreign ports. But, again, no Jews were to be sent abroad.

The only consolation was that I wasn't alone in my plight. There were two other Jewish students at the department, and all three of us ended up with the so-called 'free diplomas', which virtually left us jobless. The

89

other two chaps being forced to emigrate to America shortly after that. They were certainly forced to do so. As for me, I dragged on for another fourteen years before finally being forced to emigrate. Knowing the other two – Liosha Modorski and Yura Shkeirov – very well, I can say that we all loved our country and none of us would ever have left had we been given a chance.

After two years' rustication and forced idleness as a translator in an obscure research institute, I went to live in Moscow, where eventually I did find an interpreter's position, but this was preceded by almost a year of hopeless door-knocking. Moscow officials, I must say, were much more sophisticated than their opposite numbers in Kharkov. They rarely said that I was not appropriate for the job because of my nationality, although occasionally they would make reference to it saying 'because of your nationality we can't send you to any Arab country. We don't want you to be killed. The only place where we can send you is India, but we have no vacancies there at present.'

When several years later I turned to journalism, it was a huge relief. There was practically no anti-semitism among my colleagues, partly due to the fact that most of them were Jewish themselves. I did suffer one set-back at the beginning of my journalistic career though. The fact was that I had been writing and publishing my poems and stories since the age of fourteen under my mother's maiden name, Rapoport. It sounded so roaringly poetic to me! But when I brought my pieces to *Literaturnaya Gazeta* for the first time, the elderly bearded editor did not like my pen-name. 'Aren't you looking for fame, young man?' he asked me, jokingly. Then he added quite seriously: 'We can't publish you under this Jewish-sounding name. Our executives simply won't let it happen!' The irony was that he was Jewish himself, though he was known to the readers under a Russian-sounding pen-name. I discovered that for many years in Soviet journalism this had been common practice, and one of the most revealing books is the telephone directory of the Moscow Writers' Trade Union, where along with the writers' pen-names their real names were given too. One could know nothing about anti-semitism in the Soviet Union but after leafing through this directory one would understand its extent. No, it was not for want of something better to do that so many writers and journalists had to change their names. They wanted to live, to survive, to be published.

Here's one of the most extraordinary stories about one man's struggle with anti-semitism I have to tell.

In 1983 I was in the Soviet Far East investigating the abominable conditions under which students of one of the Institutes in Blagoveshchensk had to live. One day I had a call from the editorial director of the local publishing house. 'Come over to my office,' he said. 'I'll tell you a story.'

His office was in total disarray. Piles of books were scattered everywhere, swarms of fat Far-Eastern flies were buzzing in the air. He was an elderly bespectacled man with a thick mane of curly red hair just beginning to go grey. He had been born in Leningrad and for many years worked there as a journalist. In 1953 Stalin 'uncovered' the so-called 'doctors' plot'. The doctors, many of whom were Jewish, were said to have murdered Andrei Zhdanov, head of the Leningrad Party organisation. This was the pretext for starting another great purge, this time the purge of Jews. An unseen anti-semitic campaign was unleashed in the country, and my new acquaintance, who was Jewish, had to flee from Leningrad to the Far East, where anti-semitism was not so rampant. Here he found a good job, a wife and, after some time, has completely settled down in Blagoveshchensk.

Being active and restless, though, he was constantly in search of new publishing projects. His tiny publishing house has printed many reference books and foreign titles which would turn even big Moscow publishers green with envy. I browsed through some of these books and was amazed by their high artistic and editorial standards. Once he went on a business trip to the neighbouring Jewish Autonomous Region, which was formed in 1928 on Stalin's initiative. The dictator was planning to resettle all Soviet Jews in the Far East and it was only his death in 1953 that prevented him from realising his chauvinistic intentions. The publisher was shocked by the complete absence of Jewish culture in the region: there was only one old man there who knew Yiddish and he was the editor of the local newspaper. There was not a single Jewish school.

On returning to Blagoveshchensk he became preoccupied with a new project – to publish an ABC-book in Yiddish. 'It is not fair,' he told me. 'Even the smallest national minorities of the Far East have their schools and books in their mother tongue. But not the Jews.' In an attempt to get permission for his Yiddish primer he made innumerable trips to Moscow – at his own expense of course – knocking on doors, pleading, imploring, persuading. But, where there's a will, there's a way and at last his persistence was rewarded: a high-ranking Moscow bureaucrat, wanting to shake the dogged publisher off, said: 'Ok. Go ahead. But the paper and the money are your concerns. The state won't give you a kopek!'

The publisher sold his house and his car (salaries in the Far East being considerably higher than in the European Russia, partly due to the hardships of climate and geographic isolation), managed to acquire the first-class paper and to hire experienced editors and illustrators. He also paid all printing and typesetting expenses.

The primer came out. It was a wonderful publication: glossy cover, witty colour pictures, big clearly-printed letters. I was leafing through it in the publisher's decrepit office. 'So where was the book circulated?' I asked. 'Aha!' the publisher cried out. 'Look around you!' he said. 'It's all here!'

Cardboard boxes of ABC-books were piled on the unswept floor, on the desk and on the window sill. 'They have been here for two years. Publishing the book was only half the battle. The main thing now is to persuade the authorities to try and introduce at least one experimental Yiddish lesson a week if only in one class, if only in one school of Birobidzhan, the centre of the Jewish Autonomous Region! This is proving to be much more difficult than publishing the book itself!'

The primer could bring joy and knowledge to many kids. But instead the fruits of the selfless efforts of the publisher were doomed to rot in his crammed office. Of course, I wrote a passionate story for *Krokodil* but like the ill-fated ABC-book, it too never saw the light of day.

Another reminder of Soviet anti-semitism occurred in Dnepropetrovsk in 1987 when I was investigating the local mafia. It was then that I met Yasha Konstantinopolski, the captain of the militia and the ONLY Jewish CID detective in the whole of the Soviet Union. Yes, the militia as well as the KGB, the Foreign Ministry and the defence industries did not – and still do not! – employ Jews. What is this? A craze? An idiocy? A far-reaching strategy?

Yasha was a smiling young chap. He was physically fit and very efficient. His subordinates adored him. One day over a couple of drinks he told me how difficult it had been for him to get enrolled at the law institute where he got his degree and then into the militia. He had to apply to the highest militia bodies, and he won in the end, though his case remains the exception, which, as we all know, only proves the rule.

In November 1990, when I was already in Australia, I came across statistics on the professional status of the 82,823 Soviet Jewish emigrants who arrived in Israel between January and September 1990. Alongside the 11,500 engineers; 2578 doctors; 2530 teachers; 1452 musicians and 187 sculptors there was also one detective.[3] Was it you, Yasha?

Here I can't but remember my two friends from Perm, Alik Berdichevski and Volodya Klimov, the tandem of satirical writers. I knew them very well. They often contributed to *Krokodil* and whenever I went to Perm they used to take good care of me. They only wrote together and in fact were known as one writer with two pairs of hands and two heads, literary Siamese twins. They were also friends. The only difference between them was that Volodya was Russian and Alik was Jewish. One day they jointly applied for membership of the local Soviet Journalistic Union branch. What followed resembles a scene from an absurdist's novel: Volodya was granted membership and Alik wasn't! One writer was split into two unequal parts, an unprecedented case of social vivisection. Unwillingly, this brought analogies with the Goncourt brothers, if only to try and imagine the situation when Edmond was admitted to the French Academy and Jules wasn't. Alik and Volodya laughed but the story was not funny.

Jews have been living on the territory of the present-day Soviet Union since time immemorial. The arrival of the Jews is linked with the exile of the Ten Tribes (720 BC) or with the Destruction of the First Temple (586 BC).[4] Greek inscriptions in the Black Sea area testify to the presence of Jews in the early centuries of the Common Era (Anno Domini). Since that time they have also settled in Central Asia and the Caucasus. There were Jews in Kievan Rus in the tenth century and in the Crimea in the thirteenth.

The Russian tsars fell over themselves to keep Jews out of their territories. In 1727, all Jews were expelled from the country, and ten years later from the Ukraine and Belorussia. Much of the adverse feeling towards the Jews originally stemmed from Christian beliefs that they had killed Christ. 'From the enemies of Christ I wish neither gain nor profit!' Tsarina Elizabeth declared in the eighteenth century, banning Jewish merchants from trading in the Ukraine. After Polish partition in 1772 thousands of Polish Jews found themselves under Russian rule. They were confined to live and work in special restricted areas – the so-called 'Pale of Settlement' – and were banned from dwelling in major Russian cities and towns. The period before 1917 was alternately characterised by repression and relaxation.[5] The early twentieth century was marked by the appearance of the so-called Black Hundreds, predecessors of the present-day Pamyat, the fascist Memory Society. They organised pogroms directed against Jews and members of the progressive intelligentsia. 'Beat the Yids and save Russia!' became their slogan. The authorities tended to ignore the pogroms and Tsar Nicholas II even thanked the Black Hundreds for their support.[6]

There were five million Jews living in the Russian empire on the eve of the 1917 revolution.[7] It was not by chance that they became one of Bolshevism's main driving forces: no other national minority was oppressed by the tsarist regime as much as they. Jews occupied leading posts in the first Bolshevik government led by Lenin. They fought in the Red Army in the 1917–22 Civil War. During the twenties and the early thirties a certain revival of Jewish culture was observed in the Soviet Union. In 1927 the country had 509 Jewish schools teaching 107,000 pupils.[8]

Strange as it may seem, it was the end of the Second World War that brought about a big rise in anti-semitic feeling. People were looking for a scapegoat to be blamed for the hunger and devastation and Stalin helped them to find one. On his orders Solomon Mikhoels, a famous Jewish actor and stage director, was murdered in the street in Minsk by state security agents in 1948. After the killing, a truck was driven over his corpse to give the impression of an accident. In 1952 the members of the Jewish Anti-Fascist Committee were shot on Stalin's instructions[9] and the 'doctors' plot' continued the vicious anti-semitic campaign.

Under Khrushchev and Brezhnev public anti-semitism went into hiding, but its ugly face could be seen in the secret 'enrollment norms' for Jewish high-school students which were observed to the letter, in the ignominious virtually complete banning of Jews from government posts, diplomacy, security, defence industries, the army, the militia, the executive Party jobs. Strict norms for showing Jewish faces on TV and for mentioning Jewish names by the press were introduced. In 1967 *The Commissar*, a brilliant feature film directed by Alexander Askoldov, was banned simply for presenting a Jewish family in a sympathetic light. It was genocide all right, but a hidden, cowardly and covert one which made it even more repugnant. As to the popular, unofficial anti-semitism, it was contained as well as any other nationalistic trend in which the rulers were inclined to see an immediate threat to themselves and their powers.

What happened with the ascent of Gorbachev was that official anti-semitism was slightly curbed, though all the norms and percentages remain in force. It has simply become more cunning, less obvious and was technically no longer officially encouraged. But it was not discouraged either.

What was and is being encouraged is so-called 'unofficial anti-semitism', which has always been very easy for the rulers to manipulate. During Gorbachev's reign it has reached unseen dimensions and triggered an unprecedented exodus of Jewish people from the Soviet Union at a rate of 200,000 a year.

It all started in 1986–7 with the formation of Pamyat, an anti-semitic, fascist organisation. The leader of Pamyat, a mediocre former actor called Dmitri Vassilliev, introduced a special uniform – black T-shirts with a picture of a tolling bell on them and black knee-length boots. Masking themselves with claims that they were 'saving Russian culture', they gradually unleashed the biggest anti-semitic campaign in the Soviet history.

It is interesting to note that Pamyat was the first unofficial organisation to hold an unsanctioned rally in the centre of Moscow, shortly after its formation in 1987. The officials treated the rally with unusual restraint. They didn't disperse the demonstrators with truncheons, as they used to do with tiny groups of political dissenters. Pamyat members were even received by Boris Yeltsin, then First Secretary of the Moscow Party Committee, although this was the first and last Pamyat meeting with an official of this rank.

Pamyat agitators were sent all round the country. I saw one in the main street of Krasnodar, Caucasus. He was distributing leaflets covered with figures specifying the number of Jews in the first Bolshevik government, in Cheka (Lenin's secret police) and so on. The point was simple: the Bolshevik revolution was part of the Zionist conspiracy to destroy mother Russia. Now that destruction is complete – which incidentally is true – the Jews, having finished their historic mission, are fleeing to Israel. With all the antediluvian primitivism of this declaration, it did manage to strike a responsive chord among the Russian people, driven to extreme despair by unending shortages and growing unrest: they are eager to find culprits, even if imaginary ones . . .

The farther in, the deeper. Soon it became common knowledge that Pamyat was conducting a census of the country's Jewish population. To become a Pamyat member, one had to provide the addresses of five Jewish families (or of three Jews with Russian names) as an entrance fee. There were also numerous cases of physical violence against Jews. People were appealing to the government and to Gorbachev to do something to curb anti-semitism. There was no reaction.

It was becoming clearer and clearer that some powerful force was standing behind Pamyat, whose members were systematically breaking not only the constitution but also the Criminal Code by disseminating nationalistic information and spreading racial hatred – but not one of them had even been detained! In fact officialdom gave Pamyat the support of several fully official and highly circulated publications – *Nash Sovremenik, Molodaya Gvardiya, Kuban, Literaturnaya Rossiya* and *Sovietskaya Rossiya.* (The last one, by the way, has a circulation of about ten million copies and is the official organ of the Communist Party Central Committee!) These newspapers and magazines took up openly pro-Pamyat anti-semitic positions, insulting and cursing Jews in every issue, but the authorities stubbornly turned a blind eye while *Molodaya*

Gvardiya asserted: 'No, we do not like Jews in the USSR and we can't be forced to like them.'[10]

In May 1989 Lord Nicholas Bethell visited Moscow and met the leaders of Pamyat. The harrowing account of this meeting was published in the *Mail on Sunday* under the heading 'I meet the Soviet Nazis': 'They claim support running into several million. They have branches in thirty cities. During the meeting I was openly filmed by a young man with a video camera, an expensive Sony of a type not normally on sale in the Soviet Union. "Anti-Russian forces have captured our press, radio and TV," Vassilliev told me. "The white nations are being driven out of Europe." As he rambled on, I sat hardly believing that I was listening to the language of Hitler and Oswald Mosley in a Moscow flat.'[11]

Lord Bethell's fear is shared by numerous Western observers. 'Pamyat people believe that the Jews killed Christ and Tsar Nicholas II. They say Jews organised the Bolshevik Revolution, and masterminded Stalin's Terror. They see glasnost and perestroika as a conspiracy to allow Jewish capitalists to regain control of the country,' Carroll Bogert wrote in *Newsweek*.[12]

Here's the sad, though incomplete, chronicle of other Pamyat 'achievements': anti-semitic leaflets sent to many of Moscow's progressive newspapers and magazines; threats and pogroms; anti-Jewish rallies; raids on dachas belonging to the Jewish intelligentsia; harassing of anti-Pamyat parliamentary deputies; murders of several Jewish activists; arson attacks on flats of non-Jewish Pamyat opponents; scuffles on Moscow's Pushkin Square where people with 'suspicious faces' were severely beaten; pogrom in the Moscow Writers' Club, the appearance of an article entitled 'Russophobia' in *Nash Sovremenik* where the author, academician Igor Shafarevich, wrote of 'small people' (a euphemism for Jews) dominating 'big people' (ie Russians).

On 21 March 1990, five radical Russian nationalist groups formed a coalition under the umbrella title the Popular Orthodox Movement of Russia Pamyat. They published a manifesto saying that Russia has become 'the appendage of the world Zionist oligarchy', that the murder of Tsar Nicholas II and his family was 'a brutal Jewish ritual killing', that Russia is being systematically robbed by 'international usurious Zionist capital'. Thus Pamyat has become a real political force.

At the beginning of May 1990, two men with white bags over their heads burst into the flat of a non-Jewish Moscow writer and journalist, who was very anti-Pamyat and had more than once delivered tough speeches against it on the Russian service of the Munich-based Radio Liberty. At the time he was abroad and his flat was occupied by the family of his friend Steve Crawshaw, the newly-arrived Moscow correspondent of the *Independent* who hadn't been provided with his own flat yet. Steve was in the office and his wife Eva had just put their little daughter Ania to sleep.

The hooded invaders were brandishing knives. They kicked Eva into the kitchen and slammed the door. One of them held the knife at her throat. 'Svolotch!' – 'bitch,' he said in Russia. A rag was thrust into Eva's mouth to prevent her crying out. She started struggling. The masked attacker smashed her against the furniture, wall and door. One of her fingers was sliced through with the knife and her entire body was cut and bruised. They would certainly have killed her had a neighbour not overheard Eva's muffled screams and rung the doorbell. The intruders panicked and fled.[13] They were not found.

That was clearly the hand of Pamyat: Klu Klux Klan hoods, two untouched wallets, ignored by the attackers, and the fact that only two weeks before petrol had been spilt on the threshold outside the flat's door. This last detail is especially convincing, since more than once Pamyat has spilt petrol on the doorsteps of Jewish activists in Leningrad as a warning: if you don't move out, we'll set fire to your flat. And on many occasions they have carried out this threat.

The flat of Vladimir Pribilovski, a member of the *Panorama* editorial board, was set on fire on the night of 23 August 1990 while he was on holiday. The fire followed the newspaper's publication of an article critical of Pamyat. Three months earlier, on 16 May, the flat of *Panorama*'s editor was burnt. The arson attack occurred the day after another article in the same paper exposing Pamyat. Many *Panorama* journalists used to get threatening letters signed by 'Russian patriots'.[14] The arsonists remain unknown even now.

In August 1990, Konstantin Smirnov-Ostashvili, the Pamyat activist and bigot responsible for the pogrom in the Writers' Club in January when many Jewish authors were insulted and beaten up, was brought to trial under pressure of public opinion. He was sentenced to two years' imprisonment, but his trial was used by Pamyat to propagate their ideas. Suddenly Ostashvili, a drunkard and a hooligan, became a martyr. He was showered with flowers in the courtroom and he solemnly promised to continue his struggle with Jews even in jail. Outside the courtroom Ostashvili's supporters carried banners saying 'Zionist genocide against the Russian people is continuing' and 'Democracy in Russia is for Jews only'. One of the demonstrators shouted: 'Russian villages are dark and hungry while the Jews get rich. Who is making our gas and benzene disappear? The answer is as obvious as the sun in the sky!' A leaflet distributed outside the courtroom said: 'Zionists want to throw Smirnov-Ostashvili into prison because he told the truth. It is no coincidence that this trial is taking place at the exact moment when our anti-people government moves to a so-called market economy – which really means the conversion of our state into a colony of multi-national corporations. The Zionists seek to use this trial to divert attention from the crimes being perpetrated against the Russian people.'[15] Again the authorities didn't make even a meek attempt to curb this anti-semitic manifestation.

On 19 September 1990, Alexander Men', a Russian Orthodox priest, a theologian and a people's deputy, was killed with an axe on the way to his church in the Moscow region.[16] Father Alexander was a baptised Jew. In his sermons he preached the ideas of peace, tolerance and national reconciliation. He taught christianity in a Moscow school and was spiritual teacher to many human rights activists. Again the assassins were not found. In the first days of 1991 Hegumen Lazar, a member of the church commission set up to investigate Father Men's murder was killed in his home: he must have found a trail.[17]

So why are Pamyat's activities being stubbornly ignored by the ruling elite. They would say that it is because of pluralism. But pluralism accepts anything but attacks on pluralism itself. The real reason is that at this stage of the country's development, the rulers can retain power only in an atmosphere of social unrest, instability and mutual hatred, with the population fragmented into many small warring factions. There's no more certain way of doing this than to offer them a scapegoat. Why are the shops empty? Because of cunning Jewish cooperators. Why is crime rocketing? Because of Jewish journalists teaching the underworld how to rob poor Soviet people. They have ruined our country and now they are fleeing to Israel. Kill them! Try them before they leave! 'We won't let you flee this time like Trotsky: we'll kill you here in Russia!' one of the letters to *Ogonyok* said. 'We must try every Jew for his or her crimes against the Russian people. Even children! Let capitalist bankers pay us at least 100,000 roubles for every emigrating Jew!' Ostashvili said in one of his interviews.[18]

Or let's look at the protocols of the Sixth Plenum of the Board of the Russian Federation Writers' Union, 13–14 November 1989, where, according to tradition, high-ranking members of the CPSU Central Committee were present as guests. Here's what the so-called writers said from the rostrum with the tacit approval and applause of the Party leaders:

Anatoly Builov: Let's talk about the Jews. The Jews are evidently the only national group interested in breeding strife amongst us. Some time ago I didn't know anything about this Jewish subject. But why are they everywhere where there's a smell of profit? I was told they're clever. But why have they led us down a blind alley? [*Applause*] Let's also speak about those who've changed their names and nationalities from their Jewish ones, and whose number is three times larger than the official figure.

Tatyana Glushkova: There is an argument between Zionism – the worst form of world fascism – and humanity. We shouldn't conceal the fact that everyone who speaks out like me is risking her neck like the Palestinians or those protesting against the apartheid regime in South Africa. How long will Russian writers, the legitimate sons of the Russian land, the Russians with roots, languish under the heel of the oppressors and usurpers?

Vladimir Sharikov: I'll say a few words about the oft-cited decree of the Council of People's Commissars of 25 July, 1918, 'On the Prevention of Anti-Semitism and Jewish Pogroms'. I believe it's high time to make a thorough study of the reasons behind that decree, under which practically every citizen of Russia could become an outlaw for pronouncing a not-too-well-thought-of word. The label 'anti-semite' has been stuck to such world-famed names as Cicero, St John Chrysostom, Tacitus, Seneca, Shakespeare, Dickens, Fichte, Hegel, Kant, Gogol, Dostoevsky. Generally this label could be stuck to almost the whole culture of the world.

Vassily Bielov: I am surprised that the Secretariat of the Russian Federation Writers' Union has allowed Moscow and Leningrad writers of Jewish nationality to lead it by the nose for many years. I am ready to repeat this opinion of mine anywhere.*[19]

Two other rampant anti-semites – Valentin Rasputin and Veniamin Yarin – were appointed by Gorbachev to his Presidential Council, the country's main ruling body. Valentin Rasputin, actually a talented writer, hasn't written anything noteworthy since he joined the anti-semites. 'The foundation of anti-semitism has always been mediocrity,' said Nikolai Berdiayev, the well-known Russian religious philosopher. Rasputin does however often accompany Gorbachev on his visits abroad.[21]

Gorbachev's only public mention of anti-semitism at the Twenty-First Annual Congress of Komsomol on 11 April 1990 was demagogic and rather vague: 'We must do everything to prevent the spread of anti-semitism and all other isms,' he stated.[22] What did he mean by 'all other isms'? Zionism? Internationalism? No-one knows, but it is clear that he could stop the exodus of Jews and 'the spread of anti-semitism' by simply saying publicly just once: 'Don't leave! We need you! We'll protect you!' He has never said this and he never will.

* Bielov is close to Gorbachev, who took him on a visit to Finland as part of his official delegation.[20]

This refusal to act gives reassurance to the fascists themselves. 'Our struggle is supported by official Soviet organs and healthy forces in the KGB, the MVD [the Interior Ministry – VV], the army and the Presidential Council,' Pamyat states cynically in its manifesto.[23] And they seem to be right.

Alexandr Yakovlev, the former Politburo member, answering the question of why no criminal prosecutions had been brought against those spreading national hatred, said: 'I myself asked the Procurator General this question more than once. But it looks like even the Procurator General can't bring himself to institute such proceedings. Some powerful pressure from the top does not allow the law to be applied.'[24]

Mikhail Chlenov, a leader of the Moscow Jewish community commented: 'The trouble is that the authorities have never condemned anti-semitism openly. Gorbachev's attitude is to be silent in the face of our problems. Perhaps the leadership is frightened of being accused of being pro-Zionist. Or maybe they would far rather we all left the country, once and for all.'[25]

Oleg Gordievsky, a former KGB officer said: 'The anti-semitic campaign is being pursued with the evident connivance of some authorities in the Party and it would appear that there are even some members of the Politburo sympathetic to chauvinism.'[26]

G. Shatalov, a Soviet journalist from Baku, complained: 'I think that our statesmen have a certain interest in being lenient to extremists and very rough towards their victims.'[27]

Zeev Ben-Shlomo, the London *Jewish Chronicle* Eastern Europe correspondent wrote: 'A top Russian Communist has been named in a Soviet TV report as a supporter of anti-semitic organisations. Mr Ivan Polozkov, head of the Russian Federation Communist Party, was named by Mr Andrei Makarov, public prosecutor in the trial of Pamyat activist Konstantin Smirnov-Ostashvili. During the trial Mr Makarov said: "Serious forces are behind Pamyat." '[28]

While progressive public figures both in the Soviet Union and in the West are looking for the sources of 'the powerful pressure from the top' which supports 'Pamyat comrades', anti-semitism keeps growing. The percentage norms for quotas of Jewish applicants have been reintroduced at some faculties of the Moscow University.[29] Anti-semitic assaults, beatings and insults are becoming more and more frequent.[30] Many schools in Moscow and Leningrad are dominated by Pamyat and it is no longer unusual for schoolteachers to call any boy or girl whose nose seems to be of a suspicious shape a dirty Jewess, Yid or Kike.[31] A Moscow synagogue had to open a special school for the Jewish kids thrown out of ordinary schools. There are more than eighty children there.

In summer 1990 *Moscow News* carried the results of an opinion poll conducted among Muscovites by the Moscow Institute of open research in conjunction with Houston University: 27.7 per cent of those polled were of the opinion that 'given a choice between people and money Jews will take the money'; 26.6 per cent claimed that they would be unhappy 'if a Jew were to become a member of their family'. 'Thus,' concludes the newspaper, 'about 25 per cent of us are rabid anti-semites.'[32]

But the most eloquent development occurred on 1 February 1990, when Goskomtrud (the USSR State Committee for Labour Resources) issued instruction N56–9 as an addition to the USSR Council of Ministers decree of 6 October 1989, N825, 'On Giving War Veterans' Benefits to Former Prisoners of the Fascist Concentration Camps'. This was a long-awaited decree. Since Stalin's times, prisoners of the German labour camps have been officially treated as traitors. Now, after forty-five years – at last! – justice triumphed. But not for everyone. In the above-mentioned Goskomtrud instruction it is written in black and white: 'Citizens of Jewish nationality, who were imprisoned in fascist ghettos during the Great Patriotic War, are exempt from the benefits provided under the decree N825.'

I'd like to leave the last word on anti-semitism in the Soviet Union to the letters of relatives of some of my new friends, recent Soviet emigrants to Australia.

I don't understand Jewish communities in Western countries. It looks as if they are interested in having us victimised by the fascist mongrels. Or maybe they are waiting for the 'final solution'? I am reading yours and mum's letters from Australia and my eyes are filled with tears. I think that we are the most unfortunate nation in the world – eternally harassed and persecuted. We'll probably go mad before we get an answer from the embassy. *Minsk, February 1990*

We want to tell you that we are still alive and are just holding out, though, frankly, we don't know whether we want to. We've lost all faith in the future. The situation here is very troublesome, and we were promised a night of terror by anti-semites on May 5. If God helps us survive, then goodbye. If not, then farewell to you!. Don't think that I have gone mad. It's simply that we are living on a powder keg. *Kiev, February 1990*

We were preparing to celebrate the Day of Atonement. My daughter and grandson came to visit us from Kishinev. While my daughter and wife were busy in the kitchen, two unknown men in black masks burst into our flat. They announced that they didn't need anything from us Jews, but our lives. They left my daughter alone only after they had split her head open and she was bleeding to death. My wife, trying to save us, led them to the neighbouring room and there they dealt with her, stabbing her three times. She died on the spot. We were the last remaining Jewish family in our town. *Moldavia, October 1990*

The situation in our town of Bershad' is very critical. Many Jewish people are leaving. Two days ago a distant relative was killed. She lived alone and was eighty-two years old. She was brutally murdered: her arms and legs were twisted, her breasts were cut off – this was something unheard of. Now Jewish people are scared of going out in the evening. One man, a Jew, did go out, and was beaten up. 'We'll give you Jews a roasting!' they told him. This is all our news. *Ukraine, November 1990*

My ten-year-old son Mitya now goes to St Mary's Roman Catholic school in Melbourne. His new schoolmates are of more than twenty nationalities, of all skin-colours. My heart fills with warmth every time I meet him after classes. His dear face has become one of the strokes on the muti-coloured palet of the school crowd. Only a year ago he was chanting gibberish about 'the unbreakable Union' and now he sings religious hymns in the school church choir. A couple of times I have seen him praying silently in his room before going to bed. God help him to become a free person, a real believer, something that his father has not been able to achieve. May his ears never hear and his lips never utter the inhuman words Churki and Yids.

5

The Deep-Drilling Office*

'Fear remains one of the principle weapons of the KGB. Fear of repression is evaporating, but Soviet citizens are now being exposed to more sophisticated scare tactics.'

Soviet Intelligence and Active Measures,
Summer/Fall 1990, Washington DC

What is fear? As defined in Websters,

An unpleasant emotional state characterised by anticipation of pain or great distress and accompanied by heightened autonomic activity especially involving the nervous system; agitated foreboding often of some real or specific peril . . .[1]

Fear is experienced by all living creatures. Pigs squeal and cows moo piercingly before being slaughtered. Even cockroaches run desperately for their lives at the peril of being trampled.

But human fear is something more than just an instinct. Being one of the most powerful human emotions – on a par with love, hatred, jealousy, greed and pity – fear has been used throughout history for ages as a powerful tool to manipulate the masses. Slaves, serfs and vassals have been always kept under the rulers' thumb by fear; fear of punishment, of famine, of being imprisoned or executed. It was much more effective than chains, barbed wire or iron bars. It was inflicted by the rulers' faithful servants – guards, executioners, policemen, who also went in fear of their lives and thus obeyed Emperors, tsars, dictators and slave-masters who, being themselves scared of a popular uprising, trial and death, had to maintain a sufficiently high climate of fear to ensure their safety. The vicious circle of fear . . .

Fear has been the main cementing stuff for Soviet power since the very first days of its existence. Being inhuman and inefficient in its very nature,

* This is the English translation for the Kontora Glabokogo Bureniye, a popular Russian euphemism for the KGB.

103

the system chose terror and cruelty as its only means of survival. The Soviet Union firmly holds the sad world record in repressions and massacre of its own people. By Alexandr Solzhenitsyn's estimate the loss of life from state repression and terrorism solely for the forty-two years from October 1917 to December 1959 under Lenin, Stalin and Khrushchev was 66,700,000.[2] This many human lives were prematurely terminated only because the rulers of the 'first socialist state' deemed it necessary to preserve their power. Other estimates put the figure at 80,000,000. Whatever the total number we can definitely add thousands liquidated in labour camps and psychiatric prisons under Brezhnev and thousands more killed in ethnic clashes and street violence, mismanaged, ignored or openly provoked by the ruling elite under Gorbachev.

The reins of this monstrous machine of fear and repression have been held for more than seventy-three years by one and the same organisation – the KGB (alias Cheka, GPU, OGPU, GUGB, NKGB, NKVD, MGB and MVD). It frequently changed its name, like a recidivist criminal changes aliases, but its *raison d'être* always remained the same – to serve the rulers by infiltrating all levels of Soviet society and instigating animal fear among the people.

In this chapter I am not going to analyse the origins and development of the KGB: numerous Western historians and KGB defectors have already done this. My aim is to show how it felt for an ordinary person – neither a prisoner nor even a clear-cut dissident – to live in the atmosphere of constant fear, something almost impossible to imagine for those who live in free (or relatively free) societies. This will be a human assessment of the KGB, this bastion of fear, rather than a scholastic one. It's high time that such an appraisal was heard in the West.

In January 1990, only a few weeks before I left the Soviet Union, a short article in *Izvestia* attracted my attention. 'Forty-two years in Voluntary Exile,' the headline ran. It was the story of a Belorussian peasant called Ivan Bushilo who reappeared in his village after spending forty-two years as a hermit in the dense forest. The story began in 1947 when Marshal Zhukov, the Second World War hero, suddenly went out of favour with Stalin. Bushilo, who had fought under Zhukov's command throughout the war, was called an enemy of the people by a local militiaman. Bushilo tried to defend his glorious commander's name and 'the guardian of law and order' promised to 'send him away'. At that time it was not an empty threat. Ivan decided not to tempt fate and fled to the forest where he settled in the impassable thicket. He built a shelter and severed all ties with the outside world, living in this Robinson-like self-imposed exile for forty-two years, feeding on berries and game. Some time ago, the villagers found him and started secretly bringing him newspapers during the night. Reading them led Bushilo to believe that times had changed, and he made up his mind to return to normal life.[3]

Just a short story, presented by the paper as a curio . . . But what a human tragedy is hiding behind it! A normal healthy person has lived most of his life as an animal in the forest. That's what fear does to people: it turns them into beasts.

Under Stalin, fear was directly associated with the leather-jacketed KGB (or NKVD) men and their black cars ('little ravens' as they were popularly known). One could easily lose one's life for a casual joke, an ill-considered word, or simply for not showing sufficient enthusiasm for the words and deeds of Comrade Stalin. When he appeared on the rostrum, the applause lasted forever: everyone was afraid to be the first to stop cheering, since it was common knowledge that NKVD agents, planted in the audience, were watching vigilantly. Death was the price for the lack of enthusiasm. I remember reading a Western monograph on Stalin where eyewitnesses recalled how at state receptions some of his Soviet interpreters couldn't translate, because their teeth were clattering uncontrollably for fear of saying something which might displease the dictator.

When did I first feel this fear? It's hard to remember. Sometimes it seems like it has been with me from birth: the information carried by the genes might have included it too. But certainly among the first valedictories I heard from my parents were 'watch your tongue', 'never say what you think' and 'silence is golden'. I am not sure these had a great effect on my early life: I was an inquisitive, garrulous child and liked to say whatever I wanted. 'Your tongue will ruin us all!' my parents would complain, shaking their heads disapprovingly.

The first minor problem they faced because of me, however, stemmed not from my tongue, but from my hand. In the fifth form at secondary school, when I was twelve, we were given the assignment of writing an essay about our favourite literary hero. Despite persistent indoctrination with the fictionalised lives of revolutionaries, I wrote an essay about Ostap Bender, a witty, enterprising crook, the smooth hero of Ilf and Petrov's hilarious satirical novel, *Twelve Chairs*. As a result of this, grandpa Misha (with whom I was living at the time) was summoned by the headmistress. 'Your grandson has strange tastes!' she announced to him sternly. 'What kind of upbringing is he getting at home?' For almost an hour she dragged on about how important it was for a Soviet schoolboy to have selfless revolutionaries and brave soldiers as his heroes, as opposed to some 'miserable bourgeois machinators and smart alecs'.

This was my first encounter with censorship of which, as Bernard Shaw put it, murder is just an extreme form.

In 1970 I was savouring Solzhenitsyn's *A Day in the Life of Ivan Denisovich* all night through under the blanket (lest the parents should find out). I'd borrowed the banned book from a school friend and the following morning I was to pass it on to the next one in line. I was only sixteen but already well aware that one could go to prison for merely possessing a book like that. The feeling was daring and only added to the pleasure of reading.

When I was a senior university student with a wife to support I used to give private English lessons to earn extra money. One of my students who worked as a salesgirl in a second-hand bookshop showed me a copy of the secret weekly bulletin, published by Glavlit, the state censorship agency, a department of the KGB. It was a thick paperback listing books to be confiscated from all libraries and second-hand bookshops of the USSR. Alongside the works of dissident and emigré writers it contained hundreds of purely scientific titles in physics, chemistry and engineering. The whole 'danger' of these books lay in the fact that they had mentions of either Stalin or Khrushchev somewhere in the introductions. This was a huge section of the list, since under Stalin, say, every book – no matter how scholarly and esoteric – was supposed to have at least one quotation from the works and speeches of 'the great leader and teacher of all nations'. We had at home a bulky volume called *On Good and Healthy Food*, which was dominated by a large-print quote from Stalin – something to the effect of how essential food was for the builders of Communism ... In Brezhnev's times, when the secret bulletin in question was published, Stalin's name was not supposed to be used in print at all, as if he had never existed.

Speaking about censorship, it is interesting to note that those who controlled the literary process and published the forbidding bulletins found it quite proper to read the banned books themselves. It was pure doublethink. All major publishing houses had – and still have – special secret departments involved in publishing prohibited books for the Party and KGB elite. I've seen such books a number of times thanks to a friend's mother-in-law who worked in the CPSU Central Committee library. Each of them had its own number and the word 'Classified' rubber-stamped on the cover. One of the books I saw in the mid-seventies was *Nineteen Eighty-Four*, the other was *The Technology of Power* by Abdurakhman Avtorkhanov, whose mere mention used to drive Soviet ideologists mad. The books were thoroughly translated into Russian and very well bound, only without illustrations. At the beginning of the eighties I got hold of the 'special' edition of *Secrets of Eternal Life* by C. Northcote Parkinson. The senile octogenarians who ruled our poor country were naturally curious about the secrets of eternal life, since it was they – not the people they ruled – who were supposed to live forever. They must have especially liked one piece of Parkinsonian advice: never worry about other people's problems.

Studying at Kharkov University I became increasingly aware of some dark force which was keeping us all under strain, Jews and non-Jews alike. At the interpreters' department persistent rumours circulated about KGB informers planted in every group of students, about their full-time KGB 'curators' whom they met at specially designated places, about monthly payments the snitchers were supposedly getting for spying on their comrades. We couldn't help noticing that sensitive details from our private lives (occasional drinking sessions, girlfriends etc) became known to teachers, especially to those from the military department (we had a compulsory military training at our faculty). 'We know more about you than you do yourselves!' the military translation teacher, Colonel Akishev, liked to boast. But it was not until graduation that the whole truth came out.

A month before the final exams we had a showdown in our group. There were only ten boys in it and, as it turned out, three of them were working for the KGB. They confessed and claimed that they had been trying not to harm the rest of us, their fellow students, but were simply trying to improve their own lives. They received a paltry twelve roubles a month each for their services so it was not expensive for the KGB to buy them. The enormous proportion of KGB stooges in the group can be explained by the fact that we studied at the foreign languages department and the mere word 'foreign' incited real paranoia in our xenophobic provincial Kharkov. We were not allowed to mix with foreigners (apart from the foreign students living at the hostel) or to come close to the city's only Intourist hotel where the visitors from abroad were housed. Our knowledge of foreign languages was an additional 'risk factor' in the eyes of the local KGB. That's why they were watching us so vigilantly.

My first serious encounter with the KGB occurred four days before I had to present my diploma paper on Henry Longfellow's poetry and one day before the final exam on Scientific Communism.

A couple of weeks earlier I started noticing strange activity around me. During one of the breaks I was approached by a lad from a parallel group whom I hardly knew. He led me to a quiet nook behind the lifts and there, in a conspiratorial whisper, asked me whether I could lend him a book by Solzhenitsyn to read. It was an explicit provocation. First of all, I didn't have any Solzhenitsyn books at home and, even if I had, I wouldn't have told him. I told him I didn't have Solzhenitsyn: it was a criminal offence to possess 'anti-Soviet' literature. 'But you must have read him!' he insisted. 'I've read only those works which were published in the Soviet Union in the early sixties,' I said. And this was also true: Solzhenitsyn experienced a short period of recognition and even fame under Khrushchev when some of his works saw the light.

The informer left me alone . . .

The Dean was stubbornly refusing to give me back my character references endorsed by the regional Party Committee. I was supposed to send them to the place of my future employment in Kaliningrad, where I was to work as an interpreter for a fishing company: without the character references, according to the procedure, I couldn't start my new employment.

So four days before defending my diploma paper, I approached the Dean again asking for my references. Instead of returning them to me, she told me rather sternly to go to the University Party Committee where 'someone' wanted to talk to me. I immediately had a bad premonition.

At the Party Committee I was met by a certain Romanov, its Deputy Secretary, who produced several sheets of rumpled paper where my first wife's fellow students (she was studying at the same faculty, but at the pedagogical department) denounced her for 'sporting foreign clothes and expressing pro-Western views'. Romanov interrogated me for two hours. His main point was having a wife like that, I couldn't be given the honour of working abroad.

Both for my first wife and me it was a huge blow, like a bad dream: suddenly all our plans were turned into dust. Next morning we both hurried to the University, hoping secretly that yesterday's nightmare was either a mistake or someone's bad joke.

Again we were told to go to the Party Committee. Approaching its doors, covered with black leatherette, we suddenly saw Romanov fluttering out of them. 'Let's go to the First Department!' he said to us. The doors of this obscure department were just opposite the Party Committee. By that time, I already knew what First Department meant. It was the KGB office. First Departments were part and parcel of every single Soviet institution and enterprise. I had never been inside one before.

Romanov didn't enter the First Department himself. He opened the door and, bowing obsequiously, let in a nondescript young man who materialised out of nowhere, then beckoned us to follow and closed the door behind us.

The First Department looked like any ordinary Soviet office, only instead of the regulation portrait of Lenin on the wall there was a portrait of Dzerzhinsky, the first head of the Cheka. In the corner of the room there stood a wooden partition, half-covered by a thick velvet curtain.

The young man sat at the desk with a broad sadistic grin on his round face. 'I am not going to play hide-and-seek with you,' he declared. 'I am from the State Security Committee.' With obvious pleasure he produced his red ID which stated that the bearer was captain at the Kharkov branch of the State Security Committee and was permitted to carry firearms. I can't remember his first name now, but his patronymic was quite a rare one, Serafimovich, and his last name was Kniazhev. He was dressed in a good Polish suit and brown imported shoes. Even the fountain pen with which he was playing was of a foreign make. This was quite ridiculous for someone investigating into the 'crime' of 'sporting foreign clothes'.

'Do you know where you are? This is the First Department, the University's holy of holies.'

He interrogated us for four hours, round and round in circles. From time to time he made brief telephone calls to the local KGB headquarters in Sovnarkomovskaya Street, telling someone that he was being detained by an urgent matter at the University.

Kniazhev's arguments were as follows: since the denunciations had dates and signatures, they were documents which couldn't be dismissed. They had nothing against me personally, but my wife was a problem. He wanted to help us out of this mess (of course!), and, in his opinion, we could either confess, or they would have to call an emergency Komsomol meeting which would certainly exclude us from Komsomol and – automatically – from the University. Not a very good prospect just three days before graduation.

I was watching him closely, the first real KGB man I had ever seen. He had a very plain face and blank emotionless eyes, the eyes of a fish or of a murderer. Since that time I was able to identify KGB people in a crowd by the expression, or rather lack of expression, in their eyes. I am convinced that this is their main distinguishing feature.

As it appeared, Kniazhev was the 'curator' of our interpreters department. I had never seen him before but he had the names of all my fellow students at his fingertips. Making sudden breaks in the interrogation, he would ask me what I thought of this or that person. I said nothing. From time to time he would pose a random question like 'Do you know how to cook?' or 'Where did you meet Meyerovich?' 'Who is Meyerovich?' I would enquire. 'Oh, never mind, he's just someone.' Like in a bad spy film he was obviously enjoying himself and was pleased to see how frustrated and scared we were.

In the end I threatened to write a letter of complaint to the Politburo and he suddenly became apologetic. 'You must understand me,' he said, 'I have my job to do. My bosses will ask me to account for the time I've spent with you. So you must write some kind of an explanation – and this will be the end of it.' We both wrote short notes rebuffing all the accusations as dictated by envy and the desire to compromise us. But he made my wife add something to the effect that she considered her behaviour 'unworthy of a Soviet student'. 'You should make some kind of confession!' Kniazhev insisted. 'It's not going to affect you, but I'll have to write my report, you know. I've helped you out, so why don't you help me?' It was a bad mistake allowing this last sentence to be inserted, but we were tired and inexperienced. All we wanted was to end the nightmare as soon as possible.

'So it means that I can now get back my character references?' I asked. 'Certainly!' Kniazhev was beaming. 'You'll get them tomorrow and let's forget about the whole thing. Are you sure you've got nothing to say about your comrades from the group?'

Next morning when I came to the Dean to pick up my references she said: 'What references are you talking about? Your wife has confessed everything!'

The truth about the case only came to light a couple of years later, when I bumped into my former wife's fellow student, a woman who had signed one of the denunciations. 'Please, forgive me! I know we've ruined your life. But, believe me, we had no choice. They didn't want you to work abroad. They kept calling us – me and three other girls – to the First Department several times a day. They threatened to throw us out of the University, if we didn't denounce your wife. We had no choice. They dictated these filthy letters to us and made us sign them. It was terrible. We were afraid. Please, forgive me, if you can.'

Looking back I feel that I should be thankful to them for changing my life so drastically. Because of their actions I gained enough experience to become a journalist several years later. Even the fact that my first wife walked out on me eventually proved for the best: it helped me to find Natasha who really cares about me – not about the job I have. So I should bless my lucky stars for the KGB's first intrusion into my life, but at the time it seemed my whole existence was broken and all my hopes dashed.

It's interesting that none of my university teachers, who knew me very well and valued me highly as a student, ventured to put in a word for me. They all started pitying me afterwards, when the danger was past. The reason was simple: they were afraid. Fear made them meek, dumb and obedient. When thirteen years later in December 1989 I came to speak at my alma mater, already then a well-known Moscow journalist, they avoided my eyes. I told the whole story from the stage and hoped they felt pangs of shame.

Back in 1976 many of my fellow students did not conceal their desire to work for the KGB. One of them, who had been zealously informing on his comrades for years, went to Sovnarkomovskaya Street shortly before graduation and pleaded to be employed as a KGB agent. They didn't take this one – their criteria were always a bit of a mystery – but they did take another one who they employed as a restaurant mole in Odessa. His job was to sit in restaurants and cafés listening to what the clients were saying. Wonderful career for a university graduate! They also took a couple of humble country lads from the German department, who had only one thing in common: a blank and cold expressionlessness in their eyes.

After my divorce I started going out with a girl who lived in a neighbouring house. Galya was Ukrainian and a graduate of the foreign languages faculty like myself. Both of her parents had died and she was living alone in a two-room flat. Her English was excellent and she had many foreign friends. She was especially close to a young British woman called Cynthia who had taught English at Kharkov University some time before. Cynthia fell in love with one of her Russian students and they got married. Soon her husband graduated and was drafted. It was unthinkable for a Soviet army officer to be married to a Westerner and he was faced with a dilemma: to ruin his career at the cost of retaining his English wife, or the other way round. He chose the career and divorced Cynthia. She couldn't make herself believe in such a betrayal. When her contract expired she kept coming to Kharkov in the hope of getting a glimpse of her former husband. She couldn't afford a hotel and so often stayed with Galya.

One night Galya and I were approaching her house chatting elatedly, when all of a sudden she said: 'Don't come any further, and don't ring me for a while!' and charged inside.

I was puzzled by her behaviour and thought she had simply ditched me, albeit in a strange manner. She kept refusing to see me and didn't answer my phone calls. But after a month or so she called me herself and we met.

After Cynthia's last visit, Galya had started being harassed by the KGB. They kept coming to her flat and to the institute where she worked trying to persuade her to inform on Cynthia. Galya used to slam the door in their faces but they kept persecuting her, taking advantage of the fact that she was alone in the world and had no-one to protect her. The last time we had seen each other, she had noticed them from a distance standing near her house. 'I didn't want them to see us together,' she said. 'You've had enough of them anyway. I didn't want them to start tormenting you again because of me.'

When I came to live in Moscow in 1978, I couldn't help feeling that the atmosphere there was much more relaxed than in Kharkov. There was less fear. Once, browsing through a small bookshop in Kuznetski Most, just a stone's throw from the awe-inspiring KGB headquarters in Lubianka, I saw inside one of the books a small piece of paper with several typed lines on it. 'Read and pass on to a friend!' was written in the upper right-hand corner. I put the note in my pocket and brought it home. It was a poorly rhymed, but passionate anti-Communist poem. I don't remember most of it, but one line is clearly imprinted in my memory: 'The Communist Party is a vampire washing its ugly face with people's blood.' On my next visit to the bookshop I stuck the note into another book on the shelf. It was very reassuring to know that even KGB terror could not stop some brave people from expressing their thoughts.

And the terror was there all right. I felt the suffocating grip of its ugly tentacles many times, when working as an interpreter in Moscow. We all had strict instructions not to mention the word KGB when speaking to foreigners. The huge complex of buildings housing the KGB head-quarters around Dzerzhinskovo Square kept growing every year. It couldn't help attracting the foreigners' attention. 'What is that big building opposite the "Children's World" shop?' they would ask whenever we passed through the city centre. Under instructions we were to say that this was 'an administrative building', though I myself always said that it was the KGB. Once a driver of the Intourist car in which we were travelling denounced me to my bosses. It turned out he worked for the KGB himself. I had a hard time trying to justify myself and nearly lost my job. The fact that the KGB driver didn't know English saved me. I claimed he had just misheard me saying KGB whereas in fact it was just a similar-sounding English word . . .

In Baku my guest, an American piano player, once wanted to change her hotel room which she did not like. The hotel manager explained to me in a wheezing whisper that this was impossible since her room was 'specially equipped, you understand?'

One evening in Leningrad in 1980, I was having dinner with my 'delegate', a Canadian museum curator. She was a charming woman. We had some vodka and she told me lots of things about her life, about her house in Vancouver, about her father who had asked her to bring him three souvenirs of Russia: a copy of *Pravda*, a loaf of black bread and an empty bottle of Soviet Pepsi Cola. I felt attracted to her and suddenly told her about my university ordeal, the restrictions they imposed on interpreters and many other things. She listened eagerly with genuine interest and sympathy.

After dinner, when I found myself in my room overlooking the Neva, I suddenly felt a wave of fear. What a fool I had been to speak out when I knew only too well that all the tables in the Intourist restaurants were bugged! I clearly envisaged how after I'd seen my guest off the KGB would be waiting for me at the airport.

What precisely I was afraid of I could not understand. I was just afraid and that was all. It was something beyond me – an uncontrollable, animal fear. To subdue it, I started dialling frantically the numbers of my friends in Kharkov and Moscow, just to hear their voices. After talking to them I felt better, but when the next day in Moscow I was not arrested in the airport, I was genuinely surprised.

Ten years after this incident I found a very precise description of my state of mind in John Le Carré's *The Russia House*: 'Then suddenly the Moscow fear hit him at a gale force. It sprang out at him when he was least expecting it, after he had fought it all day.' This was exactly how I felt, though in my case it was the Leningrad fear, not the Moscow one. But it didn't make a big difference.

In September 1981 I was working as an interpreter at the Moscow International Book Fair. The interpreter's duties included preventing the foreign books from being stolen by the information-hungry visitors. Plainclothes KGB men swarmed all around the place and searched everyone leaving the pavilion. Despite this, large numbers of books were disappearing from the stands.

I was working at the stand of a British publisher, Mitchell Beazley, who had lots of colourful albums and atlases on display. The stand was one of the fair's biggest attractions. At some point I got talking with a man from the neighbouring American Jewish Publisher's Association stand. He presented me with two paperbacks by Isaac Bashevis Singer, the US Jewish novelist and winner of the 1978 Nobel Prize for Literature. I'd heard a lot about this writer, but had never read any of his works.

At the exit I was stopped by a guard and asked to open my briefcase. On discovering the two books – which I didn't try to hide – he took me to a cubicle near the door. There a short man I had seen cruising around my stand was sitting at the tiny desk. 'That's what we were looking for!' he said cheerfully pointing at the books. 'They are a present!' I tried to explain. 'And where is the signed statement to certify that? Don't you know the rules? You should be guarding the books, and you are in fact stealing them! As an interpreter, you are not supposed to take presents from foreigners!' He finally let me go, saying: 'Tomorrow we'll think what to do with you.' 'What about the books?' I asked. 'Forget them!' the man shouted. 'They have been confiscated by the KGB! This Ba ... Ba. .. shevski ... or whatever his name is is a Zionist writer!'

Next morning as soon as I took my post at the stand the shorty appeared. 'Be careful. You are under surveillance!' he hissed. In the evening he brought me a sandwich from the buffet and said: 'You can relax now. We've checked you. Surveillance has been lifted!' After humming and hawing for a while he suddenly said: 'You know, there's a very nice album on your stand with photos of naked women. I collect such photos, you see ... So could you please look the other way for a moment while I take it? After all, I've helped you out of real trouble with these Zionist books. We could have arrested you.'

Interpreting for a number of Australian delegations, I made friends with Don, the only Aussie businessman in Moscow at the time. I used to drop in at his flat in southwest Moscow and borrow books from him. There I met Irina, his Russian girlfriend. She used to be Don's interpreter and they fell in love with each other. As soon as they started going out together, she was thrown out of her job at UPDK, the KGB-run agency catering for foreign diplomats, journalists and businessmen in Moscow. When they were about to get married, the real nightmare started.

It was common knowledge that there was a special KGB section in Moscow whose sole aim was to disrupt marriages between Soviets and foreigners. Among other things, they used to send fake telegrams to would-be brides on behalf of their fiancés (or vice versa) with texts like: 'Everything is finished between us! I don't want to see you again!'

With Irina they behaved even more cruelly. A number of times she was stopped by a militiaman somewhere in the city, driven to the closest militia precinct and confronted with completed protocols (with the signatures of 'witnesses' etc) to the effect that she was, for example, making a public nuisance of herself by drunkenly accosting passers-by. They would detain her for several hours at the precinct all the while repeating: 'Think well before you marry him!' The poor woman was already pregnant and the KGB intimidation resulted in her going into premature labour. But as soon as the couple got married, the KGB left them alone. Irina and Don left the Soviet Union shortly afterwards.

A university friend of mine who had served for three years as a military translator in Ethiopia told me a story about their KGB supervisor, Alexei Alexeyevich. He was a podgy, ruddy-faced elderly man about to retire.

One of his duties was to maintain secrecy as to the true mission and status of Soviet military advisers in Ethiopia. First of all, they were all posing as civilians. My friend, for instance, being a Soviet army lieutenant, had to wear an Aeroflot pilot's uniform. Who were they trying to dupe? Only God knows.

On Alexei Alexeyevich's initiative, they were also forbidden to use the words 'Party' and 'Komsomol' while in Ethiopia. At meetings they were supposed to refer to Party members as 'trade-union members' and Komsomols as 'athletes'. But his main duty was to try and make military personnel inform on each other. He would periodically approach this or that officer, put a hand round his shoulder and, after a perfunctory question about his family, would say, staring straight into the officer's eyes: 'Please, my friend, write me a message, will you? I personally don't need it, you understand? Try and reflect, who, what, when and with whom.' He drove the officers crazy with his badgering and sometimes – just to get rid of him – they did write 'reports' of the type: 'Yesterday Lieutenant Ivanov popped into my room and in an aggressive anti-Soviet manner asked whether he could borrow my electric shaver.' Alexei Alexeyevich, though, seemed to be happy even with these reports which he kept 'studying' for hours in his room.

At the beginning of my journalistic career in 1981, I got a part-time job as literary consultant to *Literaturnaya Gazeta*. My task was to answer readers' letters and to review the poems and stories sent to the editorial office. Before I took up the job, I was briefed by the editor, who was the head of the paper's literary consultants. After explaining how to file incoming letters and how to formulate the out-going refusals, she said: 'There's one more very sensitive thing to know. You may come across some letters with – er – anti-Soviet contents. Such letters must be immediately forwarded to our First Department and they will decide what measures to take. There will also be a number of letters from demented people. In this case, if you think the author is mad, just write "clinics" on the envelope and we'll throw the letter out.'

I got the message: the editor was casually advising me how to deal with 'dissident' letters without putting the lives of their audacious authors at risk. And there were quite a number of such letters, so I wrote 'clinics' on the envelopes pretty often. (The whole procedure was such that a literary consultant couldn't have destroyed a letter himself: as soon as it arrived at the editorial office it was taken control of by the letters department – a filing card and a number were assigned to it before it was read by anyone, so that the consultant could be asked to account for missing or unanswered letters.

115

Political murders, one of the driving forces of the reign of fear, became common practice in the USSR under Stalin. Suffice it to remember the assassinations of Leningrad Party Secretary Sergei Kirov in 1934, of Jewish activist and actor Solomon Mikhoels in 1948, of Lev Trotsky in 1940 and many others – all masterminded by NKVD. In 1959 in Munich the KGB staged the murder of Stepan Bandera, the Ukrainian nationalist leader. According to some Western estimates, this was the KGB's last major political murder. But was it?

In March 1990 a KGB defector Victor Sheymov claimed that the KGB were involved in the 1981 attempt to assassinate the Pope. He said they had tried to kill the Pope the year before in Warsaw, when Sheymov himself saw a cable signed by the then KGB chief, Yuri Andropov, which ordered: 'Obtain all possible information on how to get physically close to the Pope.' In KGB slang such a phrase has only one meaning – assassinate the person. Sheymov also had grounds to suspect that the KGB was behind the assassination of Mohammad Zia-ul-Haq, the President of Pakistan, in August 1988. 'Zia was not responsive to Soviet demands,' the defector explained.[5]

Everyone in the Soviet Union remembers the enigmatic death in a car crash of wartime partisan Piotr Masherov, the First Secretary of the Belorussia Communist Party, a favourite of the Belorussian people and an opponent of Brezhnev. The crash occurred in October 1980 on the outskirts of Minsk, shortly after Masherov and Brezhnev had had a big argument over the phone. Masherov's sedan collided with a lorry which suddenly drove on to the highway from a farm track. The strangest thing was that Masherov's bodyguards' cars were almost a mile ahead at the moment of the crash. When in Minsk in 1986, I went to the place of the 'accident'. The dirt road from which the fatal lorry appeared was visible from a long way off. The landscape was completely open with practically no trees in sight. Even if someone intentionally wanted a collision, it would have been fairly difficult to achieve. It was a chain of many coincidences. The sudden death of the lorry driver several days after the crash was the last link in the chain. After visiting the scene of the tragedy, I had no doubts who Masherov's killing was carefully prearranged by. By the way, Masherov's vacated place in the Politburo was taken by a close friend of the then KGB chief Yuri Andropov – a certain Mikhail Gorbachev.

While in Frunze, investigating the murder of the republic's Social Security Minister in 1987, I popped into the office of *Sovietskaya Kirgizia* newspaper, the main republican daily, to say hello to my colleagues. We started talking about Minister Balatski's murder. 'It's nothing compared to the killing of Ibragimov at his dacha in 1981,' one journalist said. 'Try and look into that, if you can. Our paper was not allowed to do so.'

I immediately became curious and started making enquiries. This was not easy since, as I was told, all information about the case was in the local KGB archives.

The picture was as follows. Ibragimov, the Prime Minister of Kirgizia, was a progressive-minded person, a radical and a reformist. This put him at loggerheads with the republic's Brezhnevite Communist Party elite. Usubaliev, the First Secretary of the Kirgizia Communist Party, was particularly notorious for his nepotism and corruption. He owned many luxurious palaces all over the republic and a man like Ibragimov was a constant thorn in his side. The two men had a number of arguments and public clashes.

In 1981 Ibragimov was murdered at his dacha on the outskirts of Frunze under extremely suspicious circumstances. The murderer, a young Russian boy, penetrated the heavily-guarded government dacha compound unnoticed, went into the house and, after wandering around for a while, went up to Ibragimov's bedroom and shot him as he lay in bed. He quietly escaped but a couple of days later was arrested by the KGB and confessed to the murder. His motives, he claimed, were purely nationalistic: he simply hated the Kirgizes and, encouraged by his father, wanted to punish them. Several days later the murderer committed suicide by hanging himself in the train which was transporting him from one prison to another, a striking similarity to Masherov's case. His father was tried for inciting murder and in the courtroom a photograph of the murderer was shown to Ibragimov's wife, who had seen the real killer at the dacha. 'But that's not him!' she said firmly.

It all looked very fishy. The only agency which could help me to establish the truth was the KGB. After some hesitation I made an appointment with the Chairman of the republic's KGB, who, surprisingly, agreed to see me.

He was a KGB general who had recently been transferred to Kirgizia from the Ukraine. Naturally he feigned total ignorance about the case. I insisted on having a look at the files and he instructed one of his subordinates to show them to me. A room was put at my disposal and the file was brought to me from the archives. It was surprisingly thin and had nothing much in it apart from a detailed map of the scene of the crime, a photograph of the murdered Prime Minister in his bed and several protocols or statements of interrogation. It also contained two sheets of paper, torn from the murderer's diary, where he expressed a boiling hatred of the people of Kirgizia. 'These dirty Asians! I want to kill them!'

he wrote. The diary was not convincing. It was written in short, clear-cut and accurately-linked sentences with all the punctuation marks in their proper places, as if it had been dictated. The most striking details I found in the statements made by Ibragimov's driver and wife. The KGB driver, who was also the Prime Minister's personal bodyguard, received a telegram on the day of the murder saying that his father was seriously ill and wanted to see him. He took a day off and went to his father only to find that he was well and hadn't sent any telegram. By strange 'coincidence', the other two KGB men who guarded the dacha grounds were also summoned elsewhere shortly before the killing, leaving the whole place completely unprotected. The murderer's behaviour, as testified by Ibragimov's wife, was even more bizarre. After breaking into the house he hung around downstairs for about half an hour. He was smoking and reading a copy of *Krokodil* (!) as if he was in a waiting room. Finally he went upstairs, shot Ibragimov with a hunting rifle, tied his wife to a chair and, after lingering for another thirty minutes, finally left the house. Shortly afterwards the guards reappeared. This case obviously has parallels with the murder of the Leningrad Party Chief Kirov in 1934. It is common knowledge now that his NKVD murderers were working on Stalin's orders.

You must have noticed that I am recounting this story without giving any names, apart from Ibragimov's. Why?

As soon as I returned to Moscow I told the story to the head of my department at *Krokodil*. 'This requires further investigation, possibly another trip to Frunze,' I told him, 'but I have a feeling this is really big.' We decided to put the notes I'd taken into my boss's safe in our office. It was just an old metallic box where he kept his Party card and the telephone directory (our colleagues had a nasty habit of borrowing and not returning it). The key to the safe was stored in one of the drawer's of the chief's desk. When after a while I decided to refresh my memory and look at the notes, they were gone. We rummaged through the whole room but they were nowhere to be found. There was no question of either writing the story or investigating further without them: they had all the names, dates, leads, contact addresses and phone numbers without which I simply could not proceed. I was thinking of going to Frunze again, but then thought better of it: there was no guarantee that the KGB would let me have another look at the file, and even if they did, nothing would prevent them – I was sure they were the thieves – from stealing or destroying my notes once more. So we will have to be satisfied with the above brief account of this article that never was.

This was in 1987 with 'glasnost' already in full swing.

During the first two or three years of Gorbachev's power, the KGB did keep a relatively low profile, presumably trying to adjust to the new Soviet realities. There exists an opinion that glasnost itself was initiated by the KGB as a ruse to divert popular attention from questioning the viability of the whole system, from shortages, corruption and elite privileges. People had to let off steam, and there was no better outlet than to let them speak out a little. This, of course, is very hard to prove, but it is pure 'logic' that prompts such a conclusion.

Despite the massive propaganda campaign, after six years of Gorbachev the KGB remains untouched by change. On the contrary, it continues to expand its payroll.[6] The KGB are paying Gorbachev back in his own coin. David Owen, the former British Foreign Secretary, wrote in the *Sunday Times*: 'Gorbymania [in the West] is a KGB creation. Ask most people in our streets and they will tell you that Gorbachev is a democrat. They hear about the Soviet parliament and about elections which are all aimed at giving the impression of a full-blown democracy. Yet the Soviet Union is very far as yet from being a true democracy. The KGB elite in power around Gorbachev intend, as he does, to hold on to their power. They are content to project a managed democracy.'[7]

When delivering his reform package to Parliament in November 1990, President Gorbachev again made sure that the KGB would be protected from the terrible economic crisis which paralysed the country, decimated all its resources and brought it to the brink of starvation.[8]

As a journalist what struck me personally was a law – 'On Measures to Protect the Honour and Dignity of the President' – passed by the Soviet legislation in May 1990 under pressure from Gorbachev and, I am sure, the KGB. This law imposes penalties of up to six years' imprisonment and fines of up to approximately \$60,000 on those who insult or slander the Soviet President. It was a terrible blow for those who still believed in Gorbachev's democratic commitment. Its main aim was to try and fully restore the atmosphere of fear and even terror which has permeated Soviet society for decades. Peter Galliner, director of the International Press Institute, sent Gorbachev a strongly-worded protest which ran: 'The International Press Institute, representing leading journalists, editors and publishers throughout the world, is most concerned about the law. The law is vaguely worded about what kind of comments would be considered insulting or slanderous and whether it would apply to foreign correspondents and foreign publications. We believe that this law violates international standards of press freedom, including Article Nineteen of the Universal Declaration of Human Rights. We urge you to do everything in your power to see that the legislature repeal this law and that no similar limitations on freedom of expression are imposed by the government.'[9]

This law enabled the KGB to unleash a new anti-democratic campaign. Soon after its adoption several people were arrested in Moscow. Among them were Moscow street vendors who discovered the exact price of the President's honour and dignity. They offered passers-by humorous matrioshka dolls representing all the Soviet leaders from Stalin to Gorbachev one inside the other. When the militia started arresting them for 'insulting the President', the sellers faced a dilemma: to go to court trying to prove that their goods were not insulting and pay a two- or three-thousand-rouble fine as an inevitable result, or to give a militiaman a ten-rouble bribe on the spot and be left in peace. Of course they all preferred to grease the sticky palms of the protectors of the President's honour, the price of which turned out to be quite reasonable.[10]

Valeriya Novodvorskaya, the former prisoner of conscience and the courageous leader of the Democratic Union, was also arrested by the KGB on September 17 1990, charged with 'insulting the President' on the grounds of the newly-adopted law and sent to Moscow's Kashchenko Psychiatric Hospital, long known as a facility for political prisoners.[11]

I have first-hand experience demonstrating that the KGB is still alive and kicking and active in every sphere of Soviet life. When I completed the manuscript of *Special Correspondent* in Spring 1989, I had to get permission from VAAP, the Soviet copyright agency, to take it to Britain. VAAP's First Department [read: KGB] refused permission on the grounds that the manuscript was in English and they couldn't read it. They suggested that I should translate it into Russian first and that they would then consider it. This was unthinkable. There was no way I could translate almost 500 typewritten pages in the fortnight which remained until the delivery date, so I virtually had to smuggle the script out of the country. In fact, in 1990 a finished copy of *Special Correspondent*, bought by a Moscow friend of mine in London, was confiscated by Soviet customs.

When I was in London in May 1989, several Soviet KGB agents, posing as journalists, were expelled from Britain for spying. (In the Soviet Union we all know that the overwhelming majority of Soviet correspondents abroad – as well as the diplomats and trade representatives – have to work full-time or part-time for the KGB. It simply goes with the job.) As a tit-for-tat gesture, the Soviet authorities threw out the same number of British correspondents in Moscow. One of them, Jeremy Harris, told me later how the KGB were trying to provoke him shortly before the expulsion by forcing suspicious-looking parcels on him. As a sort of barbaric intimidation, a number of times on returning home he discovered pigeons flying around the rooms. It looked very sinister but he was not sure what it meant. It was only in London, when he was safely out of the Soviet Union, that I told him that, according to an old Russian superstition, a bird in the house was a very bad omen meaning imminent death.

The wife of one of my closest friends was invited by the British embassy in Moscow to attend a reception in honour of the editor of *Angliya*, the Russian-language magazine published in Britain and distributed in the Soviet Union. Several days later two KGB agents visited her office. They were interested in who the other Soviets at the reception were, what they said and so on. This was also in 1989. Just like in the 'good old' Brezhnev era.

And fear, of course, remained as well. The KGB's clumsy attempts to recruit me before we fled (chapter 8) had a huge effect on my wife Natasha. She confessed to me later that when I left for my first (and last) rendezvous with KGB agent Sergei Stanislavovich, she was not sure whether she would ever see me again. This was probably a bit of an overstatement on her part: people did not disappear in Moscow in 1989 quite as they did in 1937 – but with the terrifying image of the KGB before her eyes, the image maintained by the KGB itself throughout long years of terror, she simply couldn't control her emotions. When I came back home after the meeting I could see that she had been crying.

Walking past the ever-growing complex of KGB buildings around Dzerzhinkovo Square, watching swarms of businesslike KGB officials running in and out of the ornate heavy doors with the KGB emblem of shield and two crossed swords above them, I couldn't help thinking: 'What the hell are they all doing here now, when they don't have any more dissidents to pursue, when the Cold War with its massive spying seems to be coming to an end, when political jokes are no longer treated as an immediate threat to socialism, when everyday life in the country has become a sort of political joke in itself?' And not only in Moscow. It is enough to visit any Soviet city (or town) and you will see imposing KGB buildings still dominating the cityscape. By some estimates there are more than one million KGB agents operating in the Soviet Union at present.[12] What are they all doing? What?

'Active measures' or infiltration into religious hierarchies has always been an important part of KGB tactics. In 1985 when I was already working at *Krokodil*, I was sent to the Krasnodar region to investigate systematic embezzlement of church funds by a criminal group from

121

Moscow posing as a team of restorers. The trip was prompted by a letter I received from the church parishioners. At that time anything connected with religion (apart from lampoons or rampant criticism) was still taboo for the press, so I was instructed by the editor to get in touch with the Chairman of the Krasnodar Council for Religious Affairs , a branch of the All-Union Council which has always been popularly perceived as a Department of the KGB. I was told not to take any steps in my investigation without the Chairman's approval. So the first thing I did on arrival in Krasnodar was to visit his office, which was located in the building of the Executive Committee of the regional Soviet of people's deputies.

A large roly-poly man in his fifties was sitting at the huge desk with three telephones on it and the ubiquitous portrait of Lenin above. I spent several hours in his office and he told me everything about himself. He was a KGB colonel and his job was a kind of honorary retirement. His main duty was to curb and contain religious feeling in the region at all costs. He had extensive powers and was able to manipulate the believers by imposing exorbitant taxes on them, by denying registration to this or that religious community. Without such registration, the believers had no right to attend the church.

He was obviously trying to impress me with how difficult it was to deal with 'these fanatics' as he called the clergymen. At one point he had a visitor – a broad-shouldered, bearded giant in a black suit and black collarless shirt. Looking at him one could immediately see that he was a priest. On seeing me, the giant wanted to come back later, but the Chairman beckoned him in. 'You may trust this man!' he said, pointing at me. 'What do you have to tell me today?'

Throwing furtive looks at me the priest started speaking: 'You know, comrade Chairman, the new Blagochinny* in our district is rather a dark horse. Very persistent. People say he visits the houses of collective farmers and tries to convert them by reading from the Bible and so on. He also frequents the local youth club persuading the young people to attend sermons.'

The Chairman wrinkled his meaty red nose: 'Too bad. What shall I do to discourage him from this religious propaganda? I think I know what . . . I shall double the amount of the diocese voluntary donations to the Soviet Peace Fund. This will reduce his enthusiasm a little. And if not, we won't renew his parish registration next year and have the church closed!' He made some notes in his jotter. 'Anything else you want to tell me?'

*A senior diocesan priest.

'That's all for the present, comrade Chairman.'

'OK. Now we owe you a fee for the last two months. Here's the authorisation. Show it upstairs at the window. And see you again next week!'

'Who is he?' I asked when the door closed behind the priest.

The Chairman dismissed my question with a quick wave of his hand, 'Scum. A petty crook in a priest's robe and also one of my secret assistants. They are all crooks, these clergymen, but I have to deal with them to know what's going on in the region.'

He went out of his way to prevent me from writing a critical article. That's why he allowed me to witness his talk with the informer. He thought we were of the same mentality. And he did impress me. I became much more aware of how deeply the KGB had penetrated every pore of Soviet society. Even the church, which is formally separate from the state was under tight KGB control.

But if controlling churches and clergymen has always been a part of KGB intimidation tactics, the infiltration of national liberation movements in the USSR is a relatively new priority. The KGB is going out of its way to provoke the democratic movements into haphazard action and tries to promote ethnic violence as part of their attempted destablisation of the country. John Rettie, the *Guardian*'s Moscow correspondent, reported in March 1990 that the first pogroms of Armenians in Baku had been provoked by plainclothes Russian-speaking men flashing KGB cards. They helped the frenzied mob of Azerbaijani nationalists to pick out the flats where Armenians lived. One spark was enough to ignite the powder keg of ethnic tensions. The first attacks set off a chain reaction of violence and provided the pretext for sending in Russian troops. The free elections to the republican parliament which were about to take place became out of the question. Moscow's goal had been achieved.

The KGB masterminds social unrest in the country. It covertly supports ultra-right organisations (Pamyat among them) and blackens the names of the leaders of the democratic movement. It harasses progressive journalists either recruiting them or forcing them out of the country. What for? To create chaos, to split Soviet society into miniscule, warring factions that present no danger for the rulers. It has its hands full . . .

In September 1990 in Melbourne I interviewed Bohdan Horin, a visiting progressive politician from the Ukraine, a people's deputy, deputy head of the foreign affairs commission of the Ukrainian parliament and a former political prisoner.

The KGB is growing, and there's not the slightest indication of change in their methods. Their main aim now is to compromise us democrats. They disseminate rumours that we are anti-semites, anti-Russians, anti-everyone, whereas we proclaimed from the beginning that all nationalities living in the Ukraine should be equal and enjoy the same rights. This stand of the Ukrainian democratic movement has gained us a very good reputation all over the world. But the KGB's main strategy has always been 'divide and rule'. They keep spreading rumours that at our rallies we'll be beating the Jews, the Russians, the Poles – lest people should attend them. I remember addressing a big rally in Lvov where I asked from the rostrum: 'Who spreads rumours of our national chauvinism?' And thousands of people chanted in chorus: 'KGB!!!' This popular attitude doesn't seem to affect the KGB themselves. In Lvov they have just added a new modern building to their huge complex. They are arming themselves with the latest electronics, computers and eaves-dropping devices which they buy in the West. There's no shortage of hard currency for their needs. At a recent session of the Ukrainian parliament I tried to bring Ukrainian KGB Chairman Galushko to account. He only mumbled something incoherent about the KGB restructuring themselves in reply. We gave him a hard time in parliament, but nothing has changed in the KGB so far. The most awful thing is that they are still virtually out of control. No-one, not even a people's deputy like myself, can come to their offices and check what they are doing or how much money they are spending on what. We only know that they have instigated all the political coups in our history, that they have always been involved in terror and political killings all over the world. Only God knows what they are up to now.

This is far from being the only example of the KGB intimidating the leaders of democratic and national liberation movements. In Novosibirsk they punctured the tyres and cut the petrol supply hose in the car of Lisenko and Belov, people's deputies and members of the 'Democratic Platform' faction from Moscow, while they were speaking to the local electorate. On the same day in August 1990, an uncalled-for 'electrician' was seen fiddling about with the telephone control panel at the house of people's deputy Bogayenko, where Lisenko was staying. None of Bogayenko's neighbours had summoned an electrician that day.[13]

On the night of 3 October 1990 a car belonging to the Moscow democratic *Glasnost* magazine was dismantled into spare parts in the yard. On the same night the telephone in the flat of Sergei Grigoriants, the editor of *Glasnost*, was disconnected. The militia, to whom the journalists complained, did not react. This was done immediately after *Glasnost* published a series of articles criticising Gorbachev.[14]

I've already written about KGB tricks in the Ukraine. They are doing the same sorts of things in many other Soviet republics. In Kirgizia they terrorise the leaders of the nationalist movement, Kirgizstan, who are regularly summoned at all hours of the day or night to the KGB offices and harshly interrogated, though physical force is carefully not used against them. In Georgia they spared no effort in trying to compromise the leader of the pro-independence movement, Zviad Gamsakhurdia, by spreading the disinformation line that he was a KGB agent.[15]

Audrius Butkiavichus, a Lithuanian statesman, has asserted that the KGB employs 350,000 people in Lithuania. These agents are involved in ideological and economic destabilisation, collecting information on political leaders and activists, intimidating young men who refuse to be drafted. He also proved that it was KGB agents who recently desecrated monuments in one of the Polish cemeteries in the republic, stoking up ethnic conflicts, and that the same agents had set fire to the doors of one of the KGB buildings as a pretext for accusing Lithuanian nationalists of terrorism.[16] The Lithuanian KGB chief warned in summer 1990 that his organisation would punish anyone who tried to stop it from fulfilling its functions in the republic.[17]

A good illustration of the KGB's sadistic methods of intimidating progressive politicians was provided by Kazimiera Prunskiene, the Prime Minister of independent Lithuania, whom I interviewed in Melbourne in December 1990. In one of her speeches at the Vilnius Palace of Sport she said that the KGB should now turn into an institute of public opinion – and nothing more. Next day she was visited in her office by a high-ranking KGB official. 'I'd like to tell you a joke,' he said. 'A man was talking too much about the KGB. So one day he was invited to a KGB office where they told him they wanted to send him to Turkey. "Why?" the man asked. "I don't even know the Turkish language and won't be able to talk to the locals there." "Don't worry!" they answered. "You won't have to do much talking while you are there: we'll cut off your tongue before you go!"'

She also told me how for a long time she had been openly followed by KGB agents in the streets. 'Once I was buying an ice-cream and two of them were standing right behind me. I bought three portions and gave two to them. And they took them!'

On another occasion she was speaking at the Supreme Soviet in Moscow formulating her government's refusal to sign the Union Treaty. Suddenly a young man brought her a glass of water. With the glass came a hand-written message: 'This water is sent to you by the KGB. Vladimir Kriuchkov.' She picked out the KGB chief's face. He was grinning . . .

Moldavian leaders have accused the KGB of instigating armed clashes between Russian and Gagauzes to compromise Moldavia's peaceful breakaway from the Soviet Union and to give Moscow an excuse to send in troops, which it did in autumn 1990.[18]

Alongside stepping up their activities inside the Soviet empire, the

KGB is expanding its operations both in foreign countries and against foreign nationals in the USSR.

In March 1990, an Intourist guide complained in *Moskovskiye Novosti* that guides and interpreters working with foreigners in Moscow still have to write reports on every Western visitor, specifying his or her interests, questions, attitude to the Soviet Union, Soviet contacts (if any) and places visited.[19]

During the Second International Conference on Human Rights in Leningrad in September 1990, the KGB openly followed almost all foreign participants.[20]

In an article entitled 'Ten Months that Shook the World', Graham Barrett, the European correspondent of the *Melbourne Age*, gave evidence that all the revolutions in Eastern Europe in 1989 were part of a great KGB plot to overthrow East European dictators, replacing them with faithful 'Gorbachevites'. In East Germany and Czechoslovakia these schemes eventually failed: the plotters did not anticipate the unseen upsurge of national-liberation feelings which followed the KGB-inspired coups. In Bulgaria, Romania (and partly in Hungry and Poland) they succeeded. It is not surprising that these countries are plunging deeper and deeper into chaos and ethnic clashes – just like the Soviet Union.[21]

On the fourth day of German reunification, a senior aide to the West German Chancellor, Helmut Kohl, stated that his government had 'solid proofs' that former Stasi (East German Security) spies now worked for the KGB. He said he was expecting explanations from Gorbachev and appealed to him to stop recruiting former East German agents to spy in the new united Germany.[22]

In the first half of October 1990, Klaus Kuron, one of the foremost Stasi spymasters, was approached by KGB agents who tried to persuade him to work for them.[23] Unlike his boss, Markus Wolf, he refused to cooperate. The former Stasi foreign intelligence chief, Wolf, has simply fled to Moscow.[24]

Jan Ruml, the Deputy Interior Minister of the new federal Czech government and a former Charter 77 activist, stated in September 1990 that the 'velvet revolution' of 1989 had been set in motion by the Soviets (read the KGB) as part of a plot to put reformist Communist governments in place of the existing regimes in Czechoslovakia, Bulgaria and Romania, countries they wanted to keep within their sphere of influence. The plan was 'to bring about change in Czechoslovakia on 21 August 1989 by mounting a brutal police attack on demonstrators celebrating the anniversary of the Soviet invasion. But there weren't enough demonstrators.' The authors of the plot, Ruml continued, failed to take into account the popular hatred of Communism, which was 'so deeply rooted in Czech society that people would not be satisfied with cosmetic changes and would insist on a new regime.' He added that the Czech Interior Ministry had discovered that the KGB were still operational in Czechoslovakia, 'particularly in areas from which Soviet troops have withdrawn'.[25]

The substantial growth in KGB operations is simultaneously observed in the Western countries too. Oleg Gordievsky, a former KGB and SIS double agent, remarked in one of his *Times* pieces that for the first two years of Gorbachev's power the strength of the KGB's foreign branch increased from 3000 to 12,000 officers with the KGB stations in Washington, New York, West Germany, France, Italy, Austria and India numbering more than 100 officers each. If formerly the KGB was active in seventy countries, now it had commenced operations in more than 100.[26] Members of the Kirgiz democratic movement also claimed in March 1991 that the KGB was using torture on the arrested participants in pro-democracy rallies in Kirghizia.[27]

CIA director William Webster said in spring 1990 that KGB intelligence had become 'more aggressive, more robust' of late. He added that greater effort to recruit agents both in the US and in Europe was being made. This was echoed by Oliver Revell, the FBI's associate deputy director in charge of investigations. 'Soviet intelligence is more aggressive than it's been at any time in the last decade,' he said.[28]

On 7 March 1991 electronic listening devices belonging to the KGB were discovered in two rooms above the parliamentary offices of Boris Yeltsin, President of the Russian Federation.[29]

But worst of all is the KGB's continuing campaign against the freedom of the individual. The misery of society is made up of small miseries of its citizens. When people are desperate and frustrated, they often become obedient. In a letter to *Moscow News*, Mikhail Shevelev, a Muscovite who was brutally strong-armed and threatened by the KGB when he refused to sign up in 1984, wrote:

I don't know, and perhaps will never know, how I came to have caught the KGB's eye, what they thought I was – a money changer or a profiteer, a smart operator or a fool. I don't know how the KGB's ideas evolved, but I know the result: someone decided I would make a good secret agent, an informer, a snitcher. The only thing remaining was to secure my written consent. They tried to secure it by blackmail, intimidation and extortion – to put it mildly. When racketeers threaten you with extortion, you should go to the militia. But where do you turn when you find yourself being blackmailed by a government institution – not a housing maintenance agency, but the KGB? Five years on I still experience the fear that determined my actions in 1984. I am afraid that this quiet, low action may be repeated. Why did I decide to write about it now? Not out of an impulse to publicly recognise my weakness. I simply hope that times have changed and we can not only discuss the KGB, but finally hear what this organisation thinks about informing and about having informers on its payroll. Are they necessary? Why? Against whom? In the name of whose security?[30]

Here are the answers to your questions, Mikhail, provided by none other than Vladimir Kriuchkov, the KGB Chairman himself:

Question: Has the KGB retained its staff of secret informers and how much do you think such practices are in line with the principles of a state governed by rule of law?
Answer: We do not have secret informers, we have assistants . . .
Question: Does the KGB tap telephone conversations of Soviet citizens even in the absence of direct accusations against them or suspicions of ties with foreign intelligence services or terrorist organisations?
Answer: The tapping of telephone conversations of individuals who do not commit illegal actions is impermissible and, moreover, punishable. Of course, the USSR State Security Committee has a range of devices which it uses in its work . . .[31]

The brochure containing this Kriuchkov interview is entitled 'The KGB must abide by the interests of the people'. I picked it up on a train as we were fleeing from the Soviet Union in January 1990. By an irony of fate, this shameless lying pamphlet was the last one I got in the Soviet Union. It is with me now in Australia and serves as a constant reminder of the nightmare we have miraculously escaped.

Here's another example of the KGB perestroika. At the USSR Supreme Soviet on 6 March 1990, an official letter was circulated to delegates. 'The loud-mouthed supposed upholders of the public interest are waging a deliberate and coordinated campaign to discredit the KGB . . . [One of] those institutions of executive and judicial authority which are . . . the essential guarantors of the security of the state and society.'[32]

Incidentally, it won't sound quite so bizarre if one remembers that all the present-day KGB bosses (Kriuchkov and his deputies included) are products of the Brezhnev era. 'KGB officers who persecuted me and other dissidents are still in place,' says Father Gleb Yakunin, a Russian Orthodox priest and former dissident (now a member of the Supreme Soviet of the Russian Federation). 'KGB Major Yakovlev, for instance – who prosecuted me and was in charge of my case in 1979–80 – is now a Colonel and a Chief Prosecutor in the KGB Moscow office. Another striking example is Lieutenant General Abramov, who once served as head of the former KGB Fifth Chief Directorate, which was responsible for persecuting and prosecuting us and our families. He now occupies the extremely powerful position of Deputy Procurator General of the USSR. Colonel General Bobkov, former deputy of the late KGB chief Yuri Andropov, is now a people's deputy. In the past he sanctioned the arrest of dissidents, including myself. And he is still Deputy Chairman of the KGB.'[33]

At the same time the KGB remains merciless to any of its own members who show signs of reformism or dissent. KGB Major Oleg Zakirov, who ventured to disclose the terrible truth about the execution of 11,000 Polish officers by NKVD in Katyn and Kozyi Gori, near Smolensk, in 1940, has recently been expelled from the Party and from the KGB and stripped of his awards.[34] Yakov Karpovich, a retired KGB colonel who publicly called on the KGB to repent for all the blood they had shed and to change their methods, was stripped of his title of 'Honourable Security Man' in November 1989.[35]

The case of the dissenting ex-KGB General Oleg Kalugin stands alone. It has received extensive coverage in the West and there's no need to describe it in detail here. But I'd like to focus your attention on the governmental reaction to the affair which helps to illustrate the inseparable ties between the present-day Soviet rulers and the KGB. Oleg Kalugin retired from the KGB in March 1990 and became notorious the following summer after a daring speech he gave at the Second All-Union Conference of the CPSU Democratic Platform where he questioned the very principles and foundations of the KGB, describing it as a direct threat to reform and democracy. In further interviews with both Soviet and Western media, he developed his anti-KGB position saying that the KGB had retained its structure and strength – which for decades was the Soviet dictators' main support – practically intact; that with perestroika in its sixth year, it still remained a state within a state, an agency with formidable power, potentially capable of crushing any kind of government, responsible only to itself and acting solely in accordance with its view of what was necessary. He also claimed that the KGB had infiltrated all unofficial organisations, that it was covertly supporting Pamyat, supervised religions and used political assassinations, torture, blackmail and smear campaigns as its methods, with all the talk about its new image being no more than a camouflage.[36]

What made these allegations so iconoclastic was that they came from a KGB general, an insider, a former head of the Soviet counterintelligence. They came at a time when the KGB were frantically trying to promote their 'new image' by throwing a couple of press conferences inside Lubianka and forming their own PR department. It was unthinkable and the system immediately struck back.

By law, it is beyond KGB powers to strip someone of the rank of general. This can be done only by the USSR Council of Ministers. And it was announced by Prime Minister Rizhkov in June 1990 that the Council of Ministers had adopted such a decision and that Kalugin had been legally stripped of his rank, his twenty-two orders and medals and his pension. It turned out later that this question had never been discussed and, what is more, that the Council session itself had never taken place.[37] This enabled Kalugin to file a law suit against President Gorbachev himself.[38]

The system fought back by instituting proceedings against the rebel general through the USSR Prosecutor's office for 'divulging state secrets'! And the more the authorities pursued Kalugin, the more popular he became among the people, who soon nominated him for a vacant seat in the USSR Supreme Soviet. Kalugin won a landslide victory, defeating his main opponent, Ivan Polozkov, the new conservative head of the Russian Communist Party, and became an MP, automatically acquiring parliamentary immunity against legal proceedings. A happy ending? To some extent, yes, but many questions remain unanswered. One of them is what made the head of the Soviet Government go so far as to publicly lie to the whole country about a fictitious Council of Ministers session? Was he just another toy in the hands of the KGB?

Part of the answer can be found in the Council of Ministers decree 'On Urgent Measures to Strengthen Law and Order', adopted in October 1990 and signed by Prime Minister Rizhkov. Among other things, this decree provides for taking the fingerprints of the entire USSR population of 280 million people, and for a considerable increase in the KGB budget, huge as it already is. To support this decision, Nikolai Rizhkov claimed in an interview that 5 per cent of the country's population could be considered 'enemies of law and order', which roughly means that eight million able-bodied citizens of the USSR must be purged as such.[39] A legitimate question arises: who actually rules the country – the Soviet government or the KGB?

Further convincing proof of the firm ties between the State Security Committee and the Soviet legislature comes from the draft law on the KGB, published in summer 1990. The draft does everything to try and preserve the KGB's current status intact. It gives the KGB carte blanche to carry out secret operations against Soviet citizens and leaves the control of the legality of the KGB's actions in the hands of the KGB itself.[40]

This is not a government decree, but a document worked out by the Soviet Parliament, answering directly to President Gorbachev. What are the relations between him and the KGB?

It is common knowledge that Gorbachev was a protégé and long-time admirer of Yuri Andropov, the former KGB Chairman and the CPSU General Secretary who masterminded the crushing of democratic national-liberation movements in Hungary in 1956 and Czechoslovakia in 1968. It was Gorbachev who promoted current KGB Chairman Kriuchkov to full Politburo membership in September 1989. It was he who appointed former Latvian KGB chief Boris Pugo Interior Minister in December 1990. It was with his approval that the KGB Chairman Kriuchkov in his address on national television on 13 December 1990 threatened sweeping action against democrats by the security services to restore order at all costs and claimed in the best traditions of Cold War rhetoric that national-liberation movements throughout the country were supported and directed by 'foreign specialised services'. Kriuchkov said he was speaking 'on instructions from President Mikhail Gorbachev'.[41]

The KGB today is the Communist system's last stronghold in the crumbling and disintegrating Soviet Union. 'Our power cannot exist without such an institution,' Lenin stated with rare frankness in 1921.[42]

'Since we have such a monster as the KGB, whether we will follow the Romanian pattern and have a civil war, this is the biggest danger. The KGB will fight to preserve the old order,' Boris Yeltsin said in an interview in the *Sunday Times* in February 1990.[43] Tennent H. Bagley in the *Asian Wall Street Journal* put it even more bluntly: 'They [the KGB] will provide the excuse and clear the way for "strong-hand government" to save Mr Gorbachev's regime.'[44]

In their book *KGB: The Inside Story* Christopher Andrew and Oleg Gordievski come to the following conclusion which it is hard to refute: 'Like every major modern state, Russia needs both a domestic security service and a foreign intelligence agency. For it to possess an intelligence community worthy of its citizens' respect, however, it will have to close the KGB and to start afresh.'[43]

'KGB, you'll never wash the blood from your hands!' read the placards carried by people demonstrating near Lubianka on 31 October 1990.

'I will never forgive the KGB for forcing my friend Vitali out of the country!' said Alexandr Kabakov in an interview for Radio Liberty in April 1990. Shortly afterwards he published an article on the KGB in the *Moscow News*:

Year in year out we used to live – and still live, if we are to be honest – as if in a room whose walls were pasted with so-called photographic wallpaper. As if it's a window opening onto a beautiful landscape, but if you take a close look – it's paper, it's a wall . . . Year after year the world's most powerful organisation, no longer able to wield the axe of direct reprisals, has been painting these landscapes for us, creating as it still creates the reality it needs – by misinformation and adroitly-selected information, by discrediting people and ideas, and by smuggling out a 'truth' it finds profitable for the country and the world. Year in and year out we got accustomed to speaking without witnesses and seeing a potential stukach [snitcher] in a friend . . . So where were we living and where do we still continue to live? And what have they done to us?[46]

On 30 October 1990, a huge boulder from the Solovki Islands, where the first and largest Soviet labour camp was located in 1923–39, was brought to Moscow and installed in Dzerzhinsky Square in front of Lubianka, the KGB headquarters.

Fear persists in the Soviet Union. Special 'suggestion boxes' – 'For messages and information' – have recently been installed on the doors of all KGB offices.[47] They are waiting for new denunciations. The KGB is clinging to its half-empty prison cells all over the country and is in no hurry to hand them over to the Interior Ministry whose cells are crammed to bursting point.[48] They are waiting for new dissidents and enemies of the people.

Political prisoners are still incarcerated in Perm 35, though some of them were released after my article appeared.[49] But can quantitative parameters be applied to human beings?

What are they up to?

No-one knows.

The boulder from the Solovki will rest forever in front of Lubianka, serving as a silent reminder of the terrible crimes of totalitarianism.

The crimes which still go on.

6

Whereabouts Unknown . . .

The madmen who have made men mad
By their contagion; Conquerors and Kings,
Founders of sects and systems.

Lord Byron, *Childe Harold*, III

The letters were weird. They were written in pencil on crumpled
yellowish paper. Many lines were scored through with black ink. 'Regards
to Ivan Denisovich!' was at the end of each message.

It was the late sixties and I was still at school. The letters were shown to
me from time to time by my mother. 'Who are they from?' I would ask her.
'From a very nice and unfortunate person,' she would reply.

Sometimes the letters contained clever, well-grounded reviews of my
first essays and poems which had been sent to the writer by my mother,
but for the most part they consisted of fragmentary memories of the
author's past and occasional details of his present-day routine. Now I can
remember only bits and pieces from them.

'I will never forget how the bird cherry smelt in Luga! When you
boarded a Leningrad-bound shuttle, the carriage was brimming with this
smell, and every other passenger was carrying bunches of blooming bird
cherry with cute little flowers, something I will never see again.'

'Why never?' I asked my mother. 'Where is he now?'

'He is in prison. For something that he hasn't done.'

Judging by the few undeleted lines in the letters, it was an unusual
prison. 'We have to weave baskets here. It's a very tedious job, but better
than doing nothing. I am afraid that soon I won't be able to do even this,
since my hands have started trembling uncontrollably.'

'What is the weather like in Kharkov now? In our parts it's getting quite
warm: spring is approaching. At least, that is what those who are allowed
to go out say. I am not. But worst of all there's practically no-one to talk to.

133

Thank you for your support. I know how dearly it may cost you, but you are my only friends. Please keep sending me the magazines and Vitali's works. His writing is quite promising, I think. And also, if possible, send me a teach-yourself manual of English. This is what keeps me going. Regards to Ivan Denisovich!'

Somewhere around 1970 my mother no longer showed me the letters. 'They stopped coming,' she said, 'and all the parcels we send him are being returned without explanation. He must have died.'

It was not until several years later that she told me more about the man. His name was Yuri Vetokhin and he was an old friend of my parents. He was born in 1928 or 1929 in Leningrad to a family of St Petersburg intellectuals. His mother and father died when he was in his teens and from that point he had lived with his aunt.

After school he studied at the Navy College in Leningrad and then served as a navigator on military ships in the Pacific Fleet. It was then that he became a Communist Party member. On demobilisation he worked as chief engineer at one of Leningrad's research institutes. His speciality was computers, which had only just appeared at that time, and he can be considered one of the pioneers of computer science in the USSR. He also attended the literary studio at Mayakovsky State Library in Fontanka Street where he quickly established himself as a talented writer.

In the early sixties he became disenchanted with what was going on in the country, with the Party and its politics. Being an honest man, he made up his mind to leave the Party. The Party statute had a clause allowing every member to quit whenever he or she wanted and Yuri was naive enough to take this at face value. It was at this point that his ordeal started. He was sacked from the institute and for a long time was unable to find a job. At last he found a place as a freight handler at a bakery but he couldn't put up with the mismanagement, laxity and embezzlement. His criticism and protests against the don't-care attitude of the salespeople led to his dismissal.

Being a former sailor and keen sportsman – a marathon swimmer and a rower – he used to spend his summers on the Black Sea coast. During one of his swims he was fished out of the water by KGB boarder guards for 'being too far from the Soviet shore'. He tried to protest. The border guards beat him, then took him to the KGB office in Feodosija. When they made enquiries in Leningrad and found out that he had left the Party they decided to punish him by accusing him of attempting to illegally cross the border. It was a good chance for the local KGB to justify their existence by catching a 'defector', or maybe even a 'spy'. His situation was ideal for such a show trial since he had no relatives, apart from the aging aunt, and no-one to intervene on his behalf.

134

He was taken to Kherson and tried without legal representation. Article sixty-four – high treason. Sentence – fifteen years.

Even in prison in Simferopol Yuri did not stop struggling. He wrote appeals to the highest bodies, went on hunger strikes and became a real nuisance for the prison administration. They decided to get rid of him and he was taken to Moscow to the infamous Serbsky Institute of Forensic Psychiatry, where he was quickly diagnosed as insane and sent to the special psychiatric prison in Dnepropetrovsk. At that time of course I had no conception that someone could be sent to a mental prison for their dissenting views.

It was from Dnepropetrovsk that we received the letters. In one of them he managed to name several medicines, with which he was being 'treated': haloperidol, triftazin, tezertsin, sulfazin. I found out later that a shock course of any of these may cause depression and paralysis. It reduces one's ability to think, to write, to work and, in the end destroys one's spirit, turning a human being into a vegetable. Hence the uncontrollably trembling hands.

Yuri refused to surrender and tried to read, write letters and learn English in the cell in which he was confined for years. My father, who worked at the Physics Institute, had big problems with the First Department at his office for maintaining this correspondence. Despite this my parents kept supporting their friend until their letters started to be returned.

In July 1990 in New York I bought a book by Sidney Bloch and Peter Reddaway called *Diagnosis: Political Dissent*. At the end, there was a list of known victims of Soviet psychiatry. Among hundreds of other names was one Yuri Alexandrovich Vetokhin – 'date of birth unknown, Russian, from Leningrad, in 1971 was at the special psychiatric clinic in Dnepropetrovsk, in the beginning of 1976 – still there, after that – whereabouts unknown.'[1] So in 1976, six years after his letters stopped coming, he was still physically alive.

'Whereabouts unknown.' No-one knows where his grave is. That short reference in a foreign book is all that is left of the man.

Yuri Vetokhin's story was my first direct encounter with punitive psychiatry. The second occurred in 1977, when on a train from Kaliningrad I met a boy who had spent a month at an institution denoted OM-216-ST-2, a special hospital for mental prisoners and former SS jail in Cherniakhovsk. His revelations have haunted me ever since. He was travelling with an orderly from that notorious prison who showed me files and documents to support what the young man said. The catalogue was of daily beatings, shock courses of strong drugs, inhuman conditions, when for years the prisoners were not allowed to go outside for fresh air, the ghastly practice of keeping political dissidents in the same cell with murderers and maniacs and strict bans on inmates talking to one another. 'They all want to die, but the wardens don't let them, preferring to destroy their spirit!' my travelling companion told me. It was in that very 'hospital' that Grigorenko, a dissenting Soviet army General, was kept for several years.

Back then, in 1977, I promised myself that I would write about the victims of punitive psychiatry, a pledge I repeated in *Special Correspondent*. Ten years later, I started collecting evidence about all sorts of people thrown into mental prisons for their words and views. There was never any question of publishing the results of this investigation in the Soviet Union, even now when some separate cases of 'psychiatric abuse' have already been described by the press. But the truth is that these were not separate cases: punitive psychiatry was and still is a well-organised system for destroying the human mind and soul while managing to preserve 'the outer skin' intact. The existence of such a deliberate system has been consistently denied by the Soviet authorities who choose to speak of individual cases of 'abuse' instead. Numerous facts, however, testify to the opposite.

When we fled the Soviet Union I couldn't take all my files with me and only managed to smuggle out some recent letters and documents. They are now with me in Australia – these distant shrieks of the innocent victims of totalitarianism.

Apart from mental prisons the Soviet system has invented some other means of incarcerating people for no reason. A popular means of getting rid of the undesirables was – and still is – the so-called LTPs – medical labour institutions for alcoholics run by the Interior Ministry. People are sent there by the militia if diagnosed as alcoholics requiring compulsory treatment. They have to work and conditions in LTPs are much worse than in ordinary prisons.

In my files I had many letters from LTP patients – prisoners – who had committed no crime. The letters came from Penza and Kalinin (now Tver) regions, from Stavropol and Kirov. Their contents were in many ways similar. Most of the authors assured me that many patients in their LTP were neither alcoholics nor even heavy drinkers: they were put away for being critical of their bosses or of the authorities, sometimes even denounced to the militia by family members (mostly mothers-in-law).

In 1982 I visited several LTPs in the Kirov region. Conditions there were awful: dirt, lack of space and normal food, barbaric methods of treatment. The patients were given injections of sulfazin (just like the inmates of mental prisons), a powerful drug used by the SS doctors in their medical experiments on prisoners of war. The physical work was very hard, mainly logging and timber cutting. There were rats everywhere. There was a thick layer of loathsome slime on the floor of the toilets and washrooms. The staff were rude and even cruel to the patients, treating them like criminals though they had committed no offence whatsoever. These establishments still exist today, only the conditions there, as testified by the letters I received shortly before leaving, seem to have deteriorated substantially.

Let's now take a short look at the overwhelmingly tragic history of mental prisons in the Soviet Union. Although similar to the concentration camps for dissenters and LTPs, mental prisons were not created by Brezhnev or Stalin. The first cases of healthy people being declared insane because of their views go back to 1918–20, the first years of Soviet power, and coincide with the creation of Cheka which immediately made punitive psychiatry its own. The first two victims were women, Maria Spiridonova and Angelica Balabanova. Spiridonova was the leader of the SR, the Socialist Revolutionaries Party. After getting into serious arguments with the Bolsheviks in 1918, she was tried by the Moscow Revolutionary Tribunal and sentenced to one year in a special 'sanatorium' for the mentally handicapped. Shortly before the trial she wrote to one of her friends:

> I anticipate some dirty trick from the Bolsheviks. To kill me would be embarrassing for them, to throw me in prison for a long time would be no less awkward. They will probably declare me insane and put me in a lunatic asylum or something of the sort. They want to inflict a moral blow on me and will stop at nothing to achieve this.[2]

Balabanova was a prominent figure among the Bolsheviks and a close ally of Lenin and Trotsky. In 1920 she ventured to accuse the revolutionary leaders of making mistakes and was courageous enough to reveal her point of view to Lenin himself. The Bolshevik Party Central Committee decided to send her too to the 'sanatorium'.[3]

Throughout Stalin's rule, psychiatry was widely used as a means of suppression of the most 'obstinate' dissenters and 'enemies of the people'. Special mental prisons, though usually located in the grounds of 'normal' psychiatric hospitals, were run and administered by the now-called NKVD.[4] The number of victims of psychiatry under Stalin was relatively small and could not be compared with the numbers incarcerated and purged in the labour camps of Gulag Archipelago. It was under Khrushchev and especially under Brezhnev that psychiatry became one of the main KGB tools to crush dissent. The Psychiatry Institute of the USSR Medical Sciences Academy became the main bastion of psychiatric repression, largely in connection with the name of Professor Snezhevski, who was made a director in 1962.

Snezhevski was a monster in a white gown. Under Stalin he orchestrated purges against those psychiatrists who disagreed with the growing use of medicine for political purposes. He developed his own theory of schizophrenia, which allowed him and his accomplices to declare insane anyone whose views did not correspond to the official line. In accordance with this theory, schizophrenia was considered basically incurable and demanded massive compulsory treatment with potent medicines. It was he who diagnosed induced psychosis in a group of religious believers and declared Joseph Brodski, the great Russian poet and future Nobel Prize laureate, a schizophrenic. Thanks to him, many dissidents were sent to mental prisons rather than labour camps. He was preparing to do the same to academician Sakharov and even made up a 'scientific' scheme according to which the academician could be diagnosed as a schizophrenic. The cornerstone of his scheme was that someone must be a megalomaniac to dispute the ideas of Karl Marx. And though he failed to use it against Sakharov, the scheme was successfully applied to many others. For this Snezhevski received the honorary title of Hero of Socialist Labour.[5]

Reams have been written in the West about the terrible abuse of psychiatry under Brezhnev. Vladimir Bukovsky, Gleb Yakunin, Valeri Tarsis, Zhores Medvedev, General Grigorenko and thousands of others were tested in the crucible of punitive medicine. 'Watch your tongue or you'll wind up in psikhushka,'* was a popular saying in the seventies. Sometimes even those who were not political dissenters but just expressed minor discontent with the situation in the country or disagreement with the authorities wound up in mental prisons too. Many went there for telling political jokes or for complaining publicly about shortages of goods in the shops. Special psychiatric hospitals grew into the system's main source of fear. It was commonly understood that to be sent there was literally a fate worse than physical death.

In 1988, by special Supreme Soviet decree, they were formally transferred from Interior Ministry supervision to the Health Ministry. This was only a token change since in reality they continue to be run by the KGB.

I'd like to tell you now about three cases of punitive psychiatry which I

* Russian slang for a psychiatric clinic.

138

investigated in the USSR. The first followed a brutal murder committed in the small town of Bokino near Tambov. The local militia CID investigator, Vladimir Petrakov, came to the conclusion that a Bokino militiaman was implicated in this crime. This militiaman had a criminal record and the facts Petrakov collected convincingly testified to his being the culprit. It was an emergency not only for Tambov but for the whole country. Seeing a militiaman convicted for murder could seriously damage the reputation of the whole Tambov militia force in the eyes of their Moscow bosses, so when Petrakov submitted his report to the Tambov CID chiefs, he was casually advised to change his conclusions which 'cast a shadow over our glorious militia'. But Petrakov was persistent in his naive belief that the criminal must be tried and punished.

What was to be done with the tenacious investigator? To sack him without a plausible excuse would have been difficult, and besides he had an excellent service record. After a while the militia chiefs found the only possible solution: psikhushka – mental prison. Petrakov was ordered to undergo a psychiatric examination at the regional hospital. The examination was rigged by the militia bosses and the investigator was certified as mentally ill and unfit for service. Immediately after that, the chief of the Tambov Internal Affairs Department issued an order for Petrakov's dismissal on the grounds of bad health and 'continuous discreditation of militia operatives'. They wanted to destroy all trace of Petrakov's unfinished investigation.

Petrakov started looking for justice. He went to Moscow and on the grounds of his lack of faith in Tambov psychiatrists demanded a second opinion in the capital. Eventually he was hospitalised in Moscow's Kashchenko psychiatric clinic.

The forty-eight days and nights he spent at this hospital were the most awful in his life. Absolutely healthy normal people had to share the wards with maniacs and ever-howling or whining madmen. No-one was allowed to leave the building lest they should escape (as the nurses explained). The patients were made to clean the toilets, to sweep the dirty floors and to do monotonous manual jobs, such as making envelopes or sewing dust-covers, just like prisoners. Those who disobeyed staff orders were punished with sulfazin injections – or several in a row – after which they started running high temperatures (of up to forty degrees) and could not move for two or three days.

After nearly seven weeks of this hospital imprisonment Petrakov was set free, but with the same diagnosis: unfit for militia service due to mental handicap. In fact, in all this time he had not been examined once and was not allowed even to get a glimpse of his own medical record!

He started writing complaints to all imaginable bodies. The reply was always the same: unfit, unfit, unfit . . .

Back to Moscow for an appointment with one of the country's leading psychiatrists, Professor Polishchuk, who, after three days of examination, declared him completely healthy but refused to certify this in written form, referring to some obscure instructions. Petrakov then spent several months trying to get hold of a copy of the professor's diagnosis and, when he finally did and brought it to Tambov, Petrakov was told that they did not recognise Polishchuk's conclusion and that he should go to Kashchenko clinic again. Instead, he went to see the USSR chief psychiatrist, Churkin, who also declared him healthy but refused to certify it. On my advice, Petrakov then approached the CPSU Central Committee and got the reply that he had been certified as unfit for militia service by an expert commission and that hence there were no grounds for reconsidering this decision . . .

It was real nightmare, a vicious circle with neither beginning nor end. And what made it worse was that I could not help him: psychiatry was still very much beyond journalistic reach, and besides I could not possibly force the 'experts' to withdraw their conclusions. In January 1990, when I was leaving the Soviet Union, Petrakov was still writing complaints and getting standard rubber-stamp replies. His former bosses had achieved their goals: the murder had been almost forgotten and the nosey investigator had been taken out of the way. Society victimised him for trying to be honest in the performance of his duties at the height of the 'democratisation' campaign. But can a democracy be based on lies?

The second case concerned Victor Vertepa, an engineer from Donetsk. His only crime was to invent a device which, if introduced into industry, could have brought considerable technological gains for the country's economy. He was working at the Donetsk research institute but after making his discovery decided to quit and become a foreman at the machine-building factory where it would be easier for him to supervise the introduction of his invention into the production process. Shortly after he took up his new employment, he was robbed of his invention (and the bonus that went with it) by the factory director, who claimed that it was his own work. Vertepa tried to protest and as a result was sacked from the factory. Since he kept complaining the director decided to silence him. He persuaded the Donetsk region chief psychiatrist, who was a friend of his, to hospitalise Vertepa at the nearby psychiatric hospital.

By this stage Vertepa was living with his parents in the Voroshilovgrad (now Lugansk) region. The psychiatric chief arrived in person with a couple of burly orderlies and tried to force Vertepa into a waiting ambulance. Vertepa pulled away, dashed to the cellar, took an old unloaded hunting rifle from the wall and forced them away. He had avoided hospitalisation for the time being, but could not avoid subsequent arrest by the militia for threatening the psychiatrist.

While in prison Vertepa was subjected to compulsory medical examination and – surprise, surprise – was diagnosed as mentally ill.

This all happened six years ago. Speaking to Vertepa over the phone and reading his letters, I could see that he was an absolutely normal person with sound logic and persuasive judgments. While in Svatovskaya psychiatric hospital, he even married one of the nurses. It's amazing how he has managed to withstand all the large doses of pills and injections administered to him by the 'doctors' during these years. His wife Maria, who witnessed his sufferings, had to leave her job at the hospital. She is now writing letters to Kiev and Moscow, vainly trying to interest someone there in her husband's plight. But he was still in hospital in the end of 1989.

The third story concerns Inna Pereverzeva, a well-mannered middle-aged woman from Kiev, who came to see me in my office in 1989. She was a researcher at the Kiev High Temperature Physics Institute. Some time before she had been forcibly hospitalised in a psychiatric hospital, diagnosed as a paranoiac. She lived in the centre of Kiev, occupying two rooms in a five-room communal flat with her mother and her aged granny. Her problems started with the arrival of new neighbours in the remaining three rooms. To Pereverzeva's misfortune, these neighbours were not just ordinary people, but close relatives of the current Ukrainian Communist Party Second Secretary, comrade Titarenko himself. That's why, instead of indulging in communal scandals and kitchen squabbles, they simply added Pereverzeva's two rooms to their three, evicting her whole family to a one-room kitchenette on the outskirts of the city!

And again the familiar scenario: the victim started tolling bells, raising havoc, writing complaining letters to everyone from the chief of the district militia to the CPSU General Secretary. To get rid of the victim, Titarenko's relatives quietly and matter-of-factly made arrangements for her hospitalisation.

They succeeded. With such a high-ranking relative behind them they simply could not fail . . . Among the papers she showed me was the diary she had kept at the hospital. She asked me to publish it and I promised that I would. Having been unable to do so in the Soviet Union, I can at least keep my promise now.

DIARY
kept by I.A. Pereverzeva
in the Pavlov Psychiatric Hospital.

February 17. They took me straight from the institute – three orderlies and a doctor, all strong young men. I was returning from the canteen with a piece of cake in my hand. They were standing in my office in their white gowns waiting for me. Vika Boiko, a colleague of mine, was in the room and saw everything. One orderly blocked the door to prevent me from running away and watched my every movement. The other three grabbed me and held me tightly. One of them took my bag and my fur coat from the hanger. I started crying that the coat was not mine – just to bide time and give myself a chance to escape. They asked Vika and she confirmed that it was mine. She was scared. They dressed me forcibly and dragged me out of the room and through the lobby to the exit in full view of my colleagues. I was resisting and crying in the hope that someone would intervene and protect me. I smashed the glass in the front door with my hand on the way to attract attention. My colleagues saw this but no-one came to my aid. When we reached the car, I looked back and saw everyone in the institute glued to the windows watching. They literally threw me inside the car. On the way to the hospital the doctor told me that they were taking me away for a long time. He insulted me, calling me a bully, and was angry that I soiled his trousers with my cake. I could see that he was intentionally trying to provoke me so that he could bring me to the hospital in a highly nervous condition. I did not react to his insults. A young leather-coated orderly with refined delicate features was sitting opposite me and shamelessly staring into my eyes. The journey seemed very long.

In the hospital reception ward the orderlies warned me that if I decided to escape it would end very badly for me. All the four were standing by, holding me by the shoulders and waiting for me to be signed in. We stood like that for a long time. The real patients were being checked in nearby, but no-one was guarding them like that.

They dressed me in hospital clothes and took away all my belongings and money. I was given a man's slippers – size forty-two, I take thirty-six. Then two female nurses put on their fur coats and led me through the large yard to section four of the hospital. It was minus ten degrees centigrade out of doors and I was coatless, just wearing a thin dressing gown.

I was brought to a ward for patients with manic depressive psychoses. There were nineteen people there and one vacant bed near the window. It was evening already. I sat down on my bed and started watching the patients. They all looked quiet, nothing as terrible as I had imagined. In half an hour a nurse rushed in and told me to go to another ward, as ordered by the doctor. I refused. I found out that the ward to which they wanted to move me was for the most seriously ill people, those who are popularly known as homicidal lunatics. They have two duty nurses there all round the clock and some patients have to be tied to their beds.

142

Later I went out into the corridor. For some reason, I was sure that this was a mistake, a misunderstanding, that they would let me go next morning, when they saw that I was totally healthy. I could not leave the corridor to phone home: the doors were locked and there were iron bars on all the windows. To while away the time, I asked a nurse to give me a mop to wash the floor in the corridor. I wanted something to do as a distraction from my despair. At night I managed to take a nap. The patients told me next morning that while I was asleep the nurse had come up to my bed several times and was watching me closely.

February 18. After breakfast I was summoned to the consulting room. There were about a dozen doctors in white gowns comfortably seated there. I was shown to a chair in the middle of the room. Twenty-four eyes were staring at me from all sides. Again I was sure that they would let me go home. It can't be that all these doctors will support the reprisals against me, I thought.

The consultation was chaired by Ida Shevchuk, the assistant professor of the Kiev Medical Institute Psychiatry Department. My letter of complaint, addressed to the CPSU Central Committee, was lying before her on the table. When I saw my letter, my first thought was how come it had found its way to the lunatic asylum. Is this a branch of the Central Committee, or what? My complaint was well-grounded. I wrote how I had been thrown out of my flat, I enclosed a number of documents to support my words. I expected protection – not reprisals. And now my letter was here.

Next to me was a man with a very long nose. His nose was so close to my cheek that I leant back in my chair in revulsion. He was the one asking most of the questions, studying my reactions and every movement of my head very attentively.

'What have you got against the Communist Party?'

'Why did you complain to the KGB?'

'Why are you still a junior research worker?'

'Why haven't you moved out of your flat yet? Don't you know that your neighbours don't want you to stay there?'

The questions lasted for about half an hour. No-one was interested in my answers. I suddenly understood that this was all arranged by my neighbours' big patron. I tried to remain calm. To protest was useless.

In the afternoon, after lunch, they called me in again. In the corridor I saw the familiar face of our institute's KGB curator, Sergei Dmitriyevich. I was delighted, thinking that he had come to help me out. I was led into the same room where they introduced me to Professor Voronkov, head of the Kiev Medical Institute Psychiatry Department. Then I was asked to wait in the corridor. I stood behind the door for about an hour while Professor Voronkov and Sergei Dmitriyevich discussed something. Then the KGB man left and I had a chat with Voronkov. He was very polite, kept asking me about my relatives, my work and my private life. I was sure that this man would look into my case seriously and have me released. We were served tea. Speaking of my neighbours, Voronkov called them 'scum'. So he sympathises with me, I

143

thought, he has looked into my case properly. But all my expectations proved false.

That very evening a nurse, called Liza, gave me an injection, saying that it was 'vitamins'. I immediately fell asleep and could not wake up for a long time next day. The other patients told me that they all tried to wake me.

February 19. I had been sleeping for a long time and could not open my eyes, no matter how hard I tried: it felt as if my lids were made of lead. Then the orderly took me to a big room where a middle-aged blonde woman was sitting. She told me she was a psychologist and demanded that I vacate my flat. What business was it of hers? She then said she was going to test me. 'I am half-asleep,' I said, 'I can't.' She said that she would bear that in mind and put a black stopwatch on the table. At first I had to repeat ten words from memory, then to cross out one extra object out of four on a picture and to describe what I saw on other pictures. I noticed that the pictures were mostly of naked men. She probably wanted to check on my sexual behaviour. I thought that if I showed any interest, they might declare me a sex maniac. Then I was to sort out several proverbs and sayings. And the last test – to answer 566 questions from a book. I was answering slowly, since I felt very sleepy, and the psychologist said that I was not answering quickly enough.

February 20. This morning they took my encephalogram. They have only one Italian encephalograph for the whole hospital. It was very strange: usually they do it only to patients with brain trauma and I had none. Later a neuro-pathologist checked my nerves and said they were OK for my age.

February 28. I successfully begged permission to work with the other patients several days ago. I made 200 cardboard envelopes – much more than the norm. The doctors didn't want me to work but I was desperate for some physical exercise. Besides, this enables me to move freely inside the hospital and even to go out into the yard occasionally. I made envelopes, worked at the construction site twice, cleaned up the snow, washed the floors in the corridors. Every day I washed up dishes in the canteen and once went to the laundry to pick up clean linen.

I am adapting to the hospital atmosphere. The patients treat me with respect. To my surprise they even ask my advice whether or not to take the pills the doctors prescribe. Most of them covertly throw their pills away having no faith in their effects. They don't trust doctors. Shevchenko, one of the doctors, wears four very expensive rings on her fingers. Each time she left the patients started discussing the price of these rings. Someone said that she was the wife of the Ukrainian Deputy Light Industries Minister. Once I was walking through the yard with a group of patients and we met her half-way. She was sporting a chic sheepskin coat and a mink hat. We all greeted her in chorus. But she looked at us blankly, as if at inanimate objects, and did not reply.

In the mornings I have started conducting setting-up exercises with the patients, to keep them in shape and stay fit myself. In the evenings I sing songs to them and I have invented different games to pass the time. Winter evenings are long and they have no other distractions at the hospital. A woman patient called Maria is a believer. She has taught me how to pray. She is absolutely healthy herself and, like me, is just a victim of reprisals. She advised me to try to tolerate everything humbly and not to complain after I come out of the hospital, since it was all the will of God. God will punish the culprits himself. I should only believe in Him. He exists and He sees everything.

I suggested that we should make cosmetic masks for ourselves in the ward. I made friends with a girl called Sveta. She was a student at the Medical Institute, but was discharged for not attending lectures. Her father found connections at the hospital and put her here to get a certificate for a minor neuralgic ailment which would enable her to account for the missed classes and to get reinstated. Sveta was very young and naive. She used to sit on my bed dreaming of how she would take me to see her parents in Kozelets and treat me to something yummy, and of how her mother would get me some rare goods from the depot where she worked.

The doctors are avoiding me. They have nothing to treat me for and my diagnosis must have been completed long before they saw me. Nevertheless they try to dose me with pills – four different types. Liza, the nurse, is the most persistent one. I pretend to take the pills, but then spit them out. They say that my diagnosis hasn't been completed yet and that I shall be given a copy of it when I am discharged. My brother Boris tried to see it but the doctors insisted it was a professional secret. They keep telling me during morning rounds that my complexion is good. I reply that this is because of the cosmetic masks. At home I had no time to apply them, but here I have loads of free time. No doubt they all realise I am healthy – the doctors, the nurses, the patients, the nurses' assistants – all of them. One nurse told me: 'Don't be upset! Many would wish to be here to avoid a trial or to get a certificate of benefits or simply to save money by getting sick leave at the office.' But I was waiting to be released every moment, I couldn't understand why they were keeping me here.

I was visited by many of my colleagues from the institute. They said that everyone at the office was appalled by my detention. People were writing letters of protest, demanding an investigation. Many were refusing to work until they let me out.

I was getting food parcels. Lots of everything. Never before had I had so many oranges. My comrades must be expressing their sympathy to me with these oranges. I fed them to the whole ward. Many patients have been here for months and no-one comes to visit them.

March 10. Women's Day passed. Last week I was summoned to Professor Voronkov. He was sitting in state in his office with a huge bookcase behind his back. Ida Shevchuk, his assistant, and three other doctors were there with him. Voronkov gave me an apple and said that I looked well – the hospital was obviously good for me. It was a mean thing to say. Then he started mumbling something about my detachment from everyday life and my hypertrophied notions about certain things. He was very vague, but obviously he was speaking about my letters. I wanted to argue with him, to object, but he was not

145

interested. Then he suddenly announced that I could go on working at the institute and no-one would touch me again. Psychological tests, he said, had confirmed my attachment to my home. 'That's just what you're like. That's your character, and we can do nothing here.'

I asked Ida Shevchuk whether I would be registered as mentally deranged and she said that I would. She added that I posed a certain social danger, not in the sense that I could kill or stab someone, but . . . This 'but' was so vague and elusive that she didn't know herself how to formulate it.

For several days afterwards they kept giving me pills and tizerpin injections. They injected me with cardiamin four times and my heart started pounding like mad. I asked them to stop these injections: my heart was in order.

March 11. I have been discharged today. My brother Boris came to pick me up. I am a registered 'mentally ill' person now, and as such can only be released to a relative, like an object. They made Boris sign for me. He asked: 'And what's her diagnosis?' Pashchenko, the department head, refused to say and referred him to Professor Voronkov. Allegedly, only he knew. My brother was furious and started protesting. Doctor Pashchenko fled from the room. I started pleading with Boris to keep quiet since we were still at the psychiatric hospital and they could so easily punish him too. That was the last thing we needed. So I dragged him home. I was calm and he was wound up.

We left the hospital. It was two in the afternoon. The snow was melting.

I looked at Inna Pereverzeva as she sat opposite me in my office. Her story was less awful than Yuri Vetokhin's, she was alive and healthy after all.

But why can't I read her notes calmly?

Because her story is typical: an average woman thrown out of her home by influential bastards. Very common. This very woman being dragged out of her office in full view of her colleagues, who watch, but do not intervene. Not unusual. Her quick adaptation to the abominable conditions of her so-called hospital, her singing songs in the evenings and her frantic desire, despite everything, to work. Very Russian.

So what kind of country is this? The country where no-one is proof against being harassed by the KGB, thrown into psikhushka or declared insane any moment the system deems it necessary. The Union of Soviet Socialist Republics – what an ironic name!

Yes, Pereverzeva escaped physical tortures, but what about moral ones? To be registered as mentally ill in the Soviet Union means to be a citizen not even of the second, but of the third, class. It means no career, no family (the mentally handicapped are not allowed to marry), no voting, no trips abroad. This is a stigma for life, since once registered, it is practically impossible to get 'unregistered' from the list.

She is still looking for justice, for the restoration of her good name.

146

Having lost her flat, she wants to punish those who made her life a misery. She keeps writing letters and seeing journalists. Where is she now I wonder?

I tried to have her 'typical' story published in the Soviet Union. 'Too early to generalise!' the editors said. Is it still too early?

But let us generalise here.

The system of punitive psychiatry continues to exist in the Soviet Union. In 1987 the editor of the new avant garde magazine '*Third Modernisation*', Alexander Serzhant from Riga, was taken to the local KGB office and threatened with psikhushka if he continued to publish.[6]

In 1988 Yuri Sobolev, a 'troublemaker' from the village of Slavkino, Ulyanovsk, was forcibly hospitalised in a psychiatric clinic on the orders of V. Panasenko, the District Party Committee First Secretary, who was afraid that Sobolev would start criticising him during the pre-election meeting with the Party boss from Ulyanovsk. In hospital Sobolev was 'treated' with psychotropic injections.'[7]

In July 1990, shortly after the ignominious decree which made criticism of President Gorbachev illegal came into force, Yuri Smirnov was arrested for carrying a cartoon of Gorbachev in the centre of Moscow, near the CPSU Central Committee building. Where do you think he was taken?[8] From the KGB's point of view, anyone who ventures to joke about the country's president must obviously be mad.

On 17 September 1990 the Democratic Union leader Valeriya Novodvorskaya was arrested in Moscow. This cultivated, multilingual librarian and former prisoner of conscience was detained by the KGB for seventy-two hours and then transferred to Kashchenko psychiatric hospital. The reason? Her critical remarks about President Gorbachev. At the moment of her arrest she started a hunger strike. On 25 September 1990 she was declared healthy and discharged from hospital. But the criminal proceedings, instigated against her for 'insulting the President' remain.[9]

Kurbanberdy Karabalakov, a Turkmenian Democratic Platform activist, disseminated several dozen leaflets calling on people to join the democratic movement in October 1990. For that he was thrown into Ashkhabad psychiatric hospital without examination. A special medical commission later established that Karabalakov was completely healthy, but despite this, he was still in hospital at the end of 1990. The Moscow Democratic Platform issued a statement demanding an end be put to the vicious practice of placing dissidents in psychiatric institutions and punishment of the officials guilty of Karabalakov's unlawful hospitalisation.[10]

A growing chorus of voices – both in the USSR and in the West – is calling for an end to punitive psychiatry, this infamous disgrace of the Soviet system.

Dr Algirdas Statkevichus, a member of the Amsterdam-based International Association on the Political Use of Psychiatry (IAPUP), told a news conference in October 1989: 'After four years of perestroika, the situation hasn't changed. Soviet psychiatry is still inhuman.'[11]

The IAPUP General Secretary, Robert van Voren, stated after his return from Moscow in April 1990 that although far fewer dissidents were now in psychiatric detention in the Soviet Union, the practice of confining them to psychiatric institutions continued. According to his words, some 'strong conservative forces were opposing the change in Soviet psychiatry.'[12]

In June 1990 the International Helsinki Federation for Human Rights condemned the widespread continuing violations of human rights in the sixth year of Gorbachev's rule: imprisonment for political motives, barriers to free emigration and prisoners living 'in slavery'. The members of this independent non-governmental group were not allowed into the Serbsky Psychiatric Institute in Moscow. 'We've tried to contact the Serbsky Institute where a meeting was already fixed, but got a message that we could come only if our Russian members didn't come,' Mr von Schwarzenberg, chairman of the watchdog group, told a news conference. When the Helsinki group insisted that its Soviet representatives also attend, 'they declined to see us, telling us that our Russian members were insane.'[13]

Yes, the Serbsky Institute still remains a stronghold of punitive psychiatry in the Soviet Union. Dr Vladimir Lupandin, a prominent Soviet psychiatrist, wrote in *Moscow News* in August 1990: 'Everything happening in our country today must look like collective psychosis to the punitive psychiatry supporters. But the whole apparatus of repressive psychiatry remains intact. As before, the Serbsky Forensic Psychiatry Institute, this Bastille of punitive medicine, towers above downtown Moscow. This Institute's continued operation is impermissible. No-one can feel safe until this creation of Stalinism ceases functioning.'[14]

Here I can't refrain from quoting the words of the progressive mayor of Leningrad and people's deputy of the USSR, Anatoly Sobchak. He gave a brilliant philosophical explanation of the mechanism and origins of the repressive Soviet system in his book *Pilgrimage into Power*:

> I have discovered that there exist specific Soviet mental disorders, diseases characteristic of socialism alone. A person affronted by the system starts seeking the truth. In the beginning they are quite normal. They don't demand

much: only to correct an injustice. It is here that the system starts cornering the truth-seeker and in no time they are caught in an endless mirrored labyrinth of paperwork, refracting the tiny ray of human life and turning the person into a victim. It is impossible to find a way out of this labyrinth of circulars, instructions and circular-like rubber-stamp faces. There isn't one. And the person, who lived like a human being prior to this disaster, becomes but a walking petition, their life totally drained by the system. The seventy-odd years of the social experiment in our country have proved a continuation of the worst element of the Russian autocracy, the Russian bureaucratic machine. Communism on our Russian soil has driven people completely insane: absurd is the reality and absurd is a person in it.[15]

Until this horrible mechanism ceases to operate, it would be premature to erect a memorial to the victims of punitive psychiatry, as was suggested in *Moscow News* in November 1990.[16] Its victims still live among us, even though their whereabouts are often unknown.

7

The Ministry of Uncommunications

Let's begin by doing some simple sums. Fact: it is 2550 kilometres from London to Moscow. On 13 October a postcard was sent airmail from London to Moscow. When do you think it should reach its destination?

Let's do some calculations. The average speed of a modern aircraft is 900 kilometres per hour. Taking into account take-off and landing time, it should cover the distance in a maximum of four hours. Now add a bit extra for postal formalities, sorting, delivery etc. Given two days at each end, the card should be in the hands of its Moscow addressee on the seventeenth or, at the outside, the eighteenth.

Now let us compare our calculations with what actually happened. It appears that we are out by about fifty days, since that very real postcard, posted by myself on 13 October at London's Farrington Road Post Office, was not received in Moscow, until 6 December.

It took that card fifty-five days to cover a distance of 2550 kilometres – which gives it an average cruising speed of two kilometres per hour!

I wonder who it was who managed to turn my letter into a barely moving invalid? Maybe the fault lies with the British Post Office? It's fashionable, I gather, to blame the British post. But in this case, oh no! And I have proof. The fact is that I did not send one card that day, but two – the second one, addressed to my friend in Australia, arrived within a few days. Incidentally, a third postcard, which I also posted on that fateful day addressed to my mother in Moscow has never arrived!

You might say, perhaps, this was just an isolated case, after all, we have all heard of stories of letters taking years or even centuries to arrive at their destinations. Alas, this is no isolated case, but the result of a system. You want more examples? With pleasure!

In June 1989 the magazine *Krokodil* hosted a delegation of US satirists. One of them, a professor from the John Hopkins University in Baltimore, flew home on 26 June and, on the twenty-ninth, mailed me the usual polite letter, thanking me for the hospitality and so on. I received this letter on 31 August. Among other things, the professor informed me that he had sent me several books. Not a trace of them. In the middle of September I received another letter from Baltimore, sent on 19 July, in which the trusting professor expressed his conviction that by now (ie by 19 July) I would already have received the books he had sent on 30 June . . .

The parcel of books arrived on 30 September, three months to the day from posting. It had been opened and hastily re-wrapped with what was obviously Soviet-made string, thus ruling out blame on the American side.

At least this parcel made it, albeit three months late. I was luckier than some. The publishing house Moscow Progress was less lucky, as they are still vainly waiting the arrival of a *Fashion Encyclopedia* posted to them for translation from Paris several years ago. Obviously there are some fashion-conscious customs officers around nowadays.

My former employer *Krokodil* didn't have much luck either when, during one of my trips to London, I posted off to them an album called *The Best Of Punch* for use in a project on English caricature. It too never arrived. Evidently, in addition to fashion-conscious customs officers, there are now caricature fans among their ranks. Or more likely the reason is different, since there were some cartoons of Gorbachev in the album.

The same fate awaited the 1990 *Guinness Book of Records* posted by me to a Moscow publisher and never received. Did the book's fault lie in the entry for records in repression, firmly held by the Soviet Union? Obviously, there are not only fashion-conscious officers and *aficionados* of caricature, but also collectors of records in the Soviet customs service. If so, I would like to urge them to translate the above-mentioned book and send the text to a Moscow publisher for distribution in the Soviet Union.

Or perhaps it is the Soviet Central International Post Office in Moscow who, with the help of another organisation we've mentioned before in this book, has decided to set a few records of its own. Records for non-delivery of letters and parcels? For me the finest performance so far was achieved in December 1989 when in Moscow I received a letter from my London publisher posted in the first days of August. Now in Australia, I waited for a parcel forwarded to me from Moscow six months earlier, in July 1990. It eventually arrived, with the packaging slashed open and missing half its letters.

So who are these people, spiriting away and disembowling letters and parcels? And why? Are they looking for drugs? Do they not know that under international agreements the sender country is responsible for checking the contents of all mail?

If you talk to people in the Soviet Union about the unbelievable hold-ups in the post, they all say the same thing – that the authorities (ie the KGB) open and read the mail. It is one of the few cases where public opinion proves completely right. This was confirmed in the official letter I received at my Moscow office on 22 October 1989 after some of my postal lamentations were published in *Krokodil*. The letter was signed V. Nazarov, the deputy chief of the International Post Department of the USSR Ministry of Communications. This letter, unlike the ones mentioned above, arrived quickly. Among other things, it said: 'Judging by your description of the delayed letters and parcels, they were presented to the organs of Glavlit, where they were opened.' Glavlit, as you will remember, is the KGB-run censorship agency. I guess this is the first time that systematic tampering with foreign correspondence has been officially recognised in the Soviet Union.

This brought to mind a woman I knew at university who got a gripping job with the KGB after graduation, reading other people's letters from abroad. Why should they do it? I wouldn't have thought there are many spies left who still send state secrets by post. Besides, the Soviet constitution guarantees the privacy of correspondence.

'Are there any timescales within which foreign correspondence must be sorted and delivered?' I asked the duty administrator at the Moscow Central International Post Office in Varshavskoye Shosse. 'No.' This was also confirmed by V. Nazarov: 'Deadlines for international correspond-ence delivery are not stipulated.'

Well, as least these were frank answers. They could have complained, as these people usually do, of understaffing and low wages, but they didn't. Neither timescales nor deadlines – and that's an end to it. Very frank and very convenient, both for the Post Office and the perlustrators. And nobody will be the wiser.

In the complaints section of the International Post Office it was explained to me that in order to set in motion a search for a lost missive, one must first of all contact the sender and find out the registration number of the certificate of postage. So you write to the sender, say, on a postcard, and ask him or her to send you the registration number. Two or three months later (if you are lucky), he or she will receive your postcard. In yet another two or three months' time (if, of course, he or she has not in the meantime thrown away the certificate of postage and if your luck holds), you will receive an answer and then the postal sleuths can get to work on the trail of your missing packet. Maybe they will find it, maybe they won't.

When I put all these arguments before the people at the post office, they politely advised me to (guess what?) get in touch with the sender by telephone. Well, had I been living in Britain or Australia where you can call Vladivostok, Tananarive or Austin, Texas, within seconds of lifting the receiver in any public call box, I would gladly have followed their advice. One of my English friends assured me that he loves chatting with an Australian 'mate' on his carphone as he drives through the streets of London. It was during my first visit to the West. And when I didn't believe him, he picked up the phone and before my very eyes dialled Moscow, and I heard my wife Natasha's surprised voice answer at the other end. It was just as though she was in the back seat of the car.

In a trashy spy thriller, published in Britain but set in the Soviet Union, the crafty American, while on the run in Siberia, discovers a phone box hidden under ice and snow in a God-forsaken village. He dials the American embassy in Moscow and asks to be put through to his old buddy, the president of the United States. The president is at lunch and the spy asks to have his call returned. Eight hours later the agent hears a muffled buzzing sound from under the snow: the president!

Hopefully, in a century or so, the Russian people will be so technologically advanced and KGB-free as to be able to receive calls in public telephone boxes, and even in God-forsaken villages. At the moment it takes at least an hour to book a call to Moscow from a village in the Moscow region, let alone from Siberia. And it sometimes takes several days to get through to England or Australia – via the operator, of course. Western correspondents accredited in Moscow can easily dial direct to London or any other 'capitalist' city or town. But if an ordinary Muscovite tries to do the same thing, this will be the result: he or she will get through very quickly, provided they know the codes which are not to be found in any directory, but the very first ring will be interrupted by a metallic voice saying: 'Call the operator! Call the operator! Call the operator!'

I remember in 1980, in the run-up to the Moscow Olympics, it was solemnly announced that now we could dial direct to almost any capital city in the world from our home phones in Moscow. This did not last long:

soon after the Olympics the possibility evaporated along with Finnish sausage, Moroccan oranges and New Zealand butter.

'Who decides who is to be fortunate enough to be allowed access to direct international dialing?' I asked the supervisor at the International Telephone Exchange in Moscow in September 1989. 'I can't answer that,' she answered, 'and you probably won't find anyone who will.' Quite right. Silent as the grave. The extension is not answering.

So what are they frightened of down there? Surely they can't be concerned about mythical state secrets leaking out. Surely they know that the radio is much more convenient for spies than the telephone. But there are plenty of occasions, when one – even if he or she is Soviet and not a spy – must make an urgent call. One may have to give a partner details of a contract, inform friends about an arrival (alas, telegrams in the USSR aren't very reliable either), or simply enquire about someone's health. But the Soviet people are not allowed to exercise these basic rights. The omnipotent and invisible Ministry of Uncommunications – another euphemism for the KGB – dexterously uses postal and telephone turnpikes as yet one more means of popular intimidation. What for? To make people feel isolated, unsure and hence nervous and fearful. To make them feel like small helpless underlings at the mercy of the mighty system.

To arrive at this conclusion, I had to undertake an investigation, one of my last in the Soviet Union. The main problem was that the topic of communications terror was a totally obscure one: a small subject, but representative of the system. As you will see, this section won't have any outside references, simply because the subject has hardly ever been mentioned (let alone investigated) by Soviet or Western media. It would have been impossible for me to look into it, had one of my readers, a public communications engineer and former employee of the USSR Ministry of Communications, not ventured to help me by sharing some of his experience in the field and showing me a number of documents. For his safety, I shall call him engineer Petrov.

In the early thirties, a new internal intelligence organisation, the so-called 'organs of political control' or PCs, appeared in the Soviet Union. Their main task was to control all postal communications – both internal and foreign correspondence – and telephone conversations. Their functions were soon handed over to OGPU (later renamed NKVD then finally KGB). Letters, telegrams, phone calls, everything was monitored. Plainclothes PC officers, 'specialist-politcontrollers', posed as customs men and became part and parcel of every frontier post. Their task was to examine every out-going and in-coming piece of printed or handwritten matter. They were empowered to confiscate whatever they deemed 'dangerous to the Soviet Union' and 'immoral' as well as anything which in their atheistic eyes could pass for 'religious propaganda'.

It was at that time that the so-called 'black rooms' came into existence in all major Soviet cities and towns. They were attached to every district post and sorting office. Each was staffed with several freelance censors working under the supervision of a full-time KGB officer. The black rooms operated in such secrecy that even experienced post workers at first did not know of their existence. The letters came by conveyer from stamping machines straight to a sorting station, passing through the black room on the way. The KGB operatives were armed with long lists of names and addresses of people under constant, temporary or episodical surveillance, as well as their handwriting patterns and typewriter script specimens. If a letter seemed of any interest it was opened and photocopied. When an envelope was tightly sealed and difficult to open, they were allowed to confiscate it, ie to tear the envelope, to read the contents and to throw the letter out. Letters to and from capitalist countries were perlustrated with special zeal: they were subjected to 100 per cent control and, after being read, were usually destroyed, whatever the nature of their contents. The black rooms existed in this form until 1988, when the PC functions were officially passed over to customs, itself still under strict KGB control.

A few words about telephones. According to PC regulations, all telephone subscribers are divided into ten categories. Category zero subscribers – foreign correspondents and a handful of Soviet organisations who have dealings with the West – are allowed to dial automatically all countries of the world having communication lines with the USSR. Category one is the most widespread: it is for mere mortals – ordinary subscribers and institutions, who can direct dial the formerly socialist East European countries and, for some reason, India! (With India, though, the quality of reception is not guaranteed.) Category two is reserved for hotel telephones. Category three is mostly for rural subscribers, the most underprivileged, with no access to direct dialing whatsoever – either abroad or inside the country.

The most prestigious category is four, which is akin to special shops for the ruling nomenklatura. Category four subscribers are linked immediately with any place in the world. 'Engaged' tones do not exist here: all other conversations are disconnected to make way for them. Category four is sometimes referred to as the 'government line', though it is used by many high-ranking bureaucrats who have nothing to do with the government.

The remaining five categories are of a purely technical nature and concern public phones, intercity payphones, long-distance coin phones and so on. This graduation makes it easier for the PCs to monitor and tap telephone conversations.

If one believes the Ministry of Communications spokesman, it is a lack of available phone lines which poses the main obstacle to direct dialing. This is obviously pure nonsense. Even in tiny Bulgaria one can dial any country from a public phone. Can it really be that Bulgaria has more international phone lines than its former big Soviet brother?

Here are some more examples of state postal and telephone terror, supplied and documented by engineer Petrov.

In autumn 1987 more than 200 senior schoolchildren from Tomsk, Siberia, duped by the *Good Day, Comrade!* radio programme with its talk of 'people's diplomacy', sent letters to kids of their age in the USA. Not a single one of these letters has ever reached the Central International Post Office (CIPO) in Moscow, having been confiscated by the KGB in Tomsk. The CIPO workers testified in writing that they hadn't even seen these letters.

Buying special postage stamps for foreign-bound letters at the CIPO, engineer Petrov noticed that many of them had no glue on the reverse side and were creased. This led him to conclude that they had been removed from confiscated letters, dried, ironed and put on sale a second time. The profits must have been shared between the CIPO officials and the black rooms staff.

N, a Moscow designer, was informed by his Dutch friend and colleague that he had sent N, a book on design from Holland. Several months elapsed and the book failed to materialise. Then one day, browsing through one of Moscow's second-hand bookshops, N saw the promised Dutch book on sale there. It was inscribed to him by his friend from Holland on the title page. He didn't have enough cash on him to buy his book, which was, by the way, quite expensive, and when he returned with the money the book had already been sold to someone else. Unfortunately he failed to find out who had handed his book in for sale. The conclusion is simple: the black room people did not only confiscate (or rather steal) the book, they decided to make some money out of it.

A breed of short-wave radio enthusiasts, which expanded in the Soviet Union in the late seventies, faced big problems in trying to correspond with their 'fellows-in-the-air' from the West. Their letters either didn't reach the addressees or were returned without explanation. After a while the Moscow Association of Radio Amateurs advised its members to send registered letters. In the event of non-delivery of a registered letter, the sender could receive up to thirteen roubles in compensation. This resulted in gullible radio enthusiasts being summoned to their local KGB offices, where they were confronted with the following questions: 'Why are you interfering with our routine procedures? Do you have nothing better to do?'

Engineer Petrov himself, when leafing through *Contact*, an East German magazine, found a message from an East Berlin woman, a teacher of Russian, who wanted a Russian pen-friend. He wrote to the woman. Two days later he was approached at his office by their First Department KGB curator who led him to the smoking room and asked rather aggressively: 'Why on earth have you written a letter abroad?' 'But what's so terrible about it?' the engineer retorted. 'I have no access to any secrets. Besides, the GDR is a friendly socialist country.' 'But it is still a foreign state!' the curator insisted. Then he reached into his bag and produced the engineer's letter from it. 'This is evidence of your seeking contacts with foreigners, which is very bad! You are letting *ME* down, do you understand?' He paused and added: 'OK! I've known you for a long time. We have often drunk together – from the same bottle. Give me some matches and I'll destroy this bloody letter!' He took a lighter, and set fire to the envelope, threw the ashes down the toilet and flushed it. 'If you ever do it again, you'll have only yourself to blame!' he said. 'What about the consitution?' the engineer queried, naively. The KGB man burst out laughing: 'Are you really such an asshole? You look like a clever man but off you go: constitution, human rights – just like a dissident! Don't be naughty – that's our only constitution, so put that in your pipe and smoke it!'

In 1981, a Moscow post office director and a friend of Petrov's, confided to him in a panic: 'We have just been visited by KGB operatives in our office! They said that we had accepted a telegram for Bulgaria with an inadmissible text. They showed us a photocopy of the telegram and started interrogating us.'

P, a Moscow student, received a call one day from Canada from a chap he befriended on the Black Sea coast during his summer holidays. Next day his father was summoned to the district KGB headquarters 'to explain'.

B, a commissioned officer with the Soviet air force and a devoted stamp collector, boasted to Petrov once that he could get hold of any foreign stamp easily. 'How come?' 'Easy! My mother-in-law is a letter sorter at the International Post Office!'

M, a Moscow radio enthusiast, got a letter from a fellow ham in Africa who had put three Liberian Radio Amateurs' Association stamps on the envelope. Only one of them remained after delivery, two others were torn off with the backing, clearly not in Liberia.

On the subject of the telephone, I myself had my phone bugged, but I'll tell you about that later. Other examples abound anyway. In summer 1987 during a party at the flat of R in Moscow, one of the guests went to the kitchen to make a phone call. In the receiver he suddenly heard very clearly the voices of the people in the drawing room. He called the host and demonstrated the effect to him. It turned out an unrequested telephone repair man had visited the flat a day before the party, allegedly to service the phone.

Engineer Petrov also documented a number of cases where fake notifications of receipt of special delivery letters by foreign addressees were shown to the Soviet senders, when in fact the letters never even crossed the Soviet border having been confiscated by the black roomers.

Many more examples could be given, but I think the point has been made.

It's interesting that the system itself, through inefficiency and sheer stupidity, often provides arresting proofs of its own misdeeds. If we look into volume two, section 'International Mail Items', of the acting *'Postal Regulations of USSR'*, we find the following: 'Letters sent abroad must not contain any unconventional or uncommon abbreviations, resembling a code or a cipher, they must be written legibly, in clear and understandable language.'

So please be careful when writing letters abroad. Make sure your language is 'understandable' for the black roomers and Glavlit censors. Don't write in Amhara, Swahili or, God forbid, Hebrew. Don't hint or make understatements. Otherwise . . .

We have already had very convincing confirmation of Glavlit involvement in monitoring foreign correspondence from comrade Nazarov, the high-ranking Ministry of Communications official. More striking evidence came from Glavlit itself. In summer 1989, the weekly *Argumenti i Fakti* published an interview with B. Skorokhodov, a man with the proud title of Head of the Foreign Literature Control Department of Glavlit of the USSR. 'Foreign correspondence is not controlled by Glavlit,' he said at one point. Later in the same interview he stated that 'letters arriving in the Soviet Union by air mail are first processed . . .'

Shortly before I left the Soviet Union, I got a letter from engineer Petrov with more examples of continuing communications terror. He closed his letter:

> The more I think about it, the more puzzled I become: if the motherland doesn't trust me, then who am I for her? A beloved son or a hated stepson?

158

Who is she for me – my mother or a malicious stepmother? After all, if my motherland is a prison, does this mean that I must love this prison only because I was born there? Or maybe everything is much simpler: one's motherland is the place where one discovers oneself, not the place where one loses one's identity. And we keep losing ourselves here. From our 'beloved mother country' we get only slaps in the face and humiliation of our human dignity. What for? And for whose sake?

8

The Cursed Days

The month of October has come to symbolise the revolutionary turnover in 1917 in Russia. October 1989 for me was the month of the big decision, my own small revolution. It was then that I decided to leave my country, a place I loved and which I still love dearly.

It is very painful to recount the precise chain of events which finally led me to this decision. But I want you to understand that I had no other choice.

The month started rather routinely. I had just received and read the proofs of my first English book to be published in Britain the following March and was about to apply to the visa office for permission to go to London for its presentation (one was supposed to apply for a foreign trip half a year in advance). I was planning to go there alone for a month or so.

My last investigation into the Leningrad mafia had just been published in *Krokodil* and the usual flow of letters followed. Only this time the proportion of threats was much bigger than usual. Threats from neo-fascists, the 'heroes' of my past investigations also kept coming in. Some of them were so nasty that I decided to approach the militia to ask for protection for my family.

'What do you want us to do? Give you a gun?'

They advised me to go to the newly-formed private detective agency which provided that kind of service. The agency, one of the freshest creations of perestroika, consisted of retired militia and KGB operatives. They agreed to give me protection but, being a cooperative organisation, demanded a lofty fee that I couldn't afford.

I had also just received an invitation from the International Press Institute (IPI) to attend their conference – 'a round table' – in Moscow starting on 15 October. Of course, I felt honoured and was looking forward to meeting the world's leading journalists, my friend Martin Walker among them.

I met Martin in Moscow when he was the head of the *Guardian* bureau there. We quickly became friends since our tastes and perception of many

160

things were pretty similar. When his time in Moscow came to an end, Martin was sent to work in Washington, DC, the usual itinerary for Western correspondents.

Martin had a long-standing love affair with Moscow. He also had a number of friends there, so he arrived several days before the round table was due to start. When I took him around the city he was shocked by the changes which had occurred in his absence. The queues were longer, the shop counters were bare. He couldn't believe his eyes when in GUM (Moscow's biggest department store) we saw just one make of cup on sale in the china section. There were neither plates, nor saucers – nothing but that cup and, for some reason, a number of plastic petrol cans. Martin asked, bitterly, 'Where did it all go?'

We both knew where it all went. It went down the drain, together with meat, fruit and clothes. Down the black hole of so-called socialism which for years has been methodically killing any initiative to produce and to sell.

But the thing which most impressed him was not the shortages, nor even the unprecedented rise in crime and rampant nationalism. He was struck dumb by what he called 'the doomed expression on people's faces'.

A couple of days before the round table was to start I had a call from the organising committee saying that the gathering would take place at The Hotel Oktyabrskaya where all the foreign participants would be accommodated.

'But where is this hotel?' I asked. 'In my twelve years in Moscow I've never heard of it.'

The Oktyabrskaya, I found out later, was a special hotel used to accommodate guests of the Communist Party Central Committee. Only God (or Lenin) knows why this exclusive place was chosen as the venue for a journalistic conference. The Soviet system often does inexplicable things. The hotel was not even listed in ordinary Moscow directories or guide books. Martin Walker described it in one of his articles:

When I lived in Moscow from 1984 . . . the Hotel Oktyabrskaya was like the forbidden city. Surrounded by fences and brick guard posts, it was the Party hotel, reserved for guests of the Central Committee. We ordinary mortals could but stare and wonder as the vast electric gates purred to seal us out. There were legends about its marble floors and dining rooms where bills were never presented [this proved to be perfectly true, as Martin himself discovered – VV]. Last month I finally saw it from within, when a group of journalists, invited to an International Press Institute conference hosted by Soviets, was put up there. Our meeting took place in a conference room so grand we should have been signing the Treaty of Versailles. The sixty-foot ceiling contained so many crystal chandeliers that the antiquated Soviet TV cameras needed no

161

extra light. My room was slightly more modest. With its dark wood panelling and heavy furniture, it resembled the fifties Des Moines hotel were Khrushchev had stayed. But the TV and short-wave radio and the refrigerator all worked. There was a separate shower with two water jets, a big bath and thick towels, and curtains that actually met and kept the light out. Same-day laundry and dry-cleaning. Free haircuts. And a real treasure trove – courtesy tubes of Soviet shampoo and shaving cream and toothpaste. None of my Russian friends had seen Soviet toothpaste for months. I carried the tube around in my pocket to show people. It was like a religious relic. Touch and believe.[1]

The timing for the international journalistic gathering could not have been more appropriate. On 13 October 1989, two days before the opening, *Krokodil*'s editor-in-chief was suddenly called to the CPSU Central Committee for an unscheduled meeting with Gorbachev himself. The editors of all other national newspapers and magazines were also present. He didn't get back until the end of office hours. We journalists were chain-smoking in the corridor trying to guess what it was all about.

When our conservative, cautious editor finally entered the office, there was a smile of triumph on his face. 'I am very lucky,' he announced. 'Some of my colleagues who came to the meeting as editors left it unemployed.'

He told us that Gorbachev had launched a vitriolic attack on the editors of progressive publications for their alleged exaggeration of the difficulties faced by perestroika. His main target was Vladislav Starkov, the editor-in-chief of the most popular Soviet weekly *Argumenti i Fakti*, though the editors of *Ogonyok*, *Izvestia* and *Knizhnoe Obozreniye* (Book Review) had also been criticised.

'From now on we'll have to stop publishing any criticism of Gorbachev's course,' our editor declared gravely. 'I don't want to lose my job'.

Moscow journalists later clichéd 13 October 1989 as the black day of glasnost. Glasnost as a policy practically ended on that day. So what had happened? What was the reason for Gorbachev's sudden outburst?

In its 7 October issue, *Argumenti i Fakti* ran an opinion poll on the popularity of people's deputies, the Soviet equivalent of MPs. The list was topped by Sakharov and Yeltsin; Gorbachev was not even mentioned among the top ten. Another reason for Gorbachev's displeasure was the paper's campaign against the Party apparatchiks' privileges. In one issue they ran a letter from a group of Moscow workers complaining about a luxury house for the Party elite being built in downtown Moscow. It had all modern conveniences with imported equipment whereas ordinary Muscovites still had to wait for up to twenty years to get even a very modest flat. No other newspaper would publish the letter.

But at the meeting with Gorbachev Starkov proved a hard nut to crack. 'We are not a party publication,' he retorted to the CPSU General Secretary. 'You have no authority to sack me.'[2]

Indeed, *Argumenti i Fakti* was theoretically the organ of an obscure organisation called the Knowledge Society. Its circulation in October was twenty million, but immediately after Gorbachev's attack on Starkov, the maverick newspaper's circulation leapt to thirty million (by the end of 1990 the figure reached thirty-four million, making *Argumenti i Fakti* by far the most widely-read publication in the world; in April 1990 it was awarded the title of the world's best newspaper by the British Press Academy).

Starkov became a sort of national hero. The country was swept by demonstrations under the slogan 'Hands off Starkov'. The CPSU Central Committee was showered with telegrams supporting him. We *Krokodil* journalists sent a telegram ourselves.

Gorbachev failed to sack Starkov, so he decided to destroy him morally instead. On 21 October 1989 *Argumenti i Fakti* was made to publish an apology to the effect that their opinion poll was scientifically unsound and unrepresentative. They ran a new one instead where (amazingly!) Gorbachev was now the most popular politician. It was so obviously rigged that reading it people couldn't help laughing. To augment the point, the paper ran a long interview with Yegor Ligachev, the most ardent conservative in the Soviet leadership, in the same issue, making it absolutely plain that it was under great pressure.[3]

The attack on Starkov was a clear signal for provincial apparatchiks to try to get rid of progressive journalists. A number of pro-perestroika editors were sacked all round the country in a matter of days causing some newspapers (*Znamya Communizma* in Noginsk, Moscow, among them) to go on strike. 'When they trim nails in the capital, they cut fingers in the province.' Nazim Khikmet* once said. And he was right. For the first time in five years the whole country saw Gorbachev's real face, the face of a cunning, ruthless, vain bureaucrat who was trying to reintroduce repression.

Among the foreign participants at the IPI round table were many world-famous writers and editors: Ari Rath from Israel, Professor Paul Lendvai from Austria, Doctor Andreas Oplatka from Switzerland, Christine Ockrent from France and Doctor Gunther Nonnenmacher from West Germany. These were people who had made themselves reputations for honesty, impartiality and commitment to the idea of a free press.

* A twentieth-century Turkish poet.

The Soviet Union, on the other hand, was for the most part represented not by journalists but by functionaries of APN, the official news agency which has close ties with the KGB. I was, in fact, the only Soviet participant who was an ordinary journalist, not a functionary, and I would not have attended had I not been invited by the IPI. I was their choice and the Soviet participants could do nothing about that.

What they could do, however, was cast disapproving glances at me from time to time. Also they didn't include me in the list of participants distributed among the delegates. When I pointed this out to the organisers, they promised to correct their 'mistake', but were in no hurry to do so.

The general atmosphere at the conference was greatly affected by Gorbachev's crackdown on the progressive press. In his opening address, the British IPI director Peter Galliner said that the threat to Starkov was 'a threat to all our colleagues who have the courage to speak out, a threat to the freedom of expression'.[4]

The Soviets went out of their way to play down this adverse reaction and return to the well-worn track of mutual agreement and primitive propaganda. Seeing that the Western participants would not be easily duped, they resorted to their habitual methods of reproaching their Western colleagues for having painted the USSR 'in black colours' for decades. The whole discussion seemed rather pointless to me; there was no chance whatsoever that the Soviets would ever depart from the official line. They valued their posts with possibilities of frequent trips abroad too highly to show even a shadow of honesty or dissent (in this case synonyms).

One of the three main items on the agenda was investigative journalism. Enrique Zileri, the IPI president, approached me during the interval and said that he would like me to speak on the subject. Though I had no speech prepared, I agreed.

I can clearly see that moment from a distance in time and space. I have the floor. I can feel the hostile glances of the Soviet delegates and the reassuring ones of my Western colleagues. The participants were sitting in a large circle with a small winter garden of flowers, palm trees and so on in the middle. Though there were not many of us, about thirty all in all, I had to talk into a microphone. I decided to speak in English and could constantly hear the worried voice of a Russian woman interpreter, stammering and stumbling over this unscheduled speech of mine, in my earphone.

What exactly did I say? I'd rather not recount the speech myself, but let two foreign colleagues do it:

164

Vitaliev described his work, undertaken on his own initiative, investigating corrupt and criminal social webs in the district of Dnepropetrovsk, in the stronghold of former General Secretary Brezhnev. As a result of his publications, which threw a strong light even on connections in the political sphere, he was able to report 138 arrests and, what is more, a new existence for himself which compels him to take on a certain anonymity and to constantly change his telephone number. Vitaliev drew attention to the fact that Soviet journalists are not protected in such a case by any laws and that he often lacks the simplest technical resources – a car for example – for carrying out his investigations. How welcome such daring press people are in the Soviet Union was the dubious question posed by a Swedish editor and answered by no-one.[5]

Vitali Vitaliev, a young journalist, is regularly sued in the courts, but he is determined to persevere. He is going ahead with his plans to visit a political labour camp, something unheard of in the Soviet Press so far, and with engaging frankness he admits that he does not know whether he will be able to publish anything about this visit at all.[6]

As you see, I simply talked about my work and working conditions, but for the Soviet functionaries my address produced a considerable shock. In the interval they hurried to congratulate me but in so doing they kept stubbornly averting their eyes. A bad omen.

My apprehensions proved right. The next day one of the Soviet participants called me aside for a quick chat. Without any preliminaries he started questioning me about my salary, my trips to the West and whether or not I was pleased with my present job. I answered only briefly enough not to sound rude and returned to my lunch table.

In the afternoon on 16 October, the round table adopted the text of a declaration in support of Starkov. The document also protested against the recent growth of anti-semitic publications in the Soviet press, namely in the newspaper *Sovietskaya Rossiya* and *Nash Sovremenik* and *Young Guard* magazines.

In the evening the organisers threw a farewell banquet for participants in the Foreign Ministry Press Centre restaurant. Standing there with a glass of wine in my hand, I couldn't help feeling that someone was constantly watching me. I had to say goodbye to most of my Western colleagues who were leaving Moscow the following morning. Martin, though, decided to stay on for several days more.

They called me the next evening.

'Vitali Vladimirovich?' a velvety male voice enquired. 'This is the State Security Committee. Please excuse the late call. We know how busy you are, but could you spare a moment to come and see us some time next week, perhaps?' (I realised that I wasn't being conned: only KGB agents themselves never abbreviated the name of their organisation and talked about 'us' instead of 'me'.)

'Next Monday I am leaving on a mission.' This was really so.

'In that case,' he said, after a pause, 'could you try and meet us tomorrow at the Foreign Ministry press bar, say. We'll have a cup of good coffee and a chat.'

'What do you want to talk about? The round table?'

'Not just that, Vitali Vladimirovich, not just that . . .'

'I'll be there,' I said. I knew that if they wanted something from me they wouldn't get off my back till they got it, so it was better to finish with it quickly. Secondly I was genuinely interested in what it was they might want from me.

'Very good, very good, Vitali Vladimirovich. I'll meet you near the entrance at six p.m.'

'But I don't have accreditation*. . .'

'Don't worry. I'll take you in as my guest.'

Despite my curiosity I was slightly worried by my tomorrow's meeting, so I decided to tell Martin about it. He was furious.

'They can't risk doing anything to you.' You have too many friends in the West. But just in case, I will go to the bar at the same time and keep an eye on you.'

How wonderful it is to have friends like that. I immediately felt better.

Next evening at exactly six o'clock I was at the entrance to the press bar in Sadovoye Ring. 'Vitali Vladimirovich?' came yesterday's velvety voice from behind my back. 'Nice to meet you. I am Sergei Stanislavovich.'

A young man in his late twenties stood beside me extending his hand. I ignored the hand. His face was vaguely familiar, the face of a man you think you have seen before, but can't remember where. He had a small black moustache and was sporting a snow-white shirt and a strict brown suit and black tie.

He flashed his red KGB card to the militiaman at the entrance and we were waved in. Having mounted the steps to the second floor, we found ourselves in a brightly-lit oblong room, filled with cigarette smoke and a hubbub of voices.

This was the famous press bar, frequented by foreign correspondents, APN employees and all kinds of influential crooks.

At the far end I could see Martin chatting to Nina, his former secretary.

*Only those with special accreditation of the Foreign Ministry Press Centre can gain access to the press bar.

He cast me a swift glance from the corner of his eye and winked to acknowledge my presence.

There were no vacant seats in the bar, but as soon as we approached one of the front-row tables, two lanky young men stood up as if on command. There were only two chairs near that table, whereas all the rest had six or even eight seats, all taken. Sergei Stanislavovich pointed to one of the vacated chairs and lowered himself down on to the second, facing me. The two young men suddenly re-emerged and placed a third, vacant, chair next to me. There they put a plastic bag with something flat and rectangular inside, something which looked like a very thin book. It was probably a tape recorder. 'So that no-one will disturb us,' Sergei Stanislavovich explained with a cold smile.

'Vitali Vladimirovich,' he continued in a grave, but low voice, 'we have been admiring your courage and perseverance. Your writings are great. You have even managed to penetrate into the holy of holies, the mafia.'

'Look, I haven't come here to listen to your compliments,' I interrupted, 'I don't need them.'

'Don't try to be rude to us. Your mind must be full of stereotypes about our organisation. Are we really as bad as some of your colleagues write? Yes, we've made some mistakes in the past, but who hasn't?'

'Some mistakes. You mean millions and millions of innocent people who were purged and murdered by the KGB and its predecessors –'

'Look at me. Do I look like a murderer? Did you not hear our Chairman Kriuchkov's last speech at the Congress of People's Deputies? He said that our organisation must demonstrate a new openness of vision. It was in that spirit that we conducted the round table of journalists.'

'Wait a moment. I was naive enough to believe that it had been conducted by the Novosti Press Agency.'

The deadpan expression didn't falter. 'You misunderstood me. I meant we, our country, had hosted the round table. Anyway, we wanted to ask you a favour. At the round table we observed that you are on very friendly terms with many foreign journalists. You've also been abroad and written for Western newspapers. You must be well aware of what your foreign colleagues think about our country, what their movements and intentions are. This was only the first round table, but there will be many more for you, if you see what I mean.'

I found it hard to believe my ears: here, in the fifth year of glasnost, just one day after a conference where the Soviet representatives pledged their allegiance to the freedom of the press, they were trying to make me spy on my foreign friends. It felt like a bad dream.

'My dear Vitali Vladimirovich, don't misunderstand us. After all you are a loyal citizen, aren't you? Think it over please, don't say anything now. This is only our first meeting, the first of many, believe me.'

This was too much.

'You know what, let's make it clear once and for all: I've never been a spy and never will be. This first meeting will be our last. I am leaving now and if you don't want me to raise a really big scandal in the Western press, don't contact me again.' I threw a crumpled one rouble note on the table and pushed back my chair, more angry than frightened.

To a chance observer we must have looked an odd pair – me, pacing angrily out of the bar into the street, and Sergei Stanislavovich mincing at my heels with his plastic bag under his arm – like two friends who have just had a drunken quarrel. The pavement of Sadonoye Ring was dark and almost deserted even though it was early. A bitter October wind was blowing in our faces.

At about 100 metres from the Park Kulturi Metro station, Sergei Stanislavovich caught up with me.

'Do you believe in old superstitions?' he asked. 'I've just remembered how old people say that if ash berries are red in autumn, the winter is going to be very cold.' He paused awaiting my reaction. 'You know, Vitali Vladimirovich. I've just looked at a rowan tree across the road and the berries on it were red as blood. Doesn't that suggest that you are in for one hell of a winter?'

I turned round sharply, but Sergei Stanislavovich was no longer there. Only his straight and vigilant KGB back could be discerned, quickly disappearing towards the brightly-lit portals of the press centre.

The next morning I went to see Martin off at Sheremetyevo airport. 'Bastards,' he commented. 'Are you sure they threatened you?'

'He threatened me, Martin. Do you think they meant it?'

'You never know with the KGB. On the one hand, they are as clumsy and inefficient as the whole system, on the other – they can be surprisingly persistent at times. The way they behaved with you shows that they feel powerful again after lying low for several years. I have a feeling that they won't leave you alone. In your shoes, Vitali, I would seriously think about getting out. The tragedy here is inevitable, it's just a question of time. If you agree with me, you must act very cleverly and cautiously, so as not to arouse their suspicions. Don't tell anyone else about yesterday's meeting. We could stir up a big row, letting the IPI know what was going on behind their backs, but we'd do better to wait until you come to the West with your family. So take courage and see you there.'

The turnstile clicked at passport control and my friend was gone behind the invisible wall that separates East from West. The wall was as tall and solid as ever before, only now I had to climb over it myself.

On Martin's advice I started to keep a diary. My last three months in the Soviet Union were the most awful of my entire life. It was like living under siege. The KGB tapped my phone, intercepted my mail and pestered me with warnings and threats. In the end, they started following me in the streets. Winter was getting colder.

These too were months of revolution in Eastern Europe. Totalitarian regimes were shattered all over Europe, but not in the Soviet Union, where hypocrisy was still in power, despite the lip service to democracy paid by the rulers. Their grip on the progressive press was tightening every day, and it was becoming harder and harder to remain a journalist.

'The Cursed Days' was the title Ivan Bunin, my favourite Russian writer and the 1933 Nobel Prize laureate, gave his harrowing account of the days preceding his emigration in 1920. I couldn't think of a better title for this chapter. I was forced to leave Russia at a time when its whole future was in the balance. I had no choice, but I hope you will forgive this small plagiarism.

I am opening the tattered green notebook in which I kept my diary. It has travelled with me all the way to Australia. The pages are covered with my hasty scribbles, sometimes almost unintelligible. I often leaf through them, those last ninety days in Russia, the days of confusion, the days of despair, the days of decision . . .

November 1. Izvestia reported a demonstration near the KGB head-quarters in Moscow. The protestors organised themselves into a chain and surrounded one of the KGB buildings in Dzerzhinski Square holding candles. From there they went to Pushkin Square where they were dispersed by spetsnaz, special militia troops armed with truncheons and tear gas. *Izvestia* photo correspondents Y. Iniakin and A. Steshanov were brutally beaten and their films confiscated.[7]

Yuri Vlasov, the 1964 Olympic weightlifting champion and writer, left the Communist Party in protest against Gorbachev's attacks on the press.

Cereals, salt and macaroni are disappearing from the shops at the speed of light.

Very gloomy and slushy out of doors.

From Dnepropetrovsk came rumours that the Sailor, the head racketeer and 'hero' of *Amur Wars*, my documentary novel, had been released from jail, having served only half of the term. I got in touch with my militia contacts in the city and they assured me that it was not true. But I wouldn't be surprised if it was . . .

The new special exchange rate for the rouble has just been published. Now you can officially get ninety-eight roubles and thirty-four kopeks for ten pounds sterling, only if you are a foreigner of course. The black market rate has reached forty roubles for one pound.

November 2. The telephone in my flat gets naughtier and naughtier. It keeps switching off on its own all of a sudden. Conversations are often interrupted by pauses, echoes and strange voices commenting on what we are saying. If I want to say something important now, I have to use the public telephone in our street.

The newspapers reported on the formation of the new KGB Directorate 'to protect the USSR constitutional power'. It will be responsible for 'fighting anti-socialist groups and public unrest inside the country'.[8] The good old days are back! The new directorate is to replace the one which dealt with ideological dissent. Tweedledum and Tweedledee . . .

Today I applied for foreign passports for me and my family to go to England next January. I had to stand in line for several hours just to enter the militia visa office. Now we have to wait for a month or so until (and if) our foreign passports come through. We've decided to try and stay in the West, but one never knows. My only hope is that my KGB 'friends' won't intervene, but this hope is rather slim. Let's wait and see.

I've started smoking again after two-and-a-half years of total abstinence.

November 3. B, one of my *Krokodil* colleagues, wrote a piece on the events in Nagorni Karabakh. The article was butted [banned] by the censors. In a gesture of desperation, B decided to complain to the ideological department of the CPSU Central Committee. He rang Kapto, the deputy head of the department, who was very nice to him over the phone and promised to look into the matter 'after the holidays'. Next morning our editor-in-chief got an angry call from our curator, the instructor of that very department of the CPSU Central Committee (each official Soviet publication is effectively run by such a curator having full authority over the editor). The editor summoned B and threatened him with the sack if he ever tried to call the Central Committee again without his consent.

Academician Sakharov was banned from appearing on the TV show *Vzgliad* ('The View') where Afghan war veterans are to be interviewed.[9] It was probably connected with the point Sakharov made at a recent Supreme Soviet session. He said he had proof that Soviet generals in

Afghanistan had been ordered to fire at their own soldiers to prevent them from retreating.

November 5. At the grand meeting in the Kremlin Palace of Congresses celebrating the seventy-second anniversary of the October revolution, the main speech was delivered by KGB Chairman Kriuchkov, which was very unusual. Coincidence? Hardly . . .

Yesterday some of the top KGB brass were interviewed by *Vzgliad*. Among other things they were asked when the prison cells in Lubianka would be turned into a museum of KGB victims. 'Wait and hope!' one of them answered with a cynical grin.

November 7. Grim and grey day. Rain. The mood is far from festive, despite the national holiday. Red flags have got wet in the rain and droop sadly from the flagpoles on the houses. There's nothing much to celebrate: the country is in a shambles, in shops the shelves are bare.

Apart from the usual military parade and officially-sponsored demonstration in Red Square, there was an unofficial prodemocratic rally near Dynamo Stadium. More than ten thousand people took part. They carried portraits of Yeltsin and one of their placards read: 'Seventy-two Years On The Road To Nowhere!'

November 10. Tanks roaring along the main streets of Moscow during the night – that's what they showed at the beginning of *Vzgliad* yesterday. 'Here they go at last!' the presenter commented grimly. It turned out later they were returning to their units after the military parade in the Red Square. Yes, it is just an exercise today, but who knows what will happen tomorrow.

Tonight I had a painful showdown with my mother. When I told her that we were planning to leave, she started crying, but after a while she calmed down and said that she supported my decision. Poor old mum.

November 11. Queuing for vodka. The queuers are cursing, pushing and crushing each other. I stood there for three hours trying to read a book.

I had to buy some spirits, since we were expecting guests. But I couldn't endure that queue any longer. So I spat and went to Izumrudnaya Street where someone in the vodka line said wine was being sold . . . The crowd there was even bigger. There was no chance whatsoever of reaching the counter within three hours. Ruddy-faced unshaven spivs were swarming around the queue offering to provide the coveted bottle for a rouble on top of its price. They were in big demand. When one of them got hold of a rouble, he'd simply run back and screw himself into the crowd, elbowing his way to the counter and paying no heed to the screams and insults showered at him. In half an hour he could earn enough to buy a bottle for himself. The mob watched these transactions with doomed meekness.

Apart from having been made teetotal, we'll have to start fasting soon. Natasha asked me to buy some mayonnaise for the salad, but I failed to find it in any of the two dozen shops I visited.

This morning I had a telephone call from Channel 4 in London. They want me to be a consultant for a programme to be filmed in Moscow. In the middle of discussing the details with the producer, he was diverted by a local call and asked me to hold on. While I was waiting, I heard all our previous conversation in the receiver: my queries and his answers played back to me on a very low level. When will the KGB buy some decent bugging equipment? Or maybe they did it on purpose, just to exert psychological pressure on me. In that case, they achieved their goal . . .

November 12. Today as I took my son Mitya to his English class, I saw a big blue graffiti on a radio repair shop in Ostashkovskaya Street: 'Death to Yids!' I read somewhere that most people, when they write on a wall or a blackboard, usually do it at eye level. If so, the inscription, which was pretty high on the wall, must have been done by adults not kids. 'Who are Yids?' Mitya asked.

In the evening we entertained two English couples in our tiny flat: a diplomat from the British embassy and a Reuters correspondent, with their wives.

The diplomat's wife told me how two Russian friends had been summoned by the KGB earlier this year and asked to spy on them. The guests left at three.

November 20. I have just returned from Leningrad. My *Krokodil* colleagues and I made several public appearances in front of our readers. The city is dark, neglected and crumbling. People in the streets are gloomy and foul-mouthed, half of them are drunk. The shops are empty. Prostitutes were swarming around our hotel. Some of them were no older than thirteen.

Walking along Nevski Prospect, the main street, I tore my jacket on a nail sticking out of a fence. There are pits and holes in the pavement and the stucco is peeling from graceful classical buildings. It was hard to believe Leningrad used to be the intellectual capital of Russia, the city of Pushkin and Dostoevsky. 'The cradle of the revolution.' Subconsciously, I was bidding farewell to it.

Popular uprisings are under way in Bulgaria, East Germany and Czechoslovakia. The Berlin Wall is coming down and Honecker is about to be tried for his crimes against the people. I keep remembering how only one month ago Gorbachev was embracing and kissing Honecker on a visit to GDR, calling him the Soviet Union's best friend and a real Communist. He said that East Germany was a brilliant example of socialism in action for everyone to imitate. What would he say now?

Natasha said that in my absence the telephone kept playing tricks. One day she was phoning around trying to get enrolled on a typing course. Suddenly she heard a man's voice saying: 'Typing course! She'd better learn English instead!' She heard this voice very distinctly and immediately wrote down what she had heard. They must be aware of our plans to go to England. What can I do with this invisible enemy? Just 'wait and hope', as they say in the KGB.

November 21. Averin, the editor-in-chief of *Knizhnoe Obozreniye*, is about to be sacked. I am a subscriber and an avid reader of the *Book Review*. It was the first Soviet publication to demand Solzhenitsyn's rehabilitation and to publish his works after many years of ostracism. Its pro-democratic position must have irritated Gorbachev's ideological chieftains.

Gidaspov, the Leningrad Regional Party Committee First Secretary, newly appointed by Gorbachev, appeared on TV with violent attacks on the democratic forces. 'Our banner is as red as ever,' he said. 'There are forces who want to destabilise the country, telling us fairy tales about treacherous bureaucrats and anti-semites. People are tired of unsteadiness. Strict centralism – that's what we need.' He also sang the praises of the newly-formed United Workers Front, which incorporated many right-wing forces, the anti-semitic Pamyat among them.

November 23. Leningrad TV showed a right-wing meeting organised by the Regional Party Committee. The placards hoisted above the crowd read 'Down with cheating cooperators!', 'The Communist Party still exists!', 'Enough repentance, let's start working!' 'We won't allow the revival of private property or of the exploitation of one person by another.' At the end, Gidaspov himself climbed on to the platform. 'We'll win! Thank you!'

It all left a very ominous impression.

November 28. Today F, the Krokodil Party leader, peeped into my office and beckoned me into the corridor. 'I have just had a telephone call from the organization with the tongue-breaking name.* You understand what I

* Another popular Russian euphemism for the KGB.

mean,' he said in a low conspiratorial voice. 'Well, they asked me not to tell you, but we are friends, aren't we? They were wondering whether you would be willing to give a small consultation to them on a certain matter.'

'Why didn't they call me direct?'

'Well, you know, they wanted to test the water first. With glasnost they sometimes feel insecure. So what shall I tell them?'

'Please tell them to go to hell. I have nothing to discuss with them. Nothing at all.'

'Well, of course, it's up to you, Vitali, but in your shoes I wouldn't decide too quickly. By the way, do you know exactly who called me? *Tumanov!*'

I must have reached a pretty high level, I thought. Tumanov was a well-known Moscow journalist who had defected to the West several years before. There he made a quick career in the media and soon was appointed the chief of a big Russian-language radio station broadcasting to the Soviet Union. After a year or so he 're-defected' back to Russia and started giving interviews and press-conferences exposing his recent colleagues at the radio station. Many suspected that it was all just a carefully-planned KGB operation. Perhaps they wanted me to follow his stead.

'Give my regards to comrade Tumanov,' I said and started back to my office.

'Don't tell anyone about our talk!' F called after me.

November 29. In the morning I called my friend Sasha, who lives in Czechoslovakia with his Slovak wife, Dana. He was not in but she was very excited by what was going on in their country and told me proudly that she had left the Czechoslovakian Communist Party which she had been forced to join when she went to study in the Soviet Union in 1972. 'I hope, the Soviet Union won't give us fraternal help now, as she did in 1968,' she said wryly.

Unimaginable things keep happening to my telephone. Sometimes it buzzes in the middle of the night, but when I grab the receiver there's no-one there. It looks as if it has gone mad or contracted some bizarre disease – telephone fever. Today I spoke to Jonathan Steele, the new *Guardian* correspondent in Moscow who has replaced Martin. In the middle of the conversation I suddenly heard in the receiver a distant man's voice: '. . . and then I produce my KGB card and flash it in his face . . .' I was unable to hear what happened to the KGB card holder afterwards, since the voice died away. Maybe I am going mad myself? That's probably what they want to achieve. No, I can still rely on my eyes and ears: it's all happening.

November 30. K, an old friend of mine, called me from Kiev saying that a letter which he had sent to me three and a half months ago had just been returned to him. K is a former KGB lieutenant colonel, but a thoroughly decent man (there are some decent people even in the KGB). When I was investigating the mafia in the Ukraine, he gave me a lot of help. As head of the KGB Third Department responsible for controlling the militia, he was interested in exposing corrupt militiamen who were collaborating with the criminals. When at the last moment our editor-in-chief grew reluctant to publish my story, K made a special trip to Moscow sporting the impressive KGB uniform. 'We want this story published!' he said firmly. The story appeared. Shortly afterwards K went into retirement and started writing freelance journalism. He had written a piece on the Ukrainian democratic movement and sent it to my home address for my opinion. He wanted me to offer it to *Krokodil* for publication. 'I am a professional,' he said, 'and I am absolutely sure that my Moscow colleagues have worked on this letter. There are signs that it has been opened. Don't worry, but you must be under some kind of surveillance. This is not for the telephone. I am coming to Moscow soon and we'll talk.'

So the pressure is growing. They've besieged me and the grip gets tighter and tighter, though, if I look at the calendar, the 'hell of a winter' promised by Sergei Stanislavovich, hasn't begun yet.

December 5. For the last three days I have been in my native Kharkov with my friend Alexander Kabakov. We were invited by the local youth club to make a number of public appearances. The schedule was quite tough and we had to appear on stage three times a day. The subject of our lectures (or rather performances) was 'Will the Soviet Union live up to 1993?' The Regional Party Committee apparatchiks put obstacles wherever they could: they refused to advertise our performances or sell tickets; they were trying to discourage people from attending by hook or by crook. When we arrived for the talk to the military higher school, it turned out that one hour before all the cadets were suddenly sent out to clean the snow from the streets. 'We had a call from the Regional Party committee, and we couldn't disregard their orders,' the school's commander explained apologetically. 'The underground obkom* in action,' Sasha commented acidly.

On my last day in Kharkov, I visited my father's grave. It was covered by untouched snow. Trams rattled behind the cemetery fence. The air was crisp and fresh and no-one was around. I silently spoke to my father, to

* The Russian abbreviation for Regional Party Committee.

grandpa Misha and granny Niura lying nearby. None of them had been able to travel abroad, to see the world or to find a better life. They had sacrificed themselves for the sake of the country and what did they get in return? Illusions, a miserable existence and a tiny patch of land in the cemetery. 'I am your son and grandson. You brought me into this world, you educated me. I promise that wherever I am, I will always remember you. I will be looking at the world with your eyes and you will be travelling with me.' I was saying goodbye to them.

December 6. Ogonyok ran a striking story on the Pamyat rally in the Red Square.[10] Someone at the very top must have authorised it, since no other informal group has *ever* been allowed to demonstrate there. The meeting was of a purely anti-semitic nature. To the tune of a wartime song they chanted 'Wake up, our huge land, and go to the deadly battle with the cursed masonic power, the dark Jewish horde.'

December 9. Our foreign passports came through! Natasha and I collected them from the visa office today after paying 200 roubles each in tax. Now we have to book the tickets and exchange some roubles into pounds sterling. By the new regulations, one is entitled to no more than £200, irrespective of how long he or she plans to stay abroad. Children under sixteen are not allowed any money at all. For the £400 which are due to Natasha and me we'll have to pay 4000 roubles (the new 'special' tourist exchange rate is one pound for ten roubles, whereas the official rate is one for one. The state itself has become a black-market hard-currency dealer.

This afternoon I went to the exchange office. There's only one such office for the whole of Moscow, one tiny room in Leningradski Prospect, and the queuers are kept in the street in the snow. To have one's roubles exchanged one must stand in line for a month, coming to the office every morning at six o'clock for the roll-call. If one doesn't turn up one's name is struck from the list and one has to start all over again.

No, this was too much for me. To hell with changing money. After all, I have some money in my London bank account. The main thing now is to get there. They have eased the procedure of issuing foreign passports, but at the same time they have made it almost impossible and exorbitantly expensive to have one's money changed. Who will venture to go abroad without a penny? Very clever. And the West is happy . . .

Foreign passports are only half the battle. I still have to book the train tickets, which is no easier than exchanging money. But here I've got a small plan.

December 12. K arrived from Kiev. We sat in a seedy cooperative cafe in Bolshaya Bronnaya Street drinking oily Georgian cognac from paper cups. 'It is clear to me that you have been put on the PC – perlustration of correspondence category – by my former colleagues. The reason? I don't know. Probably it's connected with your trips abroad. My letter came back with traces of having been opened: the paper was shrivelled and uneven. They have a special device which warms up an envelope and opens it. This is outrageous. The Department [KGB] is falling over itself to justify its existence, but instead of reducing its personnel, it keeps recruiting new agents. From the first of January their salaries will be doubled. Now an ordinary typist working in the department will get about 400 roubles a month. And how much do you get? 160! You see what's happening? K paused and sipped some cognac from his glass. 'The apparat is basically bribing the Department to ensure its own survival. They are preparing for a cataclysm, possibly for a war against their own people – that's the saddest thing. The new fifth Directorate, created to protect the constitution, is much bigger than the former Third one – both in manpower and equipment, whereas its aim remains the same – fighting ideological dissent.'

I was distressed by the quietness of his tone: he spoke of the coming civil war as of something which went without saying. He also said that the new KGB Directorate was equipped with the very latest Western technology. Judging by the bugging devices, used in my phone, I must be dealing with another directorate.

December 13. Literaturnaya Gazeta published Yevtushenko's poem 'Red and Black' about Pamyat demonstrating in Red Square.'

> '. . . anti-semitic wave already
> Seems to have reached the Kremlin walls.
> The government Zils nearby were diving stealthily
> Into the Spasskaya Tower gate.
> They probably think that these anti-semitic thugs
> Are not worth taking heed of . . .
> What a terrible bog we are stuck in,
> If Red Square hears 'Beat the kikes!'
> What will anti-semites do,
> When the last Russian Jew escapes the country,
> Like grain through a sieve?
> Who will be the enemy then?
> What if, to our great shame,
> Jesus Christ, also a Jew,

Being insulted to tears
And dead tired,
Joins the queue for visas
Near the foreign embassy?'

December 14. A clergyman speaking on the fifth TV channel said: 'When Sakharov said that Gorbachev was the only acceptable leader now, I agreed. When all the delegates at the Congress of People's Deputies started saying it, I was alerted. But when Gorbachev himself said it, I got frightened.'

December 15. Awful day. In the morning I learnt of academician Sakharov's death. He died at home yesterday in the evening after a session of one of the Congress of People's Deputies' Commissions, of which he was a member. And only the day before yesterday he was attacked by Gorbachev and the others at Congress for allegedly 'speaking too often'. 'Take away your papers! I don't need them!' Gorbachev shouted at the elderly, stooped man standing on the rostrum. And the audience booed approvingly. 'I am going to fight,' were his last words.

On the day of his death, Sakharov addressed a meeting of the inter-regional group of people's deputies. Among other things he said: 'We can't share full responsibility for what the leaders are doing. They are bringing the country to catastrophe by delaying perestroika for years.'[12]

He was called 'the conscience of Russia'. Yesterday, when he died, Russia lost its conscience. What can be more dangerous than a doomed, conscienceless giant?

The day is snowy, bleak and mournful. It reminds me of the day of my father's funeral.

In the afternoon we had a meeting at *Krokodil* to discuss the draft of the new press law. The draft has lots of unimportant clauses, whereas only two basic provisions are necessary: the abolition of preliminary censorship and freedom for everyone to receive and disseminate information. That's all we need.

Earlier this month we published the special anti-Stalinist issue to 'commemorate' the dictator's centenary. We managed to include a good deal of topical anti-totalitarian satire. On the cover we had a big portrait of Stalin made of tiny human skulls. The readers' response came as a shock to us all. Out of several thousand letters only a handful supported our stance. The rest were aggressively pro-stalinist, rude and anti-semitic. 'How much money have you got, you dirty kikes, for defaming our dear comrade Stalin? Don't you dare do it again! Take your glasnost back and give us some food, like we had under Stalin!' How devastated people must be to start craving for the 'firm hand' again! Sixty million killed by Stalin are not enough for them!

One of my *Krokodil* colleagues was mugged and beaten under the bridge, 100 yards from our office at seven pm. The teenage thugs took his fur hat and fled.

In the underground I saw a gypsy beggar no more than thirteen years old. She was barefoot and had a screaming baby in her arms.

Academician Sakharov is dead, and his widowed country is weeping on his grave.

December 19. The only liquor store in our district is in Sviblovo. I went there to buy some spirits for the New Year. There was a terrible crush in the shop. Fights flared up from time to time. In the corner, a saleswoman in a greasy white gown was selling vodka to those were willing to jump the queue. She charged two roubles extra for each bottle, an impertinent example of petty corruption. And no-one objected!

As I expected, the unlimited adulation of Sakharov started the day after his funeral. In *Izvestia* he was compared to Tolstoy and Ghandi. What sort of a country is this? She booes and tortures her great sons and daughters until they die and become 'harmless' and then starts deifying them! It was like that with Pushkin, with Vladimir Vysotski and now Sakharov.

I was appalled to learn that Sakharov's funeral in Luzhniki was attended by Gorbachev, Vorotnikov, Zaitsev and other CPSU Politburo members (their names were announced in the news in habitual order – Gorbachev first, and then all the rest alphabetically – as if they were attending a state dinner.) The executioners at their victim's funeral. Vorotnikov, by the way, was in the Politburo when Sakharov was exiled to Gorky. What hypocrisy.

Leningrad TV showed another right-wing meeting, this time in support of the formation of the Russian Communist Party and of making Leningrad the Russian capital. The demonstrators stood in the frost yelling in choked voices: 'Down with bourgeois democracy!' 'Give us food!' 'We support communist Gidaspov!' An army colonel attacked the progressive press for its 'anti-military campaign'.

December 21. Pavel and Tamara Globa, the astrologists, appeared on national TV's educational channel. Among other things they predicted that England would disappear off the face of the planet next century after a powerful earthquake or a deluge. They also prophesied the end of the USSR in six years' time. It's amazing how gullible the Soviet people

179

become. It always happens at moments of social instability and uncertainty. Half-crazy healers Chumak and Kashpirovski appear on TV every day claiming to treat all imaginable illnesses by hypnotic suggestion from the screen. Things of that sort have always been branded as the tricks of 'bourgeois ideologists' contradicting the materialistic laws of nature. Now the country's leaders seem eager to forget their 'principles' and distract people's attention from the mess they have created. And they have succeeded. Standing in unending lines for food, people keep discussing the latest healing session by Kashpirovski, rather than questioning the existing order of things. Brezhnev would never have thought of something like this. Only I keep remembering Valentin Katayev's novel *Ruined Life*, where he describes the appearance of large numbers of similar gurus on the eve of the First World War and the revolution. It's interesting that many people tend to compare Kashpirovski to Grigori Rasputin and find much in common between them.

December 22. I have just learnt that Ceausescu has been toppled. Romania is rejoicing. And what's going to happen here? Gorbachev's reaction to the Lithuanian Communist Party's decision to break free from the CPSU does not promise anything good. I have the impression that his main concern now is to preserve the old dogmas and his own power. Nothing else.

An announcer on Romanian radio said: 'Today for the first time in my life I am saying what I think, and tomorrow you will receive an honest newspaper.' It's impossible to listen to this without emotion. Sad memories. Only a couple of months ago Gorbachev fraternised with Ceausescu on his visit to Moscow.

December 26. I was to go to Riga to speak there a couple of days ago. On the day of my departure, I received a worried telephone call from the tour organiser in Riga saying that they had to cancel the whole thing, since they had suddenly learnt from the local militia that a number of tickets had been bought by leaders of the Riga underworld and their bodyguards who wanted to settle accounts with me for my *Parabellum Jeans* story (This article, exposing the mechanisms of the local black market, was published in *Krokodil* a couple of years ago.) I had to go to the station and cancel my ticket. Maybe this is for the best. I have no right to run any additional risks now.

Besides, my gastric ulcer gave me trouble yesterday. Today I feel a little better, but have to stay in bed. To while away the time I am listening to my transistor radio. They have just reported the execution of the Ceausescus.

The fact that it was done covertly, without a proper trial, leaves an unpleasant aftertaste.

Yesterday on the TV programme *The Interior Ministry Informs* it was said that crime figures this year are 33 per cent higher than in 1988.

The main shock was caused by yesterday's CPSU Central Committee Plenum where Gorbachev condemned Lithuanian Communist Party separatism, calling its secession from the CPSU invalid and claiming to applaud that the Soviet leadership will not accept the disintegration of the Soviet state. His speech was very confused.

December 27. Though I am not feeling too well as yet, I had to go to the office today to collect my New Year zakaz, the modest food supply from the *Pravda* canteen. Otherwise, we'd have no food to celebrate the New Year. The biggest 'luxury' item in the zakaz was a bar of chocolate called Inspiration – what a bizarre name! A couple of years ago chocolate could be bought on every corner, but now it has become a deficit alongside vegetables, dairy products and almost everything else. There were huge snaking lines for fruit and sour milk in Maslovka Street.

The Supreme Soviet decree on combating organised crime was published in the papers. This is the first mention of organised crime in official documents and means that its existence has been recognised at last. Well, that's better than nothing.

A very apt metaphor in *Sobesednik* (The Interlocutor): our economy used to resemble a car with square wheels. Now, with the so-called reforms under way, it's the same car but with triangular wheels. It's different, but it still won't move.

The situation in the country corresponds to the weather: neither winter, nor autumn, but just a grey slush.

December 28. This evening we put a plastic fir tree in my son Mitya's room, and it immediately acquired a romantic and somewhat mysterious look. But the festive mood is no longer with us.

December 29. Another strange thing happened: I suddenly received a phone call from Oleg Bitov. Yes, the very Bitov who defected to Britain in 1983, spent a year there exposing repressive conditions in the Soviet Union and then suddenly reappeared in Moscow claiming that he had been drugged and kidnapped by British intelligence.

I've known Bitov for almost ten years. In 1981 he was the head of the foreign culture department of *Literaturnaya Gazeta* and published a selection of my poetic translations of Henry Longfellow. I am still very proud of this publication, one of my first in the national press. Bitov was a very experienced editor and a real intellectual. I was not surprised when news of his defection became public. I remember hearing him broadcast on the BBC radio from London explaining his motives in 1983. He didn't sound drugged or hypnotised. While in Britain he wrote anti-Soviet pieces for the *Sunday Telegraph* and published a book entitled *Bitov's Britain*. News of his mysterious return to the USSR was completely unexpected.

I hadn't heard from Bitov since this ordeal, then suddenly today he calls me offering to exchange videocassettes. It's interesting that I have only recently bought a video player and have only a couple of films, whereas Bitov, who I was told travels to the West frequently, possesses a huge tape library. It is clearly a pretext to establish (or rather re-establish) contact.

This afternoon's rendezvous in Bitov's office at *Literaturnaya Gazeta* confirmed my apprehensions. We did exchange films, though, as it turned out, he has already seen the one I lent him. He was very nervous and kept asking about my plans of going to Britain: when, why and for how long. I was evasive saying that I was going there for the publication of *Special Correspondent* and did not know exactly when, since I hadn't got a ticket yet.

The Radio Liberty Russian service broadcast predictions for the coming year by an astrologist from Tallinn: troubles will start at the end of January; by summer, the unrest will reach such proportions that Prime Minister Rizhkov will have to resign; strikes will have to be supressed by the army. Troops will also participate in combatting the growing crime wave. By autumn, the USSR will split into several sovereign states. Not a very optimistic prediction, I'd say. Only time will show how realistic it is.

December 31. If one believes oriental calendars, next year – 1990 – is the year of the horse. The Chinese calendar goes in twelve year cycles and each year is represented by one of the twelve animals: a rat, a rabbit, a snake, a monkey and so on. I was born in 1954, which was also the year of the horse. In 1978 (another horse year) I married Natasha and moved to Moscow. So 1990 should be my year. The horoscopes claim that horse years are favourable for moving to a new home and for travelling in general. I am not superstitious and don't fully believe in this, but strangely, it gives me some reassurance: to modify the popular English saying a little, when all else fails, read horoscopes.

The horse is certainly a fine animal, but it won't be enough to get us to Britain. For that I need train tickets. People say that the queues at the only Moscow booking office selling tickets abroad are enormous. One has to stand there for days. I have discovered that they start selling tickets thirty days before your travel date. So, if we want to go at the end of January, I must try and buy the tickets tonight. This is the little ruse I have been nuturing for a while now. The gist of it is that New Year night is the best time for queueing, the time when even the most inveterate queuers would like a break. The booking office is to open at ten tomorrow morning, so in the first hours of 1990 I will go there and wait. Hopefully, with everyone celebrating the New Year, the line will be much shorter than usual.

This will be a hungry New Year. The shops are bare. Formerly they used to 'throw out' something special onto the counters on New Year's eve to make people happier at least on this one occasion. Not this year. I even failed to buy the traditional bottle of champagne this time. So it looks like this is going to be my first champagne-less New Year for many years, since childhood perhaps.

Half an hour before midnight I went out for a short stroll. This is an old tradition of mine, saying goodbye to the old year out of doors. The snow was sparkling under the street lamps; it crunched soothingly under my feet. The windows of the big hospital opposite our house, usually pitch dark at this time of night, were brightly lit. The patients were celebrating the New Year too. Suddenly I felt a strong affiliation to those unseen hospital inmates. Sick people in a sick country. Will this really be my last New Year in Russia? I was thinking.

January 1, 1990. Happy New Year! I spent half last night and the whole of this morning queueing for tickets. Alas, I was not the only smart alec to have thought that the New Year holiday would be a good opportunity for that. When, at four am, I reached the Intourist travel bureau where the booking office was located, there was already a flock of people jumping on the snow to warm themselves up. It was minus twenty degrees centigrade. As it turned out, these early queuers were not from Moscow, but from other parts of the country. They told me that this booking office was the only place in the whole of the Soviet Union where one could buy railway tickets abroad. One of them was clutching a sheet of paper with the queueing list in his hand. My name was twenty-eighth. So far, so good.

The booking office was to open in six hours. For the first hour or two we stood in the doorway of the Intourist building. It was freezing but still a tiny bit warmer than outside. At about six am a militiaman appeared. He shooed us all out of the building, despite desperate pleas from the few women in line to let them stay inside. The militiaman was unyielding. 'You have no business here!' He kept repeating like a parrot.

By dawn the line had grown immensely and contained more than 400 people. Here I bumped into my former neighbour, Kostya. Our families used to share a communal flat several years ago, where Kostya lived in a single sixteen-square-metre room with his wife, mother-in-law and two sons and we occupied a slightly bigger room in the same flat, sharing kitchen and bathroom with Kostya's family and yet another one.

At ten o'clock the cashier appeared. She was in a bad mood. Passing by the freezing line, she snapped at us for pestering her with our stupid tickets even on New Year's Day. The doors opened and the queue surged forward. By an irony of fate (or rather of the mob), those who had come later were now much closer to the window than the people from our night patrol. The list was completely forgotten. It was unfair, but we could do nothing.

When my turn came, I produced a bottle of perfume and a bar of soap, given to me at home by the far-sighted Natasha – just in case – and shoved them through the window. 'Happy New Year to you!' The cashier grabbed them and something approaching a smile crossed her face. Perhaps there was no real need for me to do this, but after standing in line for almost nine hours I hardly knew what I was doing.

On the way home I bought a big cake to celebrate my achievement. It was hard to believe, but there was no queue at the bakery.

Now I am caressing the tickets in my hands. Our *laissez passer* to freedom. We are to go through Poland, the GDR, West Germany, Belgium, and then by ferry to England. The KGB must be aware of our forthcoming trip and are likely to stop me from going unrecruited. It means that I must dupe them into believing that we are leaving later than we actually are. I spent the rest of the day calling all my friends from my tapped telephone to wish them a Happy New Year, saying in passing that we had plane tickets for 3 February. I am not sure whether this simple trick will work, but it's better than nothing.

January 3. Moskovski Komsomolets, the popular youth daily, wrote about the sudden cancellation of *Vzgliad* on 29 December. Several hours before going on air, a group of plainclothes men came into the studio and confiscated all video cassettes. That night *Vzgliad* was planning to run a parody of *Vremia*, the main Soviet news bulletin. The newspaper reported increasing pressure on youth TV programmes which, according to the officials, 'have got out of hand'.[13]

In Pushkin Square I bought a copy of the new unofficial newspaper *Svobodnoye Slovo* ('the Free Word'), published by the Democratic Union. The print quality is very poor, but the contents are noteworthy. On the first page there's a cartoon depicting Gorbachev grasping with both hands a crumbling monument to Lenin in an attempt to prevent it falling from its pedestal. On the same page there's a letter from twelve imprisoned Moscow dissidents, in response to academician Sakharov's funeral:

> Sakharov's murderers have no right to bury him. His assassins are Gorbachev, whom Sakharov was vainly trying to interest in a list of current political prisoners (several hours before his death), all the members of the Politburo and the aggressive majority of the Congress of People's Deputies.[14]

January 5. Today I went to the British embassy to file the application for visas. From the first of January they introduced compulsory interviews for everyone wanting to go to Britain, either as a tourist or on business. The applicants are called one by one to the tiny cubicle in the consulate where two ever-smoking British women interrogate them about the reasons for their trip, whether they are planning to settle or work in the UK, how much money they have and who is going to support them. When I asked them what right they had to pose such impertinent personal questions, one of them explained that many Soviet citizens wanted to work illegally while in Britain. Some of the Soviet women who stood in line for visas with me were asked whether or not they intended to marry in the UK and how they had met the men who had invited them. What made these questions even more outrageous was that they were being asked by the English who themselves cannot tolerate any intrusion of their privacy. They treated us as potentially dangerous objects, not as human beings.

The paradox was that the interviews were bound to be futile anyway, since no-one in their right mind would disclose their real intentions to the alien interrogators with dull faces. That's the West's answer to the Soviet law on free emigration, which, by the way, hasn't been adopted yet!

Bizarrely, the only Soviet applicants spared the interviews were a family of deaf-mutes. The consulate workers probably didn't have instructions from London on how to interview people who could neither hear nor speak. The happy deaf-mute family got their visas promptly and left the consulate gesticulating elatedly.

What a coincidence: Radio Liberty tonight interviewed a couple of Soviet citizens 'illegally' living in London. One of them, a woman who wants to marry her English boyfriend, said that after they applied for the marriage registration she was summoned to the Home Office and asked to describe the location of birthmarks on her fiancé's body, just to make sure that the intended marriage was not fictitious.

I think this is the continuation of an age-long British policy towards immigrants and 'aliens'. Remember how the British government turned away a ship with Jewish refugees aboard from fascist Germany during the

Second World War; how in 1940 they rounded up and shipped to Australia thousands of German and Austrian Jews who had left their homelands for England to escape Nazi persecution in the thirties; how after the war they deported the Russian Cossacks to die in Stalin's concentration camps; and finally how they treat Vietnamese refugees in Hong Kong today. A very sad record.

January 8. On the *Seven Days* TV news programme the KGB and Interior Ministry spokesman assured the viewers (for the umpteenth time) that there were no political prisoners in the USSR, 'only speculators'. Will they ever stop telling lies?

Bitov called again asking for a meeting, ostensibly to exchange videos. 'When are you going to England?' he enquired. 'At the beginning of February,' I replied. 'Don't forget to buy a *Batman* cassette.' 'I won't!' I promised, and hung up.

January 10. I am writing these lines at ten to midnight, the moment of my birth thirty-six years ago. Yes, I am thirty-six now. This is awful, awful . . .

Earlier today Natasha, Mitya and I went to the West German embassy to get our transit visas. The embassy is beseiged by thousands of ethnic Germans wanting to emigrate to their historic motherland, standing there day and night in the snow. The West Germans haven't even built a simple shed to protect their strayed brothers and sisters. Many would-be emigrants hold crying babies in their arms and their plain peasant faces, burnt by the merciless sun of Kazakhstan or the Kirgizia steppe where 'comrade' Stalin exiled them, carry the stamp of doom and submission. This is no longer mere emigration. It's a stampede, an exodus. Once an hour the heavy ornate gates of the embassy open a little and a burly ruddy-faced German diplomat in a fur hat peeps out. He calls out the names of the lucky ten invited inside for an interview.

Having received our visas we decided to celebrate my birthday at the Moscow Hotel restaurant. The doorman tried to block our way muttering his habitual 'No seats', but we quickly got past him and found ourselves in a fairy tale: the empty restaurant hall was decorated with Khokhloma, traditional Russian wood paintings, the waiters were clad in Russian folk costumes, the tables were weighed down with exquisite Russian food. It appeared that this was the final round of a Russian cooking competition. A very important commission to judge the cooks and the service was expected at any moment. That was probably why we weren't thrown out. We enjoyed a delicious meal in solitude, broken only by smiling waitresses urging us not to hurry and asking Mitya whether he liked the food. We ordered meat in clay pots and borsch and desserts. Russian folk songs were being played. When we finished eating, the waitresses brought us some clean sheets of paper and asked to write down our impressions. 'It was a dream and I don't want to wake up!' I wrote.

A long queue of hungry people was waiting outside near the closed restaurant doors. Yes, we knew how lucky we were to get an unexpected gift from the system. But the fact that it was a once-in-a-lifetime gift, not the norm, made me feel sadder than before. My poor country gave her last birthday present to me . . .

Afterwards we visited formerly-famous Gorkovo Street shop, Souvenirs, to buy me a present, but there was nothing (literally nothing!) on sale. Only empty cardboard boxes were piled high on the counters. A return to reality.

Izvestia today ran a piece on the recent unrest in Chernigov, Ukraine. A local Party boss was riding in his black chauffered Volga limousine and both he and the driver were drunk. Suddenly they clipped another car and the impact flung the boot open. Passers-by glimpsed heaps of short-supply foodstuffs inside: caviar, cognac, smoked sausages and so on and, in a spontaneous surge of anger, the crowd overturned the limousine and dragged it to the Regional Party Committee building. An impromtu rally broke out there. Thousands of people demonstrated for days until the Party boss in question was sacked from his post and expelled from the Party. But the people did not disperse. Now they demanded the resignation of the whole bureau of the Regional Party Committee. After a couple of days the bureau had to resign.[15]

In this spontaneous, unpremeditated riot I can see the likely future of the whole country. The Soviet Union is like a powder keg now. One little spark could be enough to cause an explosion.

Literaturnaya Gazeta published subscription figures for 1990. The biggest increase (up 97 per cent) was scored by *Nash Sovremenik* (Our Contemporary), an anti-semitic monthly. The circulation of this semi-fascist magazine has reached one million copies. A very alarming sign.

January 12. Gorbachev is in Lithuania trying to persuade the republic not to secede from the USSR. His visit is widely televised. He talks to people in the streets of Vilnius, though these are monologues rather than conversations. Gorbachev is his usual self: he never listens to his interlocutors, he interrupts ('One second! I am asking the questions here!'), he blackmails: ('If you agree to stay with the Soviet Union, I am your friend, if not I am your enemy!') he cajoles: ('I've put off all my work to come here, my fate is in your hands . . .'), he threatens: ('You will get what you deserve from me!'). He looks pitiful, tongue-tied and inarticulate, but very fond of the sound of his own voice.

Natasha is happy: she has managed to buy some sausages in the cooperative shop in Prospect Mira. I haven't seen sausages for many months, to say nothing of eating them. We are all pleased as punch. It's amazing how little one sometimes needs to feel happy, just a kilo of bloody sausages!

January 13. The Communist Party is outlawed in Romania! Incredible – and a little frightening.

January 14. The Old New Year at the Kabakovs. By the Russian Orthodox calendar the new year starts today. It's an old tradition in Russia to celebrate the Old New Year with family and friends. It was a sad and moody evening. Sasha and his wife Ella are the only people (apart from our parents) who are aware of our plans. They have had their share of KGB persecution and know exactly how we feel. 'You should leave the country. You must think of your son. The state has done nothing to protect you.' Sasha is now working as a deputy news editor on *Moscow News*. Last week he wrote a piece on government dachas in a Moscow suburb. His editor demanded that all mention of Moscow City Party Committee dachas be cut: the Moscow Party Committee First Secretary Prokofiev, who also had a dacha there, was a friend of his . . . And this is the country's most progressive newspaper. At the end of the evening Sasha presented us with his newly-published collection of stories and novels with the inscription: 'To Natasha and Vitali, my dear friends irrespective of time and place, with wishes of good luck – irrespective of place and time.'

January 16. L, my friend from the Radio Moscow World Service, said they had been tipped off about approaching Jewish pogroms in Moscow and Leningrad. This was confirmed yesterday in *The Fifth Wheel* on TV.

An obscure Russian writer at a rally in Leningrad openly called on the Russian people to start killing Jews.

January 17. They called me again. The telephone rang at eight-thirty in the morning when I was still in bed. 'They always ring when you don't expect them to,' Sasha Kabakov once said.

'Good morning, Vitali Vladimirovich. This is Sorokin from the State Security Commitee speaking. We apologise for the early call, but we'd very much like you to come to our office and discuss one small matter. We just wanted you to clarify one situation, where you were involved indirectly.' 'Look,' I said, 'I have already met one of your colleagues and I think we've covered everything. Besides, I am not feeling well today.' 'No problem. It can wait, it really can. What about if we give you a ring in a week's time? Or you can give us a ring yourself, when you feel better. The number is 924–1806.' And with clear irony he added: 'We wish you a quick recovery.'

What was that? A reminder? A touchstone? Or were they about to launch a final offensive? With our visas and tickets ready I simply couldn't risk meeting them. I must try and avoid any contact with them for the remaining two weeks.

Later today another curious thing happened. I had a call from VAAP, the Soviet copyright agency, who were acting as Soviet literary agents for *Special Correspondent*. In fact, they have imposed themselves on me and instead of helping me with the book, they have constantly created problems. One of their people went to London some time ago, ostensibly to finalise some minor detail in the contract. My London publisher told me later that he (the VAAP man) behaved most rudely and unprofessionally. At one point he flashed a KGB card. (In Moscow we all know that VAAP has strong KGB connections.) This was the man who called me today. 'How is your health, Vitali Vladimirovich?' 'What makes you worry about my health?' I asked. 'I thought you were ill,' came the reply.

Am I going mad? Or is this really a conspiracy aimed at undermining my determination and pushing me into making a faux pas? Do they have nothing else to occupy them? It seems that what's happening to their opposite numbers in East Germany does not worry them in the least. In yesterday's *Vremia* it was reported that an angry crowd in East Berlin blocked the headquarters of Stasi, the East German KGB. They covered the walls with graffiti saying 'Gestapo', 'Murderers', 'Butchers'. The Stasi simply ceased to exist and its agents became jobless. I am sure the same thing will happen here sooner or later. Rather later than sooner though, I guess.

Life goes on. And death goes on as well. On *Vremia* tonight they showed a soldier who had been badly wounded in Azerbaijan. Lying in a hospital bed, he was muttering with his parched lips: 'The country is on the brink of civil war.' Then Armenian refugees were shown on their way from Baku to Armenia, coming down the gangway at Yerevan airport. Many women and children were crying. People are getting used to the growing numbers of wounded and killed, a gradual erosion of feeling. This is very dangerous.

Today I booked a cab to take us to the station on 31 January, from a public phone of course. The only way to book a cab in Moscow now is to do it two weeks in advance. It took me several hours to get through to the despatcher: the line was either engaged or no-one answered. She reluctantly agreed to book a car for me but said that my order could easily get lost during the coming fortnight. So I will have to call her again a couple of days before the trip just to confirm my booking. So far, so good.

January 18. The mobilisation of reservists is announced in regions adjoining Georgia and Armenia. It looks like the war there is just round the corner.

A revelation from V. Kondratiyev, a well-known Soviet writer, sharing his childhood impressions in an article entitled 'Let's Talk about Ideals':

> I remember our family returning to Moscow from Poltava in 1921. My father's aunt, an old Bolshevik, got us seats in a first-class carriage where the representatives of the new elite – Party functionaries, Red Army commanders and Commissars – were travelling. The carriage smelt of leather, good eau-de-cologne and expensive cigarettes. After two years of hunger, we were dressed almost in rags. The high-ranking passengers gave us puzzled looks. They drank wine, ate delicacies (whereas there was hunger all over the country), but not a single one of them offered me, a two-year-old skeleton covered with skin, even a small piece of bread, to say nothing of the chocolate which these new 'masters of life' were consuming greedily in large quantities.[16]

The old woman is picking up cat food from the plate behind my window. She is clutching her tattered string 'perhaps' bag in her hand.

January 19. Vzgliad. A piece on the 'special' maternity hospital of the Council of Ministers Medical Department (the former Health Ministry Fourth Department). A huge modern building for just fifty-six women in labour. Spacious wards for one or two, Western equipment, attentive and caring staff. Then they showed an ordinary maternity hospital, also in Moscow. Shabby, crumbling building. Women lying in narrow cots in dark corridors. Blood-stained walls. Cockroaches. Irascible nurses. Shortage of slippers. One shower for the whole hospital. Two thousand women. The reporter interviewed the chief physician of the 'special' hospital. 'What would happen if by chance or by mistake an ordinary woman, in labour, came to your hospital?' he asked. 'We have our instructions,' the chief physician answered. 'If an ordinary woman comes to us, we are to call an ambulance and take her where she belongs.' He smiled as he answered. He saw nothing abnormal in this stance. And this was terrifying. After all, he was a doctor, a member of supposedly the most humane profession on earth.

In every normal country after a programme like that, watched by an audience of 150 million, people would pour on to the streets protesting against this unseen social crime. But not in the Soviet Union. Seventy years of terror make them afraid to speak out.

Today I was shocked to read in the *Guardian* a preview of *The Repentance*, a tragic Soviet feature film which exposes Stalinist repression. When I watched *The Repentance* in a Moscow cinema some time ago, the whole audience was in tears and a number of women were openly weeping. In the *Guardian* they called it 'a red-and-black comedy in which scandal and Stalinist repression is unearthed with the exhumed corpse of a Georgian mayor.'[17] How can one be so shallow? Unbelievable callousness . . .

January 21. I haven't been writing my diary for two days. I've been recovering from the shock caused by the Soviet invasion of Baku, 'the most tragic and terrible event since the Second World War' as the presenter on *Seven Days* has just put it.

On a gloomy morning yesterday I was woken by a telephone call from Sky TV in London. 'Do you want to comment on what happened in Baku?' they asked. 'What exactly has happened?' I muttered, still half asleep. 'Gorbachev has sent in the troops.' I asked them to call me back in half an hour, grabbed my portable radio and tuned to Radio Liberty. They were broadcasting a telephone interview with their contact in Baku. 'This is awful!' their correspondent was screaming. 'The tanks are crushing people – women, children. I can see from my window a tank has just overturned a car with passengers in it. It is rolling over the car flattening it.' Suddenly he was interrupted by a female telephone operator in Baku: 'They are killing us!' she yelled piercingly in a strong Azerbaijani accent. 'They are killing us all!'

So what happened in Baku? The local Popular Front which supported Azerbaijani independence was gaining authority in that Caucasian republic. Free elections to the republican Supreme Soviet were about to take place, and it was clear that the local Communist Party was in for a shattering defeat. To avoid that, the local Party elite, in collusion with the KGB, provoked several cases of anti-Armenian violence in the Azerbaijani capital, Baku. Armenians started fleeing from the city in large numbers. Using this violence as a pretext, Moscow then sent in troops. The terrible irony of the situation was that by the time the tanks went roaring along the streets, there were practically no Armenians left: there was no-one to protect. The tanks started crushing the pro-independence movement instead. A state of emergency and a curfew were imposed and, plainly, free elections became out of the question. The Party achieved its goal and the fact that hundreds of innocent people were killed did not in the least worry the butchers.

Full responsibility for the massacre lies directly with Gorbachev. He did not have the excuse of being out of the country, as in April 1989 when the troops killed and poisoned with chemicals participants in a peaceful pro-democratic rally in Tbilisi.

Received a letter from my London publishers, posted three months ago. The envelope was torn and hastily patched with scotch tape. Why are the KGB such slow readers?

January 22. Three days ago a Jewish pogrom occurred at the Moscow Writers' Club. This is an exclusive Writers' Union institution, vigilantly guarded day and night lest some outsider should infiltrate its well-stocked bars and restaurants. Even for someone like myself, a USSR Union of Journalists member, entrance is denied.

All this security didn't stop several dozen Pamyat thugs, armed with knuckledusters and megaphones, finding their way in without any kind of union cards. Their appearance coincided with a meeting of April, a newly-formed organisation of progressive pro-perestroika writers (an alternative Writers' Union), who had gathered to discuss their internal problems.

Some of the writers were of Jewish origin, but the majority were Russian, Georgian, Ukrainian and so on. For Pamyat, anyone who does not actively attack Jews, is also branded. They produced their mega-phones and started shouting: 'You dirty Jewish mongrels, you are not Russian writers! Get out to Israel! Now we are the masters of the country and neither the Party, nor the KGB nor the militia are going to help you! Next time we'll come with sub-machine guns!'

They were right about the militia. Though summoned immediately, they took forty minutes to arrive and instead of stopping the pogrom they guarded the Pamyat thugs and politely escorted them to the lobby, ignoring the fact that they had broken several articles of the Constitution and of the Criminal Code.

Will they really come with the guns next time? I think they will.

At *Krokodil* everyone is talking about the unprecedented growth of unprovoked sadistic assaults, robberies and car thefts.

Today I had a chat with our magazine's executive secretary (this position is usually held by someone who ensures that the Party line is observed to the letter). Suddenly in the middle of our conversation, he said: 'I would welcome your decision to stay in England. You'd be a free person there, unlike here.' I didn't react and changed the subject quickly. Now I don't know what to think of this sudden outburst of his. Is this just another link in the chain of weird coincidence? I wish I knew.

An interesting thought in a Radio Liberty broadcast: the reason for all our recent disasters is lack of professionalism. The sending of troops to Baku, the events in Tbilisi, the inability to contain the bandits in Fergana are vivid examples of unprofessional behaviour on the part of the leadership and the army itself. They also called Azerbaijan 'the internal Afghanistan'.

The Azerbaijan Supreme Soviet called for the unconditional withdrawal of the troops within forty-eight hours. Otherwise, they said, the republic will secede from the USSR.

The world chess champion Gary Kasparov, who was born in Baku, criticised the invasion bitterly. He sent his personal plane to Baku to pick up his sixty relatives of Armenian origin.

The tension in the country is mounting with every passing day. Fear hangs in the air.

January 26. Recorded my last (?) interview for *Saturday Night Clive* from Moscow via satellite. It seems to have gone well, despite some minor problems with the sound.

Pogroms of Russians have now started in Baku. Thousands of local residents of Russian origin are fleeing to Moscow. And a sea-battle has taken place in Baku harbour. Soviet navy warships were trying to break through the blockade imposed by Azerbaijani Popular Front ships. Artillery was used by both sides. It looks like the country is pretty close to a national cataclysm.

Bought the *Guardian* at the Intourist hotel and read about a new war game played in England called 'Salman Rushdie'. One team has to shoot the Rushdie figure and the other has to defend him. The Rushdie figure wears a dinner jacket and carries a wooden shield labelled 'the book'. He has to reach an area called 'the publisher' to deliver the book and then hide in a 'safe house'. The paper reported that another game, 'Noriega', in which players have to kill or kidnap the former Panamian dictator, was being developed.[18]

January 29. Farewell evening party for the Channel 4 crew I've been consulting for at the Atrium cooperative restaurant in Leninski Prospect. I am deliberately trying to see as many Westerners as I can now. 'This is your salvation,' Kabakov told me the other day. 'You must show the KGB that you've got lots of influential friends in the West.' I am not sure whether I've managed to impress them with my contacts, but I am almost certain that they are following me in the street from time to time.

The West continues to be so blinded by Gorbachev that to criticise him in the Western press one has to use a pseudonym. A couple of sobering anti-Gorbachev articles which have just appeared in Britain and in the USA were signed Z . . .

January 30, morning. I stopped answering telephone calls at home. Natasha does it for me saying that I am out. Sorokin from the KGB called yesterday and today leaving messages to call him back urgently. Only two more days for me to hold out, though I am trying not to think about it. Two burly men in fur hats are standing outside my window and I am almost sure I saw one of them in the underground yesterday. Both Natasha and I are on the verge of a nervous breakdown.

Yesterday we all went for out last(?) stroll around Moscow. I tried not to look back. In the underground we saw a group of Russian refugees from Baku. Thin, sallow kids, dressed in rags, grim old women with shabby suitcases. It looked like a still from a war movie.

We were walking along Old Arbat, my favourite street in Moscow. It was swarming with people. The black marketeers were selling fake Russian icons and Easter eggs. Street artists stood by their portable easels: 'Portrait in ten minutes. Twenty roubles.' No-one volunteered to have a ten-minute portrait for almost a week's salary. Near Vakhtangov Theatre a group of Pamyat agitators distributed sheets of paper with figures indicating the number of Jews in Lenin's government and Cheka.

We had dinner at the Prague restaurant where our wedding reception took place eleven and a half years ago. This time the food was bad and the waiters rude.

I am going out now to look for a safe telephone booth to confirm my taxi booking.

January 30, evening. I spent most of the afternoon with mum in her tiny flat near Voikovskaya Metro. And again I tried not to think that this could be my last time here. I asked her to be brave and patient and promised to get her out as soon as I could. Then I had a short nap on her old sofa, which used to belong to me many years ago. It was so quiet in the flat. The telephone did not ring. My old children's books were in the bookcase. My father was half-smiling at me from the photo on the wall. My mother was sitting at my bedside and looking at me sadly, as if I'd already gone.

Later in the evening the Kabakovs came to say goodbye. 'You are doing the right thing,' Sasha said. 'But don't relax until you cross the border . . .'

194

We were sitting in the kitchen where everything was so familiar: my father's old radio on the fridge, my collection of empty beer cans and whisky bottles. How many heated friendly debates and family discussions had taken place here? We drank some vodka – not much, since no-one felt like drinking. 'I am sure, we'll be together again,' Sasha said. 'The world is small and round.' We embraced, kissed, and they left. Through the window I could see them crossing the road and starting towards the Metro.

B, a writer friend of mine, told me over the phone that most of his relatives and friends had got hold of American emigration forms. One can buy such a form for 100 roubles on the black market. People fill them in and drop them into a special box near the American embassy. Quotas for potential migrants to America are filled for the next five years. The desperate people are hoping that when the civil war starts, it will help to have the completed forms already at the embassy. There's even appeared a special slang expression in Moscow recently – 'to drop', meaning to file an application form at the embassy. People keep asking each other: 'Have you dropped already?' 'Do you think I should drop too?' B asked me.

January 31. I am writing these lines on the train. Yes, we've almost made it. Almost. We are still in the Soviet Union. The border control will be tomorrow morning.

The train wheels are rattling soothingly. I've always liked trains. The very fact that the carriage is moving gives me reassurance. We are moving in the right direction now, towards normal life, away from the impending chaos. But also away from the dear faces of our friends. Soon through this very train window I'll probably see the Western world. Probably. Before that I am in for one more encounter with the KGB: border guards in the Soviet Union are part of the State Security Committee. Now, before going to bed (or rather to berth), I am recording the events of the last day in Moscow.

Last night I had a bad dream: a KGB man in a fur hat and leather jacket was holding out his black-gloved hand to me. One more second and he would grab me. I woke up in a cold sweat. Five o'clock. No matter how hard I tried, I couldn't get back to sleep. At six-thirty, after much tossing and turning, I got up and decided to go out and buy some newspapers. Today the announcement of my Ilf and Petrov Award for satirical journalism was to appear in the press.

As I went out I saw a man wearing a big shapka (fur hat) and a black leather overcoat. Our small courtyard is usually deserted even during the day and the man looked very conspicuous there. As I turned the corner I quickly looked back. The man was following me at a little distance. When, ten minutes later, I returned with the newspapers he was not in the yard. I looked back, and there he was, about fifty or sixty metres behind me. Back in my flat I looked out of the window and saw another young man in exactly the same apparel pacing back and forth near the house.

Later in the morning we switched off the telephone in our flat. It looked very miserable, this noisy troublemaker, with its two-pin plug lying on my desk like a paralysed limb. At times I thought I could hear the silent rings it was giving as Bitov, Tumanov, Sergei Romanovich, Sergei Stanislavovich, Sorokin and others were trying to reach me . . .

Shortly before midday I went to the city, to the Union of Journalists headquarters, to pick up the badge and the diploma which went with my newly-won award. My KGB escorts were nowhere to be seen. A black Volga sedan was parked near the house. They were probably warming themselves there as I rushed to the Metro station only 100 metres away. Again it made me think that the men in the fur hats were really used for intimidation purposes.

In Pushkin Square, smack downtown, there was a very, very long line snaking towards the country's first McDonald's restaurant which opened this morning. The queue was cordoned off by numerous militiamen and separated from the rest of the world by metallic turnstiles. There were seven or eight thousand people in the line, the end of which was somewhere out of sight in Bolshaya Bronnaya Street. I calculated that it would take between five and seven hours to get inside. Nevertheless people were prepared to stand there and freeze just to get a glimpse and a taste of something Western. The happy ones came out clutching paper flags, plastic plates and glasses, the rubbish which people in the West throw out without thinking. One big Mac cost around five roubles, more than the average daily salary. 'Poor, poor people,' I thought.

On the opposite side of the square, across Gorkovo Street, a flock of fifty or sixty people were standing around a short red-bearded man, clad in black. 'Jews are not human beings!' he was screaming hysterically at the top of his lungs.

I said goodbye to Pushkin Square, that favourite Moscow nook of mine. Under the big street clock near the Metro is the most popular dating place in the city. Twelve years ago I myself waited for Natasha there, pacing the street nervously when she was late. Now other men were standing under the clock waiting for their dates to appear. Not me. I had nothing good to expect from this country any longer. Goodbye, Moscow.

Three hours before departure my mother and my in-laws came. We had an impromptu farewell dinner. It was a rueful surprise party. Who said that emigration is a rehearsal for one's own funeral? The unplugged telephone was staring at us silently from my desk – but the desk, the flat, the city, the country, they were not mine any longer. Half an hour before leaving, we put our last portion of cat food on the plate near the house for the old woman to collect.

The cab arrived. 'Are we going today, dad? I didn't say goodbye to the kids in my class.' Mitya was genuinely surprised. We couldn't tell even him the real date of our departure until the very last moment.

We kissed our parents hastily and rushed out with our suitcases full of books, papers and basic clothes. Our courtyard and our Lenskaya Street and our Moscow were absolutely deserted. It was dark and cold. No-one was in sight.

February 1. We are about to cross the border. The train is standing still at Brest, the old Brest-Litovsk on the Polish border, but both passport and customs controls are over. I can't believe it. They didn't even look into our suitcases where, among other things, were the notes, files, clippings and photographs for my next book. I was worried that they would try to confiscate them, since according to the Soviet customs regulations one cannot take manuscripts, books or newspapers across the border without authorisation.

I am writing these lines as the train crawls towards the Yuzhni Bug River, along which the border with Poland runs. We are moving past the drab outskirts of Brest: depots, log cabins, warehouses with peeling stucco slowly recede. In the distance I can already discern rows of barbed wire and the river behind them. The sky is cloudy and dull. A thin middle-aged woman in fur coat and clumsy hand-knitted cap with two bulging 'perhaps' bags in both hands is trudging through the snow alongside the tracks. Her face is grim and tired. The last human being on the Soviet side.

Barbed wire. A patch of ploughed 'neutral' land with neat regular furrows, looking like wrinkles, as if the ground itself is frowning at us. A frontier post with the sign 'USSR' on it. A small whitewashed cabin with big windows facing the track on the very bank of the river. A young Soviet border guard standing to attention with a Kalashnikov sub-machine gun on his shoulder and looking sternly at our train. The brownish gleaming surface of the Yuzhni Bug with a flock of carefree stateless ducks floating on it. A little cabin on the other bank of the river which looks like a twin of the Soviet one. The only difference: inside, instead of a stern, vigilant border guard, there's a Polish railway worker in a dirty orange vest sitting on the floor, smoking.

And suddenly, the bright sunlight bursts through the clouds and nearly blinds us. Small patches of new green grass are springing out along the track here and there . . .

Freedom.

Epilogue

Where am I? The white-clad tennis players jump forgetfully outside the windows of my Melbourne flat. They play day and night, oblivious of everything. They do not notice me standing on the balcony with a smoking cigarette stub clutched in my hand.

My mind tells me that I am in Australia, but I refuse to believe it.

From an early age I collected guide books, maps and train timetables. In my imaginary travels I endured rough seas near the Equator, I climbed the snow-capped Himalayas, I talked to Aborigines near Ayers Rock in Australia.

Like most of my compatriots, I was a typical armchair buccaneer, dead sure that I would never travel outside the borders of the Soviet Union. I was living inside myself, in an illusory and unreal world of make-believe.

A Soviet friend wrote to me: 'I think I understand what emotions are filling you now: a curious mixture of hope, doubt and apprehension. Sometimes I feel as if I experience this gamut of feelings with you, and I think you have made the right decision. You must have your fate firmly in your own hands. You must do everything for your son to grow up a free man, who knows his own value and relies only on his own strength. For you and Natasha, hindered by your Soviet past, it is going to be much more difficult.'

'There are sharks in Australia, there are snakes and spiders, there are huge angry crocodiles.' I can hear my mother's voice reading to me at bedtime from a coloured children's book with nasty hungry animals snarling from every page.

Australia for me was like the Moon. No, it was more like Mars or Venus. And though you can see the dim distant light of those planets on cloudless nights, you know only too well that there is no chance of you ever going there.

I remember talking to a Leningrad friend of mine, the Hermitage Museum curator, about twelve years ago. She was among the handful of privileged people who had visited Australia. She told me how after coming back to the Soviet Union she was called to the Communist Party Central Committee and was made to sign a statement to the effect that she would never share her impressions of Australia with anyone and would never disclose what she had seen there. 'What is so special about this Australia?' I kept thinking.

In November 1989 I was returning from Perm 35 Labour camp by train. It had neither a restaurant car nor traditional Russian tea. Tea was rationed throughout the country together with soap, sausage, meat. Flocks of ageless peasant women dressed in rags approached the train at every station asking for something to eat. There was nothing but stale bread in the station buffets on our route.

'We won't relinquish socialism!' Gorbachev kept repeating. What was so good about a system which had driven this huge country, with all imaginable mineral resources and plenty of fertile land, to starvation. One had to work hard to achieve such results. And for seventy-three years rulers have worked hard. And millions have died. And those still alive were denied the ability to travel and to say aloud what they thought.

Why did we wholeheartedly believe Mikhail Gorbachev in the beginning? Because he was talking freedom. We did not understand at that time that freedom and his socialism were incompatible.

Gorbachev wanted to give the system a facelift, to introduce some token changes to make it more presentable for Western consumption. He wanted to treat Russia like an ageing film star having plastic surgery. He miscalculated. Freedom is a peculiar substance. It has no dimensions. It is like a gas: if it is there, it fills the whole vessel. Gorbachev's reforms, no matter how timid and cosmetic, immediately came to blows with the system. The economy died. People became lost and frustrated. Everything went out of control.

There is a new shift of tennis players on the court outside my window now. Two elderly freckled women, dressed in shorts and white blouses, are waving their rackets like robots. They are so immersed in the game that it looks as if their whole existence depends on a lucky shot. I envy them.

In September 1989 I was working with an Australian TV crew in Moscow. They were making a programme about perestroika. We filmed a queue for tomatoes in the centre of Moscow. It was at least half a mile long. The people in it looked as if they were prepared to stand there forever, as if all their existence depended on a kilo of wrinkled tomatoes.

The Australian cameraman could not film. He was crying. 'Why are you living like this? We are the same people.'

Indeed, why? There is no straightforward answer. Russia has always been a land of too many whys and too few becauses . . .

From the letter from my Soviet friend: 'You are very far away now, but I am sure we'll see each other many times more. Let's strive for that like free people do. To stay in Russia, to go on living like a slave, was no longer possible for you. Good luck to you; you will really need it. Be courageous.'

I am watching the tennis players. I am in Australia and I am free.

But why do I feel so sad at times? Why do I feel like someone who is suffering from a severe heartburn? . . .

I love my country, I want it to be better. But I could not stay there. Here at least I am alive and thus able to do something for Russia. My first goal is to tell the truth. Russia is still my dateline, despite the thousands of miles which separate us. Russia and freedom . . . These two datelines of mine still seem as incompatible as ever, but I'm sure the time will come when they merge into one: dateline freedom.

In the New Era Bookshop in Melbourne, the selection of Russian books is amazing. Here I feel almost at home, among friends.

Every day I watch *Vremia*, the cable news programme from Moscow, on my TV. Yes, it is as dull and doctrinaire as always, but it is in Russian and therefore gripping.

Thank you, Australia, the teenage girl, the beautiful Mars with sharks and crocodiles, the hospitable home for the strayed and the outcast, the land where you can read Russian books and do not have to watch your tongue to survive.

The last set is completed. The players pick up their gear and go for lunch. The courts behind my window stand empty.

What time is it now? Almost midday. I am going for my daily TV date with Moscow.

The game is not finished yet.

Notes

FROM THE AUTHOR

1 *The Economist*, 20 October 1990.
2 *Age*, 7 November 1990; *AFP*, 6 November 1990.
3 *Asian Wall Street Journal*, 10 October 1990, *et al.*
4 *Los Angeles Times*, 13 July 1990.
5 *Independent*, 25 September 1990.
6 *Sunday Times*, 26 August 1990.
7 *Independent*, 1 October 1990; *Moskovskiye Novosti*, 21 October 1990.
8 *New York City Tribune*, 1 October 1990.
9 *The Times* and Reuters, 30 October 1990.
10 *The Times*, 23 June 1990.
11 *Los Angeles Times*, 18 October 1990.
12 *News Weekly*, 7 July 1990.
13 *The Times*, 26 November 1990.
14 *Moskovskiye Novosti*, 25 November 1990; *Russkaya Misl*, 16 November 1990.
15 *Asian Wall Street Journal*, 15 August 1990.
16 *Sydney Morning Herald*, 15 September 1990 (Reuters).
17 *Moscow News* 35, 1990.
18 *Moskovskiye Novosti*, 12 August 1990.
19 *The Times*, 13 October 1990.
20 *Moscow News* 22, 1990.
21 *Russkaya Misl*, 30 November 1990.

CHAPTER 1 THE TWISTS AND CRAZY TURNS OF PERESTROIKA

1 *Moskovskiye Novosti*, 11 March 1990.
2 *The Times*, 21 April 1990.
3 *Ogonyok* 2, January 1990; *Moscow News* 3, 1990; *Literaturnaya Gazeta* 3, 1990.
4 Reuters and *Washington Post*, 22 May 1990.
5 *Moscow News* 12, 1990.
6 *Asian Wall Street Journal*, 4 October 1990.
7 *Moscow News* 35, 1990.
8 *Russkaya Misl*, 30 November 1990.
9 *Guardian*, 15 March 1990.
10 Tass.
11 Reuters, 12 October 1990.
12 *Moskovskiye Novosti*, 18 November 1990.
13 *Moskovskiye Novosti*, 11 November 1990.
14 *Russkaya Misl*, 15 March 1991.
15 *The Times*, 24 January 1991; *The Economist*, 2 February 1991.
16 *Trud*, 13 February 1991; *The Economist*, 16 February 1991; *Age*, 14 February 1991.

17 *The Economist*, 16 February 1991.
18 *AFP*, 12 March 1991.
19 *Guardian*, 22 December 1990.
20 *Daily Telegraph*, 15 January 1991.
21 *Moskovskiye Novosti*, 12 January 1991; *Russkaya Misl*, 22 February 1991; *AP*, 28 February 1991.
22 *New York Times*, 5 February 1991.
23 *Independent Magazine*, 19 January 1991.
24 *Independent*, 17 January 1991; *The Times*, 17 January 1991.
25 *Russkaya Misl*, 25 January 1991.
26 *Moskovskiye Novosti*, 20 January 1991.
27 John Barron, *KGB Today. The Hidden Hand*, p. 190, Coronet Books, Hodder and Stoughton, London, 1985.
28 *Independent*, 28 January 1991.
29 *The Times*, 1 February 1991.
30 *Russkaya Misl*, 15 March 1991.
31 *Asian Wall Street Journal*, 12 March 1991.
32 *Asian Wall Street Journal*, 31 January 1991.
33 *German Tribune*, 3 March 1991.
34 *International Herald Tribune*, 26 December 1990.

9 *The Best of Ogonyok*, p. 111, Heinemann, London, 1990.
10 *Ibid.*, p. 113.
11 *Literaturnaya Gazeta* 1, 1989.
12 *Pilnioi Atklati* 1, January 1990.
13 *Moskovskiye Novosti*, 19 August 1990.
14 *Guardian Weekly*, 30 September 1990.
15 *Observer*, 18 March 1990.
16 *Sunday Times*, 7 October 1990.

CHAPTER 3 TWENTY-NINE

1 *Moscow News* 32, 1989.
2 Reuters, July 1988; *The Voice of the Martyrs*, February 1989.
3 Natan Sharansky, *Fear No Evil*, p. 359, Coronet, London, 1989.
4 *Ibid.*, p. 333–5.
5 *Russkaya Misl*, 15 June 1990.
6 *Ibid.*
7 *Ibid.*
8 *Ibid.*
9 Natan Sharansky, *Fear No Evil*, p. 456, Coronet, London, 1989.
10 *Russkaya Misl*, 15 June 1990.
11 *Ibid.*
12 *Krokodil* 5 and 6, 1990.
13 *Novi Mir* 10, 1989.

CHAPTER 2 THE SQUALL

1 *Novi Mir* 5, May 1990.
2 *Izvestia*, 10 January 1990.
3 *Sunday Age*, 7 October 1990.
4 *Dom Kino*, December 1990.
5 *Literaturnaya Gazeta* 50, 1989.
6 *Ibid.*
7 *Independent Magazine*, 21 October 1989.
8 *Listener*, 21 June 1990.

CHAPTER 4 CHURKI AND YIDS

1 *Independent*, 8 January 1991.
2 *Ogonyok* 47, November 1989.
3 *Australian Jewish News*, 9 November 1990.
4 Benjamin Pinkus, *The Jews of the Soviet Union*, p. 1, Cambridge University Press, Cambridge, 1989.
5 *Jewish Chronicle*, 13 April 1990.

6 John Paxton, *Companion to Russian History*, p. 57–8 and p. 280, Oxford University Press, Melbourne.
7 *The Economist*, 10 November 1990.
8 Benjamin Pinkus, *The Jews of the Soviet Union*, p. 109, Cambridge University Press, Cambridge, 1989.
9 Mikhail Heller and Aleksandr Nekrich, *Utopia in Power*, p. 502, Hutchinson, London, 1986.
10 *Molodaya Gvardia* 8, 1989.
11 *Mail on Sunday*, 14 May 1990.
12 *Newsweek*, 7 May 1990.
13 *Independent*, 7 May 1990.
14 *Moscow News* 35, 1990.
15 *Jerusalem Post*, 5 and 17 August 1990.
16 *Russkaya Misl*, 26 October 1990.
17 *Ibid.*
18 *Krasnoye Znamia*, 10 June 1990.
19 *Ogonyok* 48, November 1989.
20 *Guardian*, 22 February 1990.
21 *Ibid.*
22 *Newsweek*, 7 May 1990.
23 *Anti-Semitism in the USSR*, July 1990.
24 *Moskovskiye Novosti*, 15 July 1990.
25 *Sunday Times*, 18 February 1990.
26 *The Times*, 28 September 1990.
27 *Russkaya Misl*, 15 June 1990.
28 *Jewish Chronicle*, 5 November 1990.
29 *Russkaya Misl*, 15 June 1990.
30 *International Herald Tribune*, 26 June 1990.
31 *Literaturnaya Gazeta* 3, 1990.
32 *Moscow News* 22, 1990.

CHAPTER 5 THE DEEP-DRILLING OFFICE

1 *Webster's Third New International Dictionary*, volume 1, p. 831, Encyclopedia Britannica Inc, Chicago, 1986.
2 *The Guinness Book of Records 1991*, p. 216, Guinness Publishing Ltd, Enfield, 1990.
3 *Izvestia*, 5 January 1990.
4 *Moskovskiye Novosti*, 26 August 1990.
5 *Guardian*, 3 March 1990.
6 *Asian Wall Street Journal*, 4 October 1990.
7 *Sunday Times*, 15 April 1990.
8 *Asian Wall Street Journal*, 21 November 1990.
9 *International Press Institute Annual Report*, IPI, August 1990.
10 *Moskovskiye Novosti*, 16 September 1990.
11 *Moskovskiye Novosti*, 7 October 1990; *Asian Wall Street Journal*, 4 October 1990.
12 *Russkaya Misl*, 5 October 1990.
13 *Moskovskiye Novosti*, 19 August 1990.
14 *Russkaya Misl*, 5 October 1990.
15 *Counterpoint*, volume 6, number 5, October 1990.
16 *Russkaya Misl*, 5 October 1990. *Moscow News* 46, 1990 estimates 1,500,000 staff, 3,000,000 free-lance agents and 400,000 regular troops.
17 *Asian Wall Street Journal*, 15 November 1990.
18 *Ibid.*
19 *Moskovskiye Novosti*, 4 March 1990.
20 *Russkaya Misl*, 5 October 1990.
21 *Age*, 17 November 1990.

22 *Moskovskiye Novosti*, 11 November 1990; *Australian*, 9 October 1990 (Reuters).
23 *Los Angeles Times*, 11 October 1990.
24 *Australian*, 5 October 1990.
25 *Le Monde*, 21 September 1990.
26 *The Times*, 27 February 1990.
27 *Russkaya Misl*, 8 March 1991.
28 *Time*, 23 April 1990.
29 Reuters, 8 March 1991.
30 *Moscow News* 52, 1989.
31 Vladimir Kriuchkov, *The KGB must abide by the interests of the people*, p. 17–8, Novosti Press Agency, 1989.
32 *Moscow News* 16, 1990.
33 *Counterpoint*, volume 6, number 5, October 1990; *Moskovskiye Novosti*, 11 March 1990; *Ogonyok* 37, September 1989; *Ogonyok* 3, January 1990.
34 *Moskovskiye Novosti*, 16 September 1990; *Counterpoint*, volume 6, number 4, September 1990.
35 *Ogonyok* 3, January 1990.
36 *Moscow News* 25, 1990; *The Los Angeles Times*, 26 July 1990; *Russkaya Misl*, 28 September 1990; *Newsweek*, 2 July 1990 *et al.*
37 *Moskovskiye Novosti*, 28 October 1990.
38 Reuters, 31 July 1990.
39 *Moskovskiye Novosti*, 21 October 1990.
40 *Argumenti i Fakti* 30, 1990; *Moscow News* 36, 1990.
41 *Washington Post*, 3 December 1990; *The Times*, 3 December 1990; *Australian*, 13 December 1990 *et al.*
42 *Russkaya Misl*, 15 June 1990.
43 *Sunday Times*, 11 February 1990.
44 *Asian Wall Street Journal*, 15 November 1990.
45 Christopher Andrew and Oleg Gordievsky, *KGB: The Inside Story*, p. 543 Hodder and Stoughton, London, 1990.
46 *Moscow News* 31, 1990.
47 *Soviet Intelligence and Active Measures* 15 and 16, summer/fall, 1990.
48 *Russkaya Misl*, 23 November 1990.
49 *Ibid.*

CHAPTER 6 WHEREABOUTS UNKNOWN . . .

1 Sydney Bloch and Peter Reddaway, *Diagnoz: Inakomisliye*, p. 352, Overseas Publication Interchange Ltd, London, 1981.
2 *Ibid.*, p. 39.
3 *Ibid.*, p. 40.
4 *Ibid.*, p. 41.
5 *Moskovskiye Novosti*, 12 August 1990.
6 *Russkaya Misl*, 26 October 1990.
7 *Izvestia*, 8 January 1990.
8 *Moskovskiye Novosti*, 7 October 1990.
9 *Ibid*, 19 August 1990; *Russkaya Misl*, 28 September 1990; *Asian Wall Street Journal*, 4 October 1990.
10 *Moskovskiye Novosti*, 18 November 1990.
11 *Financial Times*, 10 October 1990.
12 *The Times*, 3 April 1990.
13 *Los Angeles Times*, 6 June 1990.
14 *Moskovskiye Novosti*, 12 August 1990.

15 *Ibid.*, 25 November 1990.
16 *Ibid.*, 16 September 1990.

CHAPTER 8 THE CURSED DAYS

1   *New Republic*, 4 December 1989.
2   *Financial Times*, 19 October 1989; *Argumenti i Fakti* 44, 1989; *Atmoda* 49, 1989 *et al.*
3   *Argumenti i Fakti* 42, 1989.
4   *Financial Times*, 19 October 1989.
5   Andreas Oplatka, *Neue Zurcher Zeitung*, 27 October 1989.

6   Gushrow Irani, *The Statesman*, Calcutta, India, 16–8 October 1989.
7   *Izvestia*, 31 October 1989.
8   *Ibid.*, 2 November 1989.
9   *Atmoda* 48, 1989.
10 *Ogonyok* 49, December 1989.
11 *Literaturnaya Gazeta* 50, 1989.
12 *Moscow News* 52, 1989.
13 *Moskovski Komsomolets*, 30 December 1989.
14 *Svobodnoye Slovo* 30, 1989.
15 *Izvestia*, 10 January 1990.
16 *Literaturnaya Gazeta* 3, 1990.
17 *Guardian*, 11 January 1990.
18 *Ibid.*, 17 January 1990.

Index